ATA

ENCYCLOPEDIA
OF
PARAKEETS

Kurt Kolar & Karl Heinz Spitzer

A Caboclo boy from the upper Rio Negro with his pet parakeet. The bird is free-flying and has attracted dozens of other birds which rely upon the family to feed them. Photo by Dr. Arthur Topilow, Rio Unini, Brazil.

Encyclopedia of Parakeets is an updated translation of the German book *Grossittiche: Haltung, Verhalten und Zucht* which was copyrighted in 1982 by Eugen Ulmer Gmbh & Co., Stuttgart, West Germany. TFH claims copyright 1989 for the translation, captions, additional illustrations, additional text, index and other original materials.

English translation by Christa Ahrens.

PHOTO CREDITS
The original German text does not specifically credit each photo to a specific photographer. Instead the authors thank Horst Bielfeld, Wolfgang de Grahl and Hans Reinhard for their contributions. Those illustrations which TFH has added are easily identified, since they are the photos in which credits are given to the photographer.

Distributed in the UNITED STATES by T.F.H. Publications, Inc., One T.F.H. Plaza, Neptune City, NJ 07753; in CANADA to the Pet Trade by H & L Pet Supplies Inc., 27 Kingston Crescent, Kitchener, Ontario N2B 2T6; Rolf C. Hagen Ltd., 3225 Sartelon Street, Montreal 382 Quebec; in CANADA to the Book Trade by Macmillan of Canada (A Division of Canada Publishing Corporation), 164 Commander Boulevard, Agincourt, Ontario M1S 3C7; in ENGLAND by T.F.H. Publications Limited, Cliveden House/Priors Way/Bray, Maidenhead, Berksi 9L6 2HP, England; in AUSTRALIA AND THE SOUTH PACIFIC by T.F.H. (Australia) Pty. Li 149, Brookvale 2100 N.S.W., Australia; in NEW ZEALAND by Ross Haines & Son, Lt Elizabeth Knox Place, Panmure, Auckland, New Zealand; in the PHILIPPINES by E search, 5 Lippay Street, San Lorenzo Village, Makati Rizal; in SOUTH AFRICA by Multip Pty. Ltd., Box 235 New Germany, South Africa 3620. Published by T.F.H. Publications, Inc Manufactured in the United States of America by T.F.H. Publications, Inc.

TABLE OF CONTENTS

Measurement Conversion Factors

When you know—	Multiply by—	To find—
Length:		
Millimeters (mm)	0.04	inches (in)
Centimeters (cm)	0.4	inches (in)
Meters (m)	3.3	feet (ft)
Meters (m)	1.1	yards (yd)
Kilometers (km)	0.6	miles (mi)
Inches (in)	2.54	centimeters (cm)
Feet (ft)	30	centimeters (cm)
Yards (yd)	0.9	meters (m)
Miles (mi)	1.6	kilometers (km)
Area:		
Square centimeters (cm²)	0.16	square inches (sq in)
Square meters (m²)	1.2	square yards (sq yd)
Square kilometers (km²)	0.4	square miles (sq mi)
Hectares (ha)	2.5	acres
Square inches (sq in)	6.5	square centimeters (cm²)
Square feet (sq ft)	0.09	square meters (m²)
Square yards (sq yd)	0.8	square meters (m²)
Square miles (sq mi)	1.2	square kilometers (km²)
Acres	0.4	hectares (ha)
Mass (Weight):		
Grams (g)	0.035	ounces (oz)
Kilograms (kg)	2.2	pounds (lb)
Ounces (oz)	28	grams (g)
Pounds (lb)	0.45	kilograms (kg)
Volume:		
Milliliters (ml)	0.03	fluid ounces (fl oz)
Liters (L)	2.1	pints (pt)
Liters (L)	1.06	quarts (qt)
Liters (L)	0.26	U.S. gallons (gal)
Liters (L)	0.22	Imperial gallons (gal)
Cubic centimeters (cc)	16.387	cubic inches (cu in)
Cubic meters (cm³)	35	cubic feet (cu ft)
Cubic meters (cm³)	1.3	cubic yards (cu yd)
Teaspoons (tsp)	5	millimeters (ml)
Tablespoons (tbsp)	15	millimeters (ml)
Fluid ounces (fl oz)	30	millimeters (ml)
Cups (c)	0.24	liters (L)
Pints (pt)	0.47	liters (L)
Quarts (qt)	0.95	liters (L)
U.S. gallons (gal)	3.8	liters (L)
U.S. gallons (gal)	231	cubic inches (cu in)
Imperial gallons (gal)	4.5	liters (L)
Imperial gallons (gal)	277.42	cubic inches (cu in)
Cubic inches (cu in)	0.061	cubic centimeters (cc)
Cubic feet (cu ft)	0.028	cubic meters (m³)
Cubic yards (cu yd)	0.76	cubic meters (m³)
Temperature:		
Celsius (°C)	multiply by 1.8, add 32	Fahrenheit (°F)
Fahrenheit (°F)	subtract 32, multiply by 0.555	Celsius (°C)

Platycercus eximius, the Eastern Rosella, originally from eastern Australia. It has been introduced into Hawaii.

Preface

Man has been fascinated by parrots from time immemorial. To many contemporaries the interest in these birds has only been superficial and lacking in empathy. The popular belief is that every parrot is able to talk (although it must not shout) and distinguishes itself with its striking colors. This widespread assumption has condemned many of these birds to become decorative splotches of bright colors, caged in inadequate housing simply as live talking machines. Relatively few fanciers endeavor to keep (let alone breed) these birds in correct conditions for the species concerned. Some parrots lead monotonous existences as ornamental cage birds. Apart from a few exceptions, a large group of parrots, commonly known as "large parakeets," are totally unsuited for life in a cage. These are species that thrive only in a spacious enclosure, where they attach little value to the company of members of their own species or to contact with their human keeper. Anyone who keeps large parakeets needs to derive enjoyment from the observation of his birds.

This volume is concerned primarily with the keeping of large parakeets, in accordance with their needs as animals, and with the affectionate and humane treatment of these birds. It is our responsibility to assist in the continuation of those species which have grown endangered due to man's progressive destruction of nature. By learning more about these birds' needs and by successfully breeding them in aviaries, bird fanciers can contribute to the preservation of earth's precious, natural life forms. In this manner the fancier fulfills a task that is accomplished in an exemplary way by zoological gardens, where the preservation of larger animals is of greater concern. It is not difficult to keep large parakeets; however, every species has its own special demands for climate, nutrition, and the artificial environment in the aviary. This fact is often ignored or taken too lightly by some bird keepers—those who expect too rapid an acclimatization of their animals and try to keep species from tropical ranges in unheated accommodations throughout the winter. Manufacturers who market seed mixtures for "large parakeets" ignorantly produce feed that does not meet the nutritional requirements of these birds. Knowledge of the bird's requirements must be learned by everyone who keeps large parakeets.

With the growing interest in bird keeping, the number of books and pamphlets that deal with this topic has also greatly increased. Some of this literature provides no more than a rough outline and is of little use, even to the novice, when it comes to specific questions on keeping. Other, more comprehensive books on parrots and their care do not fulfill the expectations of parakeet keepers who are looking for a handy reference. For the friends of this interesting group of parrots, we have provided a summary of experiences gained by ourselves and by breeders and keepers from all over the world, and have presented this information in clear format. At the same time, we have pointed out any gaps that still exist in our knowledge of the keeping and breeding of large parakeets. Surprisingly, many species of large parakeets have never been bred in captivity. Consequently, detailed breeding reports and behavioral observations are fairly rare. This leaves plenty of scope for every fancier of large parakeets to make his own observations and carry out his own breeding experiments.

We wish to thank the publishers and their expert adviser, Dr. J. Steinbacher, for the suggestion that this book should be written, and for the invitation to compile it. To Horst Bielfeld, Wolfgang de Grahl, and Hans Reinhard our gratitude for kindly placing at our disposal the color photographs. We would also like to thank Prof. Werner Frank of Hohenheim University for his critical perusal of the chapter on diseases and his valuable suggestions.

Large parakeets

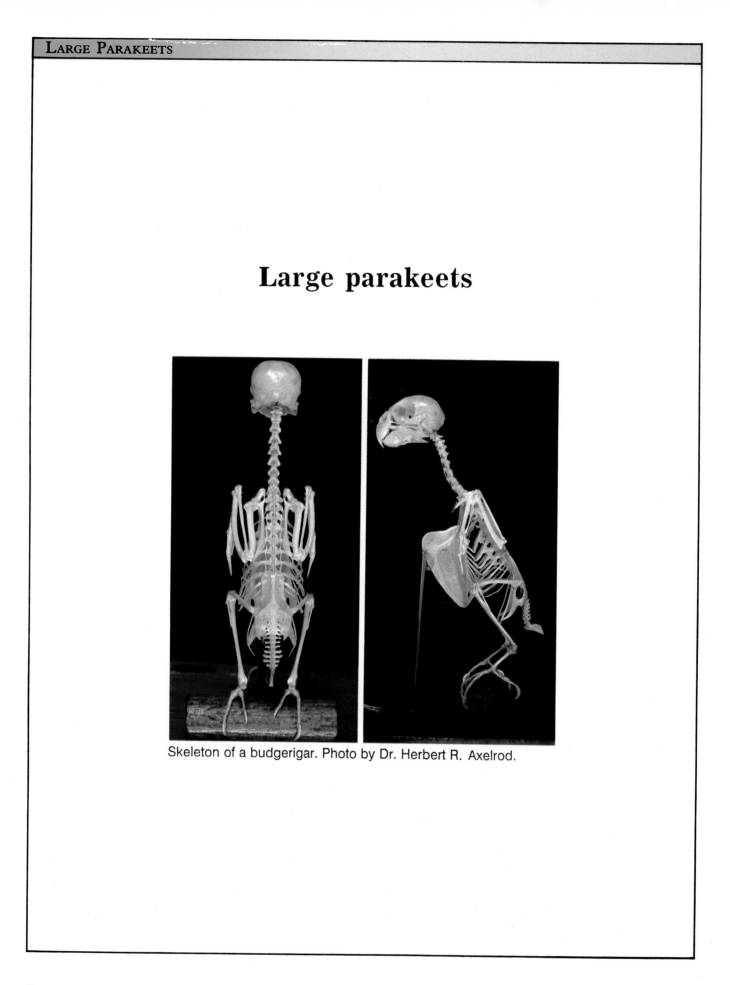

Skeleton of a budgerigar. Photo by Dr. Herbert R. Axelrod.

Their position among birds in general and in the parrot family

The characteristics of a parrot are so unequivocal that even an ornithological lay person can recognize them without difficulty; therefore, providing a definition of "parrot" is relatively simple. One important distinguishing mark shared by all species is a curved beak. In the same way, all species are distinguished by a zygodactyl position of the toes: the outer or fourth toe points backwards and, together with the first toe, works against the second and third. This turns the foot into an effective gripping tool whose function is not only to facilitate climbing, but also to enable some parrots to hold objects.

In nearly all parrot species, the beak can virtually be employed as a "third foot" used in climbing. In fact, a useless leg resulting from injuries or diseases, not uncommon in birds kept in captivity, is largely compensated for by the beak. First and foremost, however, the beak is specifically designed for removing husks and breaking up plant food. This is achieved through the special mobility of the upper mandible, which can be moved around a joint in a vertical direction. The lower mandible can be moved in a sledge-like way. Along the hard transverse ridges on the underside of the upper mandible (filing grooves), its edge is kept smooth and sharp. The thick and muscular tongue, richly covered in tactile and gustatory papillae, assists the beak in taking up food. The food is soaked inside the crop and processed with enzymes from the glandular part of the stomach. An appendix is absent in the parrots. Some groups, including the Broad-tails, possess an oil gland; in parrots that do not, its function of protecting the plumage from getting wet is then carried out by the powder-down.

Providing a clear-cut definition of the term "large parakeets" is more difficult, since this is not a zoological term but one that has been coined by practicing bird keepers. It refers primarily to Broad-tails or Rosellas (Platycercini), a few representatives of the genera forming the Loriini group such as King Parakeets, *Polytelis* species, and *Psittacula* species, as well as most species belonging to the group of genera described as Araini. If the term "parakeet" is taken to mean a parrot with a long tail, one would consequently have to include the Macaws (*Ara*) and leave out the Parrotlets (*Forpus*), which also belong to the Araini. With the practicalities of bird keeping in mind, we have omitted the Macaws from this book but incorporated the Parrotlets, despite their lack of the parakeet characteristic of long tail feathers.

Survey of genera dealt with in this book (indicated by italic type) and their position in the parrot family.

Order Parrots (*Psittaciformes*)
  Family Parrots (*Psittacidae*)
    Subfamily *Nestorinae*
        Psittrichasinae
        Kakatoeinae
        Micropsittinae
        Trichoglossinae
        Strigopinae
        Psittacinae

    Tribe Platycercini
    Genus *Geopsittacus* (Night Parrot)
      Pezoporus (Ground Parrot)
      Cyanoramphus
      Eunymphicus (Horned Parakeet)
      Melopsittacus (Budgerigar)
      Neophema (Grass Parakeets)
      Psephotus
      Purpureicephalus (Parakeet)
      Platycercus (Broad-tails or Rosellas)
      Barnardius
      Nymphicus (Cockatiel)
      Lathamus (Swift Parrot)

    Tribe *Loriini*
    Genus *Alisterus* (King Parrots)
      Aprosmictus (Red-winged Parrots)
      Polytelis
      Prósopeia (Shining Parrots)
      Psittacella
      Bolbopsittacus (Guaiabero)
      Psittinus (Blue-rumped Parrots)
      Geoffroyus
      Prioniturus (Racket-tailed Parrots)
      Lorius (Lories)
      Tanygnathus

Psittacula
Agapornis (Lovebirds)

Tribe *Loriculini*
Psittacini
Araini
Genus *Forpus* (Parrotlets)
Nannopsittaca (Tepui
Parrotlet)
Brotogeris
Bolborhynchus
Myiopsitta (Monk or Quaker
Parakeet)
Enicognathus (Conures)
Pyrrhura (Conures)
Aratinga (Conures)
Cyanoliseus (Patagonian
Conure)
Rhynchopsitta (Thick-billed
Parrot)
Anodorhynchus (Hyacinth
Macaw)
Cyanopsitta (Spix's Macaw)
Ara (Macaws)

Parakeets in the wild

Range and climate
In the perception of many contemporaries,
all parrots are "children of the tropics." At
the other extreme there is the tendency of
some bird keepers to "acclimatize" their
animals with more or less gentle force. Both
these extremes are wrong. Large parakeets
are represented in the most diverse
environments and climatic ranges. Among
them is the Derbyan Parakeet, a parrot
from the northernmost range, while the
genus *Cyanoramphus* from the Antipodes
Islands and the genus *Enicognathus* from
Tierra del Fuego constitute the
southernmost species. At altitudes of over
4000 meters in the mountains of South
America lives the Mountain Parakeet. This
species is adapted to low, fluctuating
temperatures. The Northern Rosellas, Pale-
headed Rosellas, and Golden-shouldered
Parakeets from northern Australia are
exposed to high temperatures all year
round, with temperatures not dropping
significantly during the night. A bird
keeper is under obligation to take the
climatic requirements of his animals into
consideration. It would be both untenable

and cruel to keep species from equatorial
ranges in unheated accommodations during
cold winter months.

It is generally supposed that the original
habitat of our birds were forests. Indicative
of this, particularly in the parrots, is the
adaptation to climbing that is still present
(beak, position of the toes). Changes in the
climate led to a decline in forests long
before there was any human intervention.
The animal world was forced to gradually
adapt to changing living conditions. Sparse
dry woods, savannahs (plains dotted with
trees), and extensive grassy steppes became
the parakeets' environment. Bourke's
Parakeet penetrated far into the driest
Mulga shrub steppe; the Night Parrot,
Budgerigar, and Princess Parakeet
colonized in semiarid countryside with a
growth of porcupine grass. In order to
survive on such terrain, the birds must have
the ability to migrate temporarily during
periods of severe drought. An adaptation to
these living conditions is the particularly
well-developed flight capacity of these
species. In captivity, such parakeets are not
normally satisfied with a small enclosure in
which they are only able to climb about, but
must have adequate flying space available
to them. Characteristic of steppes and
semiarid terrain are the drastic differences
in the day and evening temperatures, which
often drop below freezing. Therefore, while
these birds are able to tolerate low
temperatures for short periods, they are not
able to adjust to longer spells of cold
weather that occur during the winter
months in many countries. To expect our
parakeets to spend the winter without a
heated shelter is most certainly inhumane.

South Australian species, such as some
populations of the Crimson Rosella; species
from the southernmost extreme of South
America; or pronounced mountainous
forms, such as the Derbyan Parakeet, have
to contend with prolonged periods of ice
and snow in their native range. Provided
with some form of shelter from the wind
and damp, they can be left in unheated
outdoor aviaries in the winter.

A few representatives of the large
parakeets (e.g., certain conures) are
encountered in the tropical rain forest. This
habitat is distinguished by high

The King Parrot, *Alisterus scapularis*, is a very common parakeet in Australia. It occurs mostly in large trees and along the coast. Photo by L. Robinson.

temperatures which show little fluctuation, as well as by a humidity which rarely falls below 70%. The annual rainfall is at least 1000 mm. The rich vegetation offers adequate nourishment all year round. Consequently, no rhythm is forced upon the birds through external influences; even breeding can take place at virtually any time of the year. As a result, the birds often have several broods in succession, repeating this behavior in aviaries. Species from such environments do not always adapt to normal keeping conditions; some have to be acclimatized in suitable accommodations for a long period before they can be allowed into outdoor aviaries for a couple of warm summer months.

In dry areas, the vegetation, hence food resources and reproduction, are influenced by rainfalls concentrated over a short period of time. Species from such regions usually breed at specific times of the year and tend to retain this habit in aviaries as well, at least in the early stages. This is exemplified by the Thick-billed Parakeets, which breed in August in their Mexican home. Animals kept in Britain and the United States also did not start breeding until around this time.

As in other groups of birds, a migratory behavior pattern has evolved in adaptation to special environmental conditions. More precise information is not, however, available as yet, since only comparatively few birds have been ringed. Blue-winged Grass Parakeets, Orange-billed Grass Parakeets, and Swift Parakeets migrate in the fall from Tasmania via the Bass Strait to the Australian mainland, presumably to evade the extreme winter temperatures in their breeding range. Similar migrations, between Mexico and the southern USA, are known in respect to the Thick-billed Parakeet. Varieties that occur high in the mountains descend to lower altitudes with the onset of the cold season (northern race of the Austral Conure, Mountain Parakeet, Slaty-headed Parakeet). Not to be confused with these regular migrations is the roaming of many Australian Broad-tails or Rosellas that usually occur during a prolonged drought. Often these birds may be absent from their former breeding ranges for years. Budgerigars are well

adapted to these changing conditions. When roaming the countryside, they settle down in any area that provides food after rainfalls and proceed to breed there.

As a result of human intervention, the habitats of many species have decreased. In individual cases, albeit unintentionally, the living conditions of some species have been improved and their distribution and increase promoted. Due to the clearing of forests near the coast, the habitats of steppe-dwelling species have been expanded. Artificial irrigation and the provision of watering places for grazing livestock enables many parakeets to settle, for the whole year, in those areas in which they had previously only been able to live for limited periods. Grain fields and fruit plantations offer additional food resources. This fact has, however, led to many species developing into agricultural pests.

Enemies, dangers, and protective measures
The most important natural enemies of parakeets, apart from parasites, are probably reptiles, birds of prey, and large and small beasts of prey. None of these carnivorous enemies has ever threatened the existence of a species, or even that of a population. It was only human intervention that upset this balanced situation between the parakeets and their enemies. In Australia, the ground-dwelling Night Parakeets and Ground Parakeets were severely decimated by introduced foxes and feral dogs and cats, as well as by brush fires. The European starlings that have become naturalized in Australia have, in many localities, developed into serious rivals for nesting places—and not just of the smaller species of parrots. Even Galahs occasionally get driven out of their breeding cavities by starlings.

Most at risk, due to the progressive destruction of natural landscapes, are the woodland-dwelling species. Birds of the genus *Cyanoramphus*, native to New Zealand, are threatened by the destruction of forests, as are the Rose-ringed Parakeets from the island of Mauritius and many other species as well. The Masked Parakeet from the Fiji Islands was seriously reduced by mongooses that had been returned to the wild. The Orange-billed Grass Parakeet

The parakeet standing erect is *Pyrrhura molinae restricta* while the squatting conure is *Pyrrhura frontalis chiripepe*. Photo by Fred Harris.

from southeast South Australia is affected by a shortage of nesting trees. A few species were also threatened by the uncontrolled animal trade.

The parakeets invading agricultural land, often in huge flocks, are frequently controlled by drastic methods. In South America, control measures are directed mostly against the Monk Parakeet, which becomes rather troublesome in areas where cereals are grown on a vast scale; its large nests, constructed from twigs, are even destroyed by fire. In Australia, even protected species are rarely affected by the conservation measures. On the other hand, the export of animals of any species, apart from very few exceptions, has been strictly prohibited for 20 years. The release of certain numbers of birds of unprotected species would not endanger stocks and might put an end to the smuggling of these birds, which are highly sought after in Europe and the USA.

Species of parakeets that are particularly at risk have been incorporated in the list of internationally protected species. The following species are under strict protection and can now only be exported from their native countries in very exceptional cases:

  Yellow-fronted Parakeet;
  Red-fronted Parakeet;
  Night Parakeet;
  Ground Parakeet;
  Orange-bellied Grass Parakeet;
  Golden-shouldered Parakeet (including Hooded Parakeet);
  Paradise Parakeet;
  Rose-ringed Parakeet;
  Blue-throated Conure;
  Golden Conure;
  Thick-billed Parakeet.

In accordance with a resolution made at the International Conference on Species Protection in June 1981, all parrots not already included in List I (species that are particularly at risk) are entered on List II of protected species. Only three species—Budgerigar, Cockatiel, and Rose-ringed Parakeet—form exceptions to this rule. The export of all other varieties is dependent on special permission from the relevant authority in the country of origin. Since certain species, among them some large parakeets, continue to be regarded as agricultural pests in their native range and to be persecuted accordingly, one cannot entirely approve of this resolution. In fact, not all countries agreed to it.

National regulations banning the export of the Australian and New Zealand species mentioned have already been in force for many years. The international agreement is intended as an additional safeguard to prevent the trading of animals that have been illegally exported from their native countries.

Due to the progressive reduction and destruction of the birds' environments, the lists of endangered species will rapidly grow longer. Unfortunately, no international agreement exists to stop the main causes of the decline in numbers affecting the majority of wild animals. More than ever before, it is the duty of every responsible bird keeper to contribute to the preservation of as many species as possible by propagating the birds in his care.

It is highly likely that cages and aviaries already contain more Turquoise Grass Parakeets (for example) than are found in the birds' Australian home. However, individual parakeet fanciers are already losing interest in certain species, particularly where the sale of animals bred in captivity is failing to bring expected rewards. Bird keepers who consistently describe themselves as idealists should not be guided by such mercenary considerations. A pressing and wonderful task for all bird fancier associations is to give top priority to planned breeding so that the species are preserved.

Habits

The family of parrots has remarkably uniform characteristics, which are not only physical but also concern its social behavior. All species are gregarious, but what form the social links take can vary from one species to another. Always of significance, in this respect, is the environmental situation. Impressive flocks of Budgerigars fly en masse in search of water and areas that might provide food. Outside the breeding season, many species

Color mutations of *Psephotus haematonotus*, the Red-rumped Parakeet from southeastern Australia. Besides other differences, the females have yellow bills while the males have blue-grey bills. Photo by Harry V. Lacey.

form flocks and assemble in specific roosting trees at night. In such groups, individual animals can function as sentries. Some observations have also been made on individual pairs that retain their bond within the large group. More detailed information on the social structure within such massive assemblages is not yet available.

The flocks of Superb Parakeets are small, and their composition as to the sex and age of the birds varies with the season. The members of such small groups know one another, as can be deduced from a number of observations on social defensive action. The Monk Parakeets living free at the Institute for Behavioral Research, on the Wilhelminenberg in Vienna, reacted to the calls of fear uttered by a member of the group (for instance, when a bird was being netted) by immediately advancing on the bird catcher to within one meter of him. The corresponding calls by Monk Parakeets that did not belong to the group were ignored. Similar examples are also known with regard to other species. Reports exist, for instance, on the defensive behavior in the Varied Lorikeet and in the Peach-faced Lovebird.

A great deal of information is available on the mating behavior of parrots; many such observations have been made of parrots living in captivity. Polygamy has only been proved in the New Zealand Kea. All other species live monogamously, with some appearing to mate for life. When keeping Monk Parakeets, Cockatiels, Nanday Conures, and Maroon-bellied Conures in groups, I observed that the birds remained mated to the same partner for years.

Feeding of the partner and mutual preening demonstrate the bonding between a pair. Apart from copulation, there is no opportunity for closer contact between two individuals than direct feeding from beak to beak. In all social creatures, including man, the offering of food is valued as a positive sentiment that breaks down the contact-inhibiting barriers between members of the same species. In parrots, mutual feeding is of particular importance during the incubation period and when the young are being reared. Incubating is usually done exclusively by the hen, who only leaves the nest very briefly in order to defecate. Her food is supplied to her by the cock. After hatching she provides the young with food the male has supplied. A little later the cock will also feed his young.

For better comprehension of the birds' digestive process, let us take a brief look at the morphological and physiological facts. When food is consumed, it initially stays inside the crop, an anterior protrusion of the gullet which is present on the left and right. The food soaks, expands and is predigested, due to the effect of saliva and presumably drinking water as well, but most particularly to the enzymatic gastric juice rising up from the glandular stomach. Immediately before being passed to the partner, the pap is propelled upwards out of the crop by means of voluntary muscular action, accompanied by a violent jerking of the head. The beaks of the two animals clasp one another in such a way that a connection is formed and the food can get inside the oral cavity of the partner. Nestlings trigger the feeding behavior of the parents by uttering begging calls and probably also by means of tactile stimuli; in fledged young birds, the conspicuous begging movements are also of great importance. In a crouching position, the head slightly raised, young Monk Parakeets flap their wings, whereby a particularly striking optical effect is achieved by the splaying of the primaries. The feeding of the female by the male does not begin with egg-laying but constitutes an important component of courtship. After introductory action, such as courtship flights (Cockatoos, Cockatiel) or song (many Broad-tails), other forms of behavior follow which strengthen the bond between the partners, the most important being mutual feeding. This is always initiated by the male, whose regurgitating movements often induce the female to immediately adopt the copulatory position.

Of particular interest is a behavior which resembles that seen in mutual feeding but which occurs outside the breeding season, and at the end of which no feeding actually takes place, the introductory head jerking also being omitted from the ritual. The beaks of the two partners clasp one another

This young Budgerigar can be recognized by the bars on its head. As the bird get older, the stripes disappear. There are more Budgerigars in captivity than in Australia. Budgerigars are probably the most popular cage birds. Photo by Vince Serbin.

as in feeding, but the action is purely symbolic. It is significant that this type of behavior can be observed particularly where squabbles occur within a group. In Monk Parakeets, which often attack other members of the group, two partners employ this behavior to assure one another of their mutual sympathy.

Mutual grooming has been observed in many of the higher vertebrates that live socially and probably had a purely functional significance at its origin. Preening, however, does not result in cleaning of the plumage but rather in a tidying up of the feathers, the removal of skin and feather parasites, or the mechanical peeling off of the feather sheaths during the molt. Mutual preening is usually confined to the head and neck region, i.e., to parts of the body that are readily accessible only to the partner. Conures often scratch the partner's whole body and even pull the latter's tail feathers through the beak.

Such actions become possible only after the dissolution of barriers that normally separate individuals. Hence they will predominantly occur between parents and their children (the initiative taken solely by the parents), between siblings, and between animals that are mated to each other (in captivity these animals need not necessarily be of the opposite sex or even belong to the same species). This behavior, therefore, not only serves the purpose of personal hygiene but also functions as a gesture of tenderness designed to strengthen the social bond. Tame parrots display this tender behavior even towards the human friend. A tame Grey Parrot and a tame Hyacinth Macaw were known to scratch my eyebrows from time to time (structurally, of course, the eyebrows resemble the head plumage of the parrot more than anything else). Such tame birds also like being scratched by their human keeper and invite these attentions by coming close, lowering the head, and slightly ruffling their feathers.

The close bond between spouses can be demonstrated by Macaws, who have been known to follow hunters considerable distances after a partner had been shot down and its body taken away. When the explorer Lumholtz shot the male of a pair of Paradise Parakeets, the female at first flew off to a tree but then came back to the male and lifted up its beak. Later she brought grass seeds and put them in front of the male. Again she lifted his head, trampled about on his body, and once more flew off to perch among the branches of a tree. I observed similar behavior in Maroon-bellied Conures. The female of a pair that had been living in my care for a considerable time died suddenly. The widower sat by his dead mate and tried to scratch her. Only when I removed the dead bird, two hours later, did this behavior come to an end.

If two partners grow this close, it is not surprising that the widowed animal will often take a great deal of time to make contact with another animal; in most cases, the animals will dislike each other at first. It would seem feasible, therefore, that a gradually increasing mutual affection is of considerable significance in the mating behavior of parrots. Thus the keepers of such birds often only succeed in matching a pair after having made a number of attempts. It should also give them the empathy not to sever existing partnerships unless it is absolutely unavoidable.

As can be seen, the observation of the social behavior of large parakeets and their allies is by no means uninteresting. Yet the many reports on keeping these birds that appear in specialized literature almost always give scant attention to this topic.

Reproduction
Nearly all species are cavity breeders. Strictly speaking, this applies to the Monk Parakeet as well, although it does not normally nest in a hollow tree trunk or branch but uses brush wood to build its own breeding cave. As opposed to the well-known nests of European Woodpeckers, the breeding caves of parakeets are not always located in vertical tree trunks but can also be found in horizontal or slanted decaying branches. Therefore nest boxes don't necessarily need to be of the "grandfather clock" type. Some species build their nests in termite constructions and will not accept conventional nest boxes in the aviary. In such cases, supply an artificial termite nest

Millions of Budgerigars are bred annually, all over the world. Consequently, many color varieties appear. There are literally dozens of color varieties which are genetically fixed and available at petshops. Photo by Harry V. Lacey.

composed of compressed chunks of leaf mold or a wooden box. It should be open at the front and packed with trampled loam.

Some species nest in rock crevices or choose loamy walls as their breeding caves. Night Parakeets and Ground Parakeets breed on the ground in a nest constructed from grass blades. Such observations made in the animals' natural environment serve to provide ideas for improving the keeping conditions of the captive birds. Some parakeets are adaptable—they breed in the open as well as in tree cavities, rock crevices, or decaying wooden posts. Little, if any, nesting material is collected. The eggs lie on the damp, rotten wood at the bottom of the cavities. This must be taken into consideration when it comes to breeding in captivity.

For some species, including the Conures, the nest can (to use an expression coined by Prof. Hediger) "have the significance of a home of the first order," not just during the breeding season but all the year round. Even the young that have already fledged return to it regularly to roost. The free-flying Monk Parakeets on the Wilhelminenberg in Vienna lived in their nest chambers in fours or fives in the winter, presumably in adaptation to the low temperatures. In the spring, each pair moved back into its own cavity.

The number of broods per annum is determined by the environmental situation. Species from tropical ranges often have two broods, but if food resources are adequate after the rain falls, Budgerigars and Eastern Rosellas may also have two successive broods. By and large, however, the Australian species only manage a single brood since the heat of the summer very quickly kills off all of the food plants.

The eggs of all species are white. Between two and seven are laid as a rule, generally at 48-hour intervals. Some species deposit one egg per day; in a few others the intervals between laying span several days. As with many other birds, the eggs are usually laid in the morning. In many cases the incubating starts once the first egg has appeared, which results in different hatching times and later in different sizes among the young. In the domestic hen, with regard to which detailed research has been

carried out, every egg is fertilized 72 hours (on an average) after copulation. The male sperm cells can, however, remain fully fertile for over two weeks inside the hen's oviduct. Normally, several copulations take place during the laying period. It is highly likely that similar conditions prevail in the parrots.

The incubation period extends over 18 (Budgerigar) to 28 days (Thick-billed Parakeet). A few days before hatching, the egg tooth, a hard calciferous structure, is formed at the tip of the upper mandible. By this means, the chick cuts through the egg membrane and later the egg shell, which has already been slightly weakened. The first down feathers, if present, occur where the tips of the contour feathers will eventually form. The second down plumage, generally light gray and dense, precedes the growth of the contour feathers. The young large parakeets open their eyes on or around the tenth day after hatching.

The incubating hen is supplied with food by the male. Truly shared incubation, as in the Cockatoos, is likely to occur only in the Cockatiel (with the cock sitting during the day). Reports on shared incubation in Conures are probably based on inaccurate observation. While male Conures often spend time in the nest with the brooding hen, they do not, in fact, sit on the eggs.

As soon as the young have hatched, they are fed by the hen, who is supplied with food by the cock. The male does not feed his children directly until approximately two weeks later. Once the young parakeets have fledged, they are fed predominantly, often exclusively, by their father.

Soon after fledging, the young parakeets often display typically puberal forms of behavior. In some species the younger siblings or the young of the subsequent brood are fed. First attempts at copulation, which are not, however, preceded by courtship, are made. Monk Parakeets, at this developmental stage, show an interest in nesting material. They gnaw off twigs and pull them apart.

Feeding habits in the wild
In the majority of cases, it would be wrong to conclude that the diet birds receive in captivity is necessarily the same as the food

Mueller's Parrot, *Tanygnathus sumatranus*, from the Philippines and nearby islands. Photo by Stan Henschel.

available to them in the wild. The standard food for parrots (i.e., sunflower seeds) has little if any part to play in the nutrition of wild birds, whereas grass seeds and man's contribution of various cereals (which the birds, however, prefer to eat in a half-ripened, milky white condition) are very

A pair of Cockatiels, *Nymphicus hollandicus,* preening. Photo by H. Reinhard.

important. Although the strong beak enables the parakeets to get into hard-shelled fruits, soft fruits, blossoms, buds, and leaves are preferred. Animal food is likely to be of greater significance than is commonly supposed. In most cases, examination of the stomach contents of wild parakeets that had been shot revealed the presence of insects at various stages of development.

In seed-eating species, the ingestion of sand and small stones, to aid the digestive processes inside the gizzard, is of great importance. Sand was found in the gizzards of the following species: Yellow Rosella, Mallee Ringneck Parakeet, Red-rumped Parakeet, Blue-winged Grass Parakeet, Elegant Grass Parakeet, Rock Grass Parakeet, Swift Parakeet, Budgerigar. Charcoal was found in the stomachs of Adelaide Rosella, Yellow Rosella, Eastern Rosella, Mallee Ringneck Parakeet, and Red-rumped Parakeet. Charcoal is readily available to the Australian species because of the frequent forest fires and brush fires. Its therapeutic action in cases of digestive upsets is well known.

Life expectancy
The question of the life expectancy of an animal species can seldom be answered satisfactorily. How old parrots get in their natural habitat is virtually unknown. The prerequisite for the clarification of this question would be extensive ringing, which so far has not been undertaken. Furthermore, so many factors affect the life span of birds in the wild that few if any individuals reach their potential maximum age. With regard to birds kept in captivity, it is known that the larger species normally attain a greater age than the small species. Budgerigars live to an average age of 10–12, but I have also come across several 17-year-old birds and even one individual that lived to the age of 20. The maximum age limit of Green-rumped Parrotlets is thought to be about 15 years. Most species of large parakeets can be expected to live an average of 20 years. A life span of over 30 years was reached by Alexandrine Parakeets, Derbyan Parakeets, and Jandaya Conures.

A wild-colored adult male Cockatiel, *Nymphicus hollandicus.* Photo by Ralph Kaehler.

Keeping

The outdoor aviary

THE INDOOR PORTION Many large parakeets inhabit open savannahs with a sparse growth of trees; therefore, they are mostly good fliers used to covering large distances quickly. As opposed to some species of parrots, whose habitat is the tropical rain forest where they merely fly from one tree to another in their search for food, the Australian parakeets are forced to constantly change their location and to bridge long distances, not only to get food but also to find water. Consequently, they are poorly suited for life in the cage and require a spacious outdoor aviary if they are to feel healthy and happy.

As we shall see, the keeping of large parakeets in mixed aviaries is only a limited possibility. A description of that type of accommodation is superfluous. The mixed aviary is suitable only for display, not for breeding, and must be spacious enough to enable the individual specimen to find somewhere to hide if necessary. With the exception of collective breeders, each pair demands and defends its own territory. To build a flight room on that scale is too expensive for most hobbyists.

Since most large parakeet fanciers will also wish to propagate their birds, there is no real alternative to keeping the latter in pairs and providing each pair with its own aviary. To save space and money, several individual boxes can be arranged in a row, producing a large mixed aviary with separate compartments. The size of the individual compartments depends mainly on what species will be kept. Generally speaking, the length of the outdoor aviary represents the straight-ahead flying space and should not be less than 6 meters. Anyone who wants to keep large species, such as the Australian King Parakeet, and has sufficient space should not hesitate to increase the length to 8 or even 10 meters. For the indoor aviary, a length of 2 meters is sufficient. The width of each individual enclosure is not as critical, since large parakeets usually fly straight ahead. It should not be less than 1 meter, however, and 1.5 meters would be wide enough even for large species.

The problem of access into the individual enclosures can be solved in various ways. The simplest solution would be an exterior door leading into the first enclosure, with another door on its opposite wall leading to the next, etc., thus facilitating access from one enclosure to another. The disadvantage of this arrangement is that all the enclosures must be passed through to get

The typical aviary consists of an indoor portion designed to offer protection from the elements, along with an outdoor portion enclosed by wire mesh.

into the one at the end. Inevitably, every single pair must be disturbed in the process. This is a serious drawback, particularly during the breeding season, because some pairs cannot cope with constant disturbances of this nature and may end up deserting their brood. If, for reasons of space, this arrangement is necessary, a safety porch outside the first door is strongly recommended. This can consist of a simple wire box that enables the entrance door to be closed before entering the room in which the parakeets are accommodated. Many a hobbyist has lost a valuable bird because he did not think his birds would be able to get past him and escape through the door!

Undoubtedly a better solution is a so-called feeding passage, either at the front, going past all the individual enclosures, or at the back, leading off the closed room. Both solutions have their advantages and

This aviary is constructed so that there is space for three flight-and-shelter units.

disadvantages. If the feeding passage is at the front, it is imperative to provide additional roofing so that the food is kept dry. Furthermore, the extra layer of wire netting obstructs observation. On the other hand, it is an advantage in the winter, as the birds can easily be moved from the outdoor to the indoor shelter so that the flight windows can be closed for the night.

Although the feeding passage in the indoor room is the best solution, it is also the most expensive. The birdhouse needs to be at least 1 meter deeper to make this passage possible. A box which is closed on all sides, including that facing the passage,

is recommended. A small, glass-covered spy hole, through which the birds can be observed without being disturbed, can be built into the box. The food can be supplied through a flap from the passage so that disturbances caused by entering the birds' environment can largely be avoided. Particularly in the winter, it is very convenient to offer food and water in the sheltered indoor room.

To be prepared for all eventualities, one can fit additional connecting doors (made of wire) in the outdoor aviaries so that one has access from there as well. This is particularly advantageous when it comes to cleaning the individual compartments.

The outdoor portion
Let us start with the foundations. Concrete foundations that sink at least 80 cm into the ground, having a minimum breadth of 10 cm, are ideal. These are certain to keep out mice and other rodents and will not be affected by frost. For added security, galvanized wire netting of a narrow mesh can be installed over the ground and covered with a layer of sand or, better still, fine gravel about 20 cm deep. Before that is done the earth must be removed and the wire connected to the foundations so that no loopholes develop. Despite all of these measures, one will never be able to keep mice out of the aviaries altogether, but one can effectively keep out rats and moles as well as the weasel that comes in their wake. Rats are more of a danger, to the brood in particular, than is commonly supposed. If one uses ready-made concrete tiles for the foundation, protective wiring becomes imperative. More recently, plastic tiles have also come into use for the foundations. Where these are employed, it is important not to use them as a supportive element in the construction of the aviary. However, if buried deeply enough, they too are durable and secure.

Supporting frames for the wire netting can consist of squared timber, angle iron, or tubular metal. Undoubtedly, the cheapest and easiest building material to work with is wood. The lumber used for the framework must be durable, the length of the edges measuring at least 8 cm to withstand the weight of snow in the winter.

Vertical props, arranged at maximum intervals of 2 meters, provide necessary support, making it possible to use rolls of wire that are 1 meter broad. These are nailed down on all sides and pulled tight in the middle by means of binding wire so that the wire netting has the correct tension. In every case, the wood should be given a protective coating of paint, which comes in many different types and shades. Avoid all paints containing lead, as parakeets gnaw at the wood. Ingestion of toxic lead compounds will, sooner or later, inevitably result in their death. Harmless synthetic enamels are widely available.

For all its advantages, wood has two definite drawbacks. As mentioned, the larger species, in particular, enjoy gnawing at it, weakening not only the transverse strength but also reducing the life span of the frames. Over and above that, these chewed frames are not exactly a delight to the eye. Chewing can be reduced by nailing on strips of sheet metal, but it can never be prevented entirely. Wooden outdoor aviaries rarely withstand the exposure to the weather for longer than ten years. The life span can, however, be prolonged slightly by nailing strips of plastic onto the surface or by inserting an iron girder between the wood and the concrete foundations, which enables the timber to dry out; these precautions should also be taken with the underside. The foundations should be slanted so that the rain water can drain off easily. If one has the necessary skill, one can even use round timbers. While more difficult to work with, these generally last several years longer than squared timbers. The latter should be planed to become slightly more resistant.

The use of angle irons, of course, ensures that one has an aviary for life, provided one is not stingy with paint, removes rust, and applies a coat of enamel paint at least every other year. The latter is equally essential with regard to wood. The iron aviary is more expensive and requires greater manual skill, but it looks better and is more advantageous in every respect. If one drills small holes into the sides of the angle irons, the wire netting can conveniently be attached by means of wire ties. A particularly secure method of fastening the wire mesh is to screw a flat iron on to the inside of the angle, with the netting wedged between the two. I would like to point out once more that no medium or paints that contain lead can be used, not even for the undercoat of the iron parts. If one wants to avoid having to deal with rust, there remains only the alternative of building the framework from galvanized tubular bars, which do not rust, look very good, and are readily obtainable everywhere. While this is the most expensive method, it is also the most rewarding in the long run. What is saved on maintenance over a prolonged period more than makes up for the initial outlay.

Different kinds of suitable wire netting are available. It is important that the width of the mesh makes it impossible even for young mice to squeeze through; the thickness of the wire should not be less than 1 mm. Ordinary wire netting is rarely able to withstand the strong beaks of large parakeets. Best suited, therefore, is quadratic wire mesh, spot welded and galvanized, which can be purchased in wire thicknesses of 1 mm and upwards and mesh widths of 10 mm and above. The ideal choice would be a thickness of 1.2 mm, as this would eliminate every element of risk.

If the entire outdoor section including the wire netting is painted with a green synthetic enamel, it looks very pleasing and displays up the birds considerably better than unpainted mesh. Plastic coverings on wire and tubular bars should be avoided, as the birds quickly nibble at the plastic and the exposed wire not only rusts but tends to be thinner as well.

The birdhouse
Birdhouses come in all variations. Before supplying a detailed description, therefore, it is necessary to make it clear what types of birdhouses are suitable for the breeder and fancier of large parakeets. Taking the term "birdhouse" in its general sense, it can be understood to include glass flight halls such as those in the Walsrode Bird Park and in some other zoological gardens. Such constructions are designed purely for exhibition purposes. Equally unsuitable for the breeder of large parakeets is a small

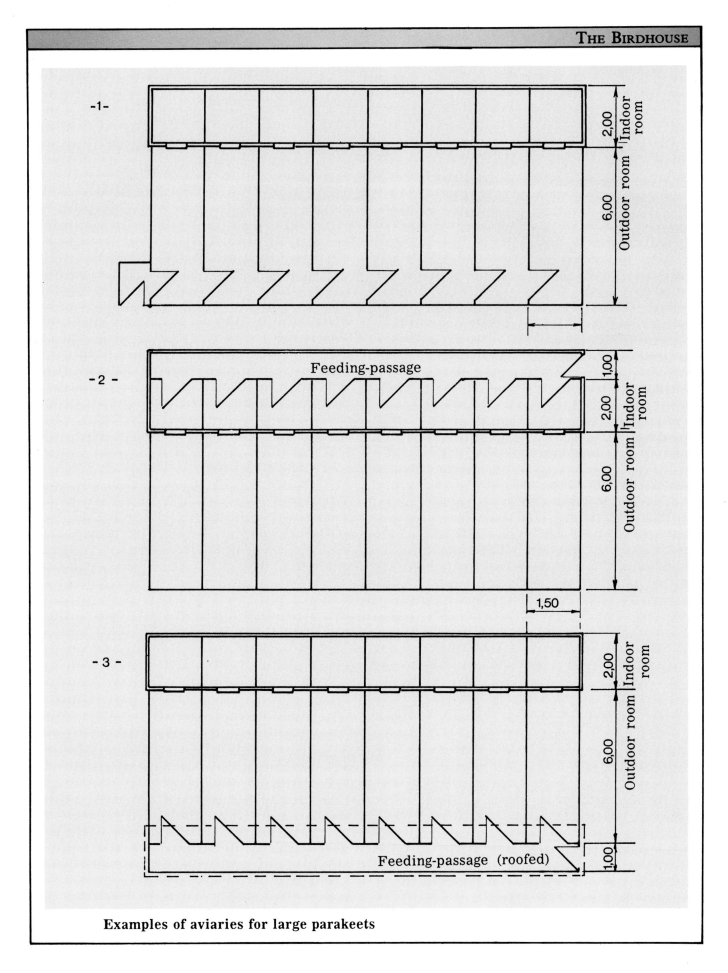

Examples of aviaries for large parakeets

round pavilion in the garden which houses a few birds. What is needed for breeding is a birdhouse or a large bird room that has been divided into a number of individual compartments, making it possible to keep the birds in pairs. While this type of enclosed house gives the breeder control over the temperature, there are often problems with daylight. If the birds are dependent on artificial illumination, they lack the ultraviolet rays that are vital for parakeets. Furthermore, an enclosed room looks rather sterile and rarely has the necessary dimensions that are required by large parakeets.

Bird rooms are well suited for waxbills or species that originate from truly tropical regions. In these cases, it is also possible to keep birds of several different species together, with an added opportunity to decorate with green and tropical plants, cacti, etc., so that the room overall is harmonious to the eye. When large parakeets are involved, none of these options can be considered since, with the exception of a few species, the birds would destroy the vegetation in no time at all.

An enclosed birdhouse or, subject to certain reservations, bird room can only be recommended for the acclimatization of newly imported parakeets. But when is this situation likely to arise where the ordinary fancier is concerned?

Over the course of the last few decades, it was invariably the combination of the enclosed room and the outdoor aviary that proved the most suitable birdhouse for large parakeets. It is essential, in every case, that solid foundations are provided. The outer foundations should at least reach into a frostfree depth, i.e., not less than 80 cm deep. To prevent invasion by rodents from below, a firm floor is required, either of concrete or of closely fitted stones (bricks, concrete tiles, etc.). Below the flooring there should be a layer of coarse gravel or cinder, at least 20 cm deep, to prevent excessive dampness. Heat insulation from below by means of polystyrene tiles, plastic sheets, etc., while having some advantages, is not absolutely essential.

Once this kind of foundation has been laid, one must decide what kind of building material to use for the actual birdhouse. As already mentioned in respect to the outdoor aviary, the most suitable accommodations in which to keep large parakeets consist of rows of individual compartments. This means that inside the birdhouse there must be enclosed compartments that are completely separated from the neighboring compartments. Merely separating each section by means of wire mesh is highly inadvisable. We shall therefore assume that the individual compartments are separated from each other by means of wooden boards with mortise and spring, by means of plastic or hardboard, or by means of a brick wall. The latter, rough cast or consisting of pointed Dutch clinkers, is of course the most elegant solution as well as being the most expensive. On the other hand, since heat insulation is not required between individual compartments, wooden or plastic boards would do equally well. The latter should, however, be fitted without gaps or cracks so that drafts and small vermin cannot enter.

In a heated birdhouse, the outside walls and the roof are crucial. If hollow or honeycomb blocks are used, there will not be any problems; the building is protected against the cold, heat, and vermin; is reasonably burglarproof; and is not only pleasing to look at but will require little in the way of maintenance and repairs for years to come. A birdhouse consisting entirely of a wooden construction is also possible. In that case, it is, however, always advisable to have double walls on the outside areas of the house; alternatively, an inner lining of the outside wall, at a distance of 5 cm, can be built so that a cavity is formed, which can be filled with insulating material.

Building materials for insulating purposes come in so many varieties nowadays that one will always be able to find something suitable. For the inner lining of a wooden outside wall, one can use ordinary pressed or hardboard tiles, or even asbestos cement tiles (Eternit, etc.). A double wall along the outside areas is not only needed to protect against cold and heat but to keep the birds inside the enclosure as well since, in the long run, wood is not a serious obstacle to the beaks

The Ring-necked Parakeet, *Psittacula krameri,* has the most extensive distribution of any parakeet. Photo by Harry V. Lacey.

of parakeets; the birds can often escape from uninsulated enclosures before the damage has been noticed.

When constructing the roof, a double layer is also advisable. Here, in fact, good insulation is absolutely essential for the birds' health. For that reason alone one should never opt for a glass roof. Suitable roofing materials include bricks,

A design of this sort has proved to be the most convenient arrangement for breeding Budgerigars, *Melopsittacus undulatus*.

corrugated asbestos cement (Eternit), as well as roofing felt, if this is put on top of a solid wooden roof that has been insulated. From below, the roof can be lined with hardboard or some other material of one's choice. The construction of the roof requires care from beginning to end. Trying to cut corners here usually leads to problems later on. Rafters that were too weak have resulted in many a roof collapsing in the winter under the weight of the snow. If one is lacking in experience, it is best to seek the advice of an expert.

The front of the birdhouse should be provided with a large window that leads into the outdoor aviary. This window can be taken out or left open in the summer and kept closed in the winter. In addition, a flight hole is required, with a flap that can also be closed. Remote control from the feeding passage, while not strictly necessary, is practical, particularly in the winter when one wants the birds to get used to spending the nights indoors. This flap should always open downwards to exclude the possibility of accidental closure. It is essential for the birds to be able to recognize the window; otherwise they may fly into it. The best solution is to use wired glass, with the wire being clearly visible.

Before the construction on these birdhouses can begin, it is necessary in most areas to obtain a building permit. The reader is urged, therefore, either to turn to an architect for advice or to go straight to the local zoning department.

Bear in mind that each pair of a species must have unlimited access to the indoor and outdoor section and must have an enclosed room at its disposal into which it can retreat; not only from unfavorable weather but where it is also invisible to its enemies, real or imaginary, and can rest peacefully away from other members of its species.

Planting shrubs around the outside of the aviary helps to make the birds feel more secure as well as making the whole construction look more attractive. All large parakeets are valuable pets. Anyone who is not willing or able to provide his pets— living creatures entrusted to our care—with optimal accommodation should refrain from keeping large parakeets.

Roosting site and perch

When the outdoor aviary is ready, the next question is where to fit branches and rods in order to offer suitable perches and roosts to the birds. Nailing on a few branches, decoratively but indiscriminately, is not the answer. The birds must have adequate flying space, unrestricted by a tangle of branches. It is sufficient to fit a perching rod at each end of the outdoor section; these rods should be fixed about 30–50 cm from the wall and wire netting respectively and in the top third of the enclosure. The best are hardwood rods derived from broadleaf trees such as oak, beech, or apple. Less suitable are conifers such as spruce, pine, etc., which contain too much resin. It is not necessary to remove the bark, as the parakeets like nibbling at it.

Dowels or round timbers that have been turned are not as good as naturally shaped branches, since they force the birds to continuously grip the same thickness, causing the gripping organs to suffer a certain loss of mobility as a result. After all, in its natural environment the bird also flies onto branches of varying thickness. Furthermore, a rod that has been turned is difficult for the parakeet to grip when it lands. For this reason, metal rods are even less appropriate. In the winter these have the added disadvantage of almost inevitably causing frostbite of the toes. Again, the most appropriate perch is a natural branch. Be certain that the wood has not been sprayed with chemicals, especially wood taken from branches of fruit trees; one cannot stop parakeets from gnawing at all the wood they can get their beaks on.

Perches should be replaced at least once a year. If this is done more often, so much the better. To make the replacing easier, wedge-shaped pieces of sheet metal can be fixed to the wire or wall so that the branch or rod can simply be inserted and is kept in position by the wedge shape, irrespective of its thickness.

Particular attention and care must be devoted to the roosting place. Ofttimes one wonders why a bird is sitting about with fluffed up feathers when there is no reason to suppose that it might be ill; very often this is due to an inadequate or unfavorable roosting place. Every bird endeavors to sit as high up as possible. If the perching rods in the outdoor aviary are placed higher than the ones indoors, no bird will voluntarily go indoors for the night. Usually it will hang suspended from the wire netting in some corner of the aviary, which is undesirable. There the bird is exposed to wind and rain, becoming vulnerable to cats or owls that may injure it from outside. In the winter there is particular danger of frostbite. It is, therefore, always best for the birds to spend the night in the indoor shelter, and this should be encouraged by installing the appropriate rods.

The indoor perches should be hung at right angles to the warm wooden wall so that the birds can lean against it. Walls that are cold or, worse still, damp should be insulated. The distance from the ceiling should be just sufficient to enable the birds to sit in an upright position, the rod being fixed as high up as possible. The roosting place and perch must not be exposed to any drafts whatsoever, not even minor ones coming through cracks in the wall. Drafts are always dangerous, particularly to roosting birds. Since parakeets have the convenient habit of always returning to their usual roosting place (this can easily be confirmed by the accumulation of droppings under the permanent roost), it is sufficient to shut the birds into the indoor shelter every night for one week to encourage them to establish their permanent roost there. Once they have grown used to this spot, no further measures are required. The windows or the flight hole can be left open again, especially during the summer, since the birds' day begins at sunrise.

Feeding place

The easiest but also the worst feeding method is to simply scatter the food on the ground. Although most species of parakeets prefer to look for their food on the ground, as this is what they do in their natural habitat, we know that this increases the risk of infection and particularly of worm infestation. If need be, one can scatter small quantities of food in the outdoor aviary during the breeding season from time to time. The dampness of the ground softens the seeds and might even cause them to germinate slightly, which is definitely an advantage. If they lie about for too long, however, they can grow moldy, which is a serious disadvantage. The aviary must always be clean if one occasionally throws a little food on the ground.

Another major drawback to feeding on the ground is that rodents are greatly attracted this way. It is therefore essential to make every major feeding place inaccessible to mice. This is certainly not guaranteed in the case of feeding houses or feeding boards that have been fixed to the wall. There are only two ways of keeping a feeding place relatively mouseproof: by fixing the feeding board to a wire suspended from the ceiling or by simply putting it on top of a tube well away from the walls. It is also important that there are no branches above the feeding tray, from which the mice can jump down or the food can become contaminated by the birds' feces. Cleanliness is the first commandment when it comes to feeding. Feeding places should, therefore, always be arranged in such a way that they are easy to clean.

If the feeding place consists of a wooden board, a landing platform should be fitted around the edges so that the bird does not land in the middle of the food and knock it off or cause it to scatter. Hard food is best served separately in round earthenware or china bowls. There are some very suitable earthenware bowls on the market that have a narrow margin at the top. Tin cans are inadvisable; they rust and can cause serious injuries to the toes. Plastic bowls are not well suited but are more acceptable than tin cans. Earthenware bowls are easily cleaned in hot water so that pathogenic organisms are killed, and they are less likely to get knocked over than lighter plastic bowls.

The water bowl does not belong on the feeding board, as placing it there exposes the food to unnecessary dampness. The birds like bathing and splashing about, so the food would inevitably get wet. Water bowls should be large but not deep and should always be placed on the ground.

Mixed housing

During the breeding season and often over a number of years, large parakeets live in pairs. They need a breeding territory that is invariably more extensive than the space they can be allotted in an aviary. Consequently, the cocks in particular fight each other until one of them is killed. Of necessity, the fancier and aviculturist will therefore prefer to keep them in pairs rather than in communal accommodation. This applies mostly to birds of the same species. Birds of different species, provided certain conditions are met, may tolerate one another, particularly when the other species is not regarded as a rival and there is adequate space available.

For instance, the Cockatiel gets on exceedingly well with the Budgerigar. The Budgerigar's behavior represents an exception since, being a colonial breeder, this species is suitable for communal housing in any case. It is, however, not possible to keep different species of the genus *Platycercus* (Rosellas) together. *P.e. ceciliae* and the Pale-headed Rosella are so closely related that their hybridization presents no difficulty whatsoever. Consequently there is direct competition between the two and absolute intolerance. This can go so far as to make it impossible even to keep them in separate compartments that are next to each other. Although this cannot result in fatal injuries, damage to the toes and bleeding heads are not unusual, and general harmony of the aviary is often upset. During the breeding season the squabbling never ends, and this makes the successful raising of young birds very difficult. Therefore, communal housing for these birds should, not be contemplated if one intends to propagate them successfully.

Matters are different where immature birds are concerned. A large flight of young parakeets of the same and of different species can be associated without any great risk. The prerequisite is plenty of space, which allows weaker specimens to hide when necessary. It is, however, essential to keep such a mixed population under constant observation. There is always the possibility of a "scapegoat" being chosen

In captivity, the male Superb Parakeet, *Polytelis swainsonii,* will benefit from ample bathing facilities. Photo courtesy of Midori Shobo.

from among them, which will get attacked by everyone if it is not rescued and rehoused.

The aviculturist should go by this principle: one aviary for one pair. If one has several aviaries in a row, closely related species should be housed as far apart as possible. Speaking from practical experience, never house two species of the *Platycercus* group (Rosellas) next to one another. Suitable neighbors would be birds of the *Neophema* group (Grass Parakeets such as the Turquoise Grass Parakeet, Scarlet-chested Grass Parakeet, etc.). Birds of the *Polytelis* group (Regent Parakeet, Princess Parakeet), being peaceable species, can always be used as buffers and put between the aggressive species. The same applies, for example, to the South American Araini. Here, too, just as with the Asian *Psittacula* species, immediate housing in the same neighborhood should be avoided.

Agapornis species behave differently. Provided the aviaries are of sufficient size, one can even breed birds of the same species in communal conditions since these charming little Africans usually live gregariously in the wild. Although not colonial breeders in the strict sense of the word, they live and breed together in fairly close association.

When keeping these birds in communal accommodation, one should, wherever possible, stock the aviary with pairs only and put them all in at the same time. Animals that are added later are not always accepted. Single birds, particularly cocks, can disturb the community and the breeding process. Young birds which have become independent should be removed from the community before they attain sexual maturity. As not to lose track, it is advisable to ring the young birds when they are still in the nest. Later it will become impossible to distinguish them.

If you still wish, despite the restricted space, to set up a mixed aviary simply to enjoy a colorful assortment of birds, you must adhere to certain fundamental rules. Initially combine just one pair of parakeets, a few waxbills, and perhaps one pair of small pigeons. The ground can be livened up with a pair of small quails. Never associate parakeets and starlings with one another, since both are cavity breeders and will start squabbling when claiming their nesting hollow, if not before. The starlings, regardless of what species they belong to, usually emerge as the winners.

It goes without saying that large parakeets such as the Australian King Parakeet or Derbyan Parakeet are not always suited for this type of mixed community. Grass Parakeets (*Neophema* species) adapt very well to mixed aviaries, and, since they do not do any excessive gnawing, the aviary can even be planted with conifers. Cockatiels are very peaceable, as is the Plum-headed Parakeet. If the keeper is not concerned about breeding, there is no reason not to stock the mixed aviary with different parakeets, cocks only if possible. These should not belong to the same group of species; different Rosellas, for instance, should not be kept together.

Again, it is important to put all the birds into the aviary at the same time, if possible, so that none of the birds will have had a chance to establish a territory. Furthermore, the birds should not be put in at night but in the morning; this gives them sufficient time to become acclimatized. On the first and second days, it is particularly important to keep an extra eye on the birds so you can intervene if any serious fighting breaks out. A well-assorted collection is delightful to observe, and if some feathered singers are added as well, a small exotic world has been created.

Keeping free-flying birds

The reports that occasionally appear in journals about free-flying parrots must not make one forget that this form of keeping is only possible with regard to a few species and, even then, only if some quite specific conditions are met. Free flight all year round in most areas is feasible only for species that are genuinely resistant to cold weather. Another important prerequisite is the certainty that the birds will return to their permanent quarters year round. In this, virtually all the Rosellas are excluded, since, due to climatic influences and the

A female Blue-winged Grass Parakeet, *Neophema chrysostoma,* feeds her youngsters at the entrance to the nesting cavity. Photo by L. Robinson.

changing food supplies in the wild, they do not remain in one locality for any length of time. The South American Rosellas, which are more favorably placed ecologically and therefore stay in one locality are, with very few exceptions, not hardy enough to cope with our winters. This leaves only the possibility of periodic free flight during the warm season.

Another drawback to free flight is the damage that such parrots do to orchards throughout the year: buds, blossoms, and fruit at whatever stage of maturity fall victim to them. For this reason, virtually every attempt at allowing free flight to parakeets was only successful for a limited period. Such experiments are tolerated more readily if carried out by a research institute or a zoological garden rather than by private bird fanciers.

The species that is best suited for free flight all the year round is the Monk Parakeet (*Myiopsitta monachus*). It is so attached to its large colonial nest, which is constantly being repaired and extended, that it invariably returns to it even after excursions involving distances of over 5 kilometers. In the winter, the nest provides adequate shelter from wind and cold. At this time of year, the parakeets do not occupy the individual nest chambers in pairs but in bigger groups, as an additional protection against the cold. In extremely cold weather, rare excursions are confined to visits to the feeding places. According to my own observations, temperatures to as low as -25°C are tolerated without adverse effects in such conditions.

Before liberating the birds, wait until a larger group of Monk Parakeets has started nest building in the aviary. A further precaution is not to open the doors until there are young in the nest. Since the nests will now remain inhabited for a while, the timing is ideal, as the animals can be locked in again without difficulty at any time. Thereafter, however, the birds invariably choose their nesting site higher up in a treetop. This happened not only during the free flight experiment begun by myself in 1953, at the Institute for Comparative Behavioral Research on the Wilhelminenberg in Vienna, but also in 1974 on the Laaerberg in Vienna. The

feeding places must be adequately supplied; however, a loss of food through songbirds, mice, or squirrels needs to be allowed. Food shortage induces the Monk Parakeets to migrate.

Occasional free flight during the warm season is a possibility with regard to many species. Results are best if one exploits the bonding of parent animals to their offspring which are still in the nest. Young birds that have become independent should not be liberated, as they often have a very strong tendency to migrate. In practice it has repeatedly proved successful to release only one partner of a pair, initially enabling this bird to get back inside the enclosure through a basket-like opening. Several days later the other bird is given the opportunity to go out on orientation and acclimatization flights. After another few days, both birds are allowed out.

This kind of free flight was accomplished successfully with Grey-cheeked Parakeets (*Brotogeris pyrrhopterus*), Plain Parakeets (*Brotogeris tirica*), and Nanday Conures (*Nandayus nenday*). The Carolina Parakeets (*Conuropsis carolinensis*), which have since become extinct, were kept in free flight conditions on several occasions in the 19th century.

Exceptions to typical Budgerigar (*Melopstittacus undulatus*) behavior have been known, as successful free-flight experiments with these birds have been carried out; usually these birds migrate instantly. Dr. Schlapp from Sprendlingen was successful with free-flying Budgerigars for many years. They bred within a distance of up to 6 kilometers from where they had been released, even in the nest boxes of tits. A sudden invasion by Magpies resulted in a severe decimation, however.

The Crimson Rosella, *Platycercus elegans,* is a good example of a parakeet species that is notably inclined to gnaw and therefore must be amply provisioned with branches. Photo by Fritz Prenzel.

Feeding

Staple food

Individual species of birds select their nourishment from the rich palette that nature offers them. Just as variant as the species and genera themselves are their basic nutritional requirements. We can differentiate between two major categories: seed eaters and soft food eaters. Parakeets are predominantly seed eaters but by no means despise fruit or even animal food.

While the staple food the fancier offers his birds does not need to be identical to the food available in the wild, it should contain the same basic substances. This requirement is largely met by millet and canary seed, which are suitable for all parakeets. Both contain carbohydrates and proteins similar to the grass seeds that form the bulk of the diet in the wild. In addition, one offers sunflower seeds, which contain oil and are an absolutely essential component of the birds' basic diet. With these three seed varieties, one is able to feed every parakeet or, rather, to keep it alive for a certain length of time. They constitute the staple or hard food, in addition to which should be provided suitable supplementary food.

The different kinds of food are best served separately in individual bowls or automatic food dispensers, to which the birds should have ready access at all times. As birds have a tendency to drop the empty husks back into the food bowl, one needs to remove the husks every day by blowing them out of the bowl.

Other suitable seeds are niger, hemp, and whole oats. Niger and hemp have a high oil and calorie content and are fattening. Hence these seeds are only offered on cold winter days or during the molt for extra energy. A strict regulation of the dose is advisable in every case.

When purchasing the staple food, it is of the utmost importance to be certain it is in perfect condition. Wherever possible, it should be derived from the latest harvest,

Parakeets may be supplied a seed mixture by means of automatic food dispensers such as these.

stored dry; it should also smell fresh. Musty or moldy food frequently causes high bird mortalities. Mouse droppings in the food are also a cause for concern; such food should, of course, be rejected as firmly as inferior old food that has outlived its shelf life (mouse droppings can become a dangerous source of salmonellosis infection). It is wise for the fancier to find out the exact origin of the food and to select the food himself.

Drinking water

The second basic nutritional requirement is drinking water. Without an adequate supply of water, every bird will die within a very short period. Parakeets are not big drinkers by nature, as many of them originate from warm dry zones where water is not available in abundance. Nevertheless, even those native to the savannahs are not able to survive without water; they need their daily drinking ration. It is, therefore, of the utmost importance for every bird fancier to supply his birds with fresh water each day.

How this is done is up to the individual fancier. It is vital, however, that feces and other pollutants are removed from the drinking vessels and that the latter are given a thorough washing as soon as they show deposits of algae and moss. Cleanliness is crucial if the parakeets are to be kept healthy. Water that has grown old and polluted can become a dangerous

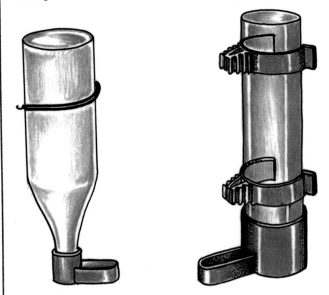

Automatic water dispensers contribute to hygiene because the water is not so easily fouled. Because they depend on a vacuum to function, fittings are necessary to keep them in position.

source of infection. The bird does not have a choice, as it has to drink bad water if it is not given anything else.

Drinking water is generally supplied in earthenware vessels which are placed on the ground. Tin cans and similar articles should be avoided. Plastic bowls can be used but must be designed in such a way that the bird can get at the water easily, since the walls are very smooth as a rule. Every parakeet loves a bath from time to time; consequently, the bowls should not be too deep. They should be shallow and big enough for the bird, when standing inside, to just get the plumage on the underside wet, while on the other hand it must be able to get at the water with the whole body.

Bathing is necessary for the birds to feel happy, look after their bodies and plumage properly, and remain healthy.

In conclusion, a few words about the use of an automatic water dispenser. If the latter does not supply running water but consists of a water depot supplying stored water as required, then this water should be changed daily. In this case, however, it is necessary to provide a separate bath.

Running water is the ideal solution but, because of the cost, can only be considered by a few aviculturists. The next best solution is a drop system along the lines of a dripping tap. This ensures that the water in the bowl remains considerably fresher and is gradually replaced or topped up once the bird has splashed some out while bathing. It goes without saying that with this method, the water bowl still requires cleaning, though only every third or fourth day.

Greenstuff and food plants

Greenstuff, fresh green plants as opposed to hard food, do not keep and need to be supplied fresh each day. However, since green plants are not available all year round, the bird fancier needs to provide a suitable substitute for them to ensure that the birds get the necessary vitamins.

Throughout the year there are two excellent foods available that are particularly well suited: apples and carrots. Carrots in particular are first-rate sources of vitamins, notably vitamin A, which promotes fertility. These are given all year round, especially in the spring, during the breeding season and molt, and when the young are being raised. Only in the winter, during periods of severe frost, should they be administered with care—the birds only being given as much as they can consume within two or three hours. This applies even more where apples are concerned. When they are slightly frozen, perhaps lying on the ground and defrosting or growing moldy, they become a dangerous food. For this reason alone it is advisable to stick both apples and carrots on a nail or wire hook so that the parakeet can reach them easily and nibble at them from its perch. This kind of food should always be served in the indoor shelter rather than in the outdoor aviary.

In the winter and early spring, one can give pleasure to almost all parakeets by letting them have fresh twigs to nibble. Particularly well suited are the twigs of apple trees, which the birds prefer above all the buds. All broadleaf wood is suitable, whereas conifer woods are not. Care needs to be taken with poisonous shrubs and with fruit trees that have been sprayed. If one is fortunate enough to own lilacs, one can use their twigs; those of willow catkin or hazel are also well received. The twigs of fruit trees are favored. Another supplementary food is germinated seed, which can be prepared at any time by the fancier. In the wild, birds find seeds at varying stages of maturity all year round, and germinated food is a good substitute for these. Through the process of germination, seeds are enriched with nutrients and vitamins which are not present in the hard form.

Greenstuff can also be obtained when needed by growing spinach or cress in small wooden trays. When the greens have grown sufficiently, the tray is deposited inside the aviary and the birds can eat as much as they want; the roots are often pulled out and eaten as well. In the summer, the culture of such greenstuff presents no problem. In the late fall and early spring, however, a warm room with plenty of light is required to get the seeds to germinate.

It should also be mentioned that parrots will accept tropical fruit such as bananas, figs, oranges, grapes, dates, etc. Feeding them with tropical fruit is expensive, however, especially where larger bird populations are involved. Commercial lettuce, spinach, apples, etc., should always be washed before being given to the birds so that any remnants of insecticide are removed. Lettuce goes bad very easily and quickly. Leftovers should, therefore, be removed daily.

Wild food plants are deserving of our special attention. They have the disadvantage that they are not available all the year round, but they do constitute by far the most natural type of food for our birds. For this reason, they should be provided whenever the opportunity exists. There is absolutely no doubt that for good breeding results, seeding weeds at various stages of maturity are of vital significance.

Chickweed (*Stellaria media*) shall be mentioned first of all. This so-called weed grows in gardens, vineyards, by the wayside, and in fields all year round, and it usually has the additional advantage of bearing seed heads at all times. Chickweed can be found from the early spring to the onset of winter, and the parakeets enjoy not only its seed heads but also the leaves and stalks. Another very good supplementary food is shepherd's purse (*Capsella bursa pastoris*). This can be found in the same places as chickweed and again nearly all the year round.

Depending on the season, the following food plants can also be found and are very popular: groundsel (*Senecio vulgaris*); sow thistle (*Sonchus oleraceus*); redshank (*Polygonum persicaria*). The seed heads of chicory (*Cichorium intybus*); ribwort plantain and greater plantain (*Plantago*); orache (*Atriplex*); and, above all, dandelion (*Taraxacum officinale*) are very popular. After dandelion flowering, but before the seed heads open up and when the white tips of the spermatophores show at the top, they are just right for feeding to the birds; only the small heads with the semimature seeds are collected. The parakeets nibble the heads open, eat the seeds, and drop both the white spermatophores and the sheath to the ground. It is delightful to watch the parakeets perched on the rod with one foot while holding the dandelion heads in the other, eating the contents with such obvious enjoyment.

Needless to say, the birds are partial to all the different cereals, in a half-ripe (milky) condition, and to meadow grass (*Poa annua*). Corn on the cob in a ripe or nearly ripe condition is not only a very good but a much appreciated supplementary food; however, it can only be offered to the parakeets for a short time. In the fall, the red berries of the rowan tree grow ripe. These berries can be kept for a while; stored dry after they have been picked, they can be fed to the birds all through the fall. It goes without saying that the parakeets also like other native berries such as currants, for example, red as well as black ones.

Nature offers a great variety of plants all year round in this respect, and the fancier only needs to make use of them to guarantee his pets an optimal diet. While this involves a lot of time and trouble, the birds reward their keeper with their good health and longevity.

Rearing food

The importance of greenstuff and food plants applies even more strongly to the rearing of the young. Anyone who wants to breed parakeets must be prepared to take the trouble of offering the adult birds a constant supply of suitable rearing food; otherwise they will not be able to raise healthy young. Natural rearing food, in the form of semimature seeds and fruits, is and will always be the best food for young birds.

Parakeets feed from the crop; it is obvious, therefore, that the adult bird cannot feed the young brood successfully on hard food alone, since the latter takes too long to be sufficiently predigested in the crop. With half-ripened seeds, the pap inside the adult bird's crop grows more quickly. Particularly during the first few days of the chicks' life, when, with the aid of the crop secretion (crop milk), the adult bird needs to produce a very fine pap, it is important to add "soft" food components to the diet. In a good pair of breeders, the cock gathers the food, predigests it inside the crop, and passes it on to the hen, who, after a further digestive process in her crop, feeds the pap to the young. Consequently, the food ingested by the adult birds must contain all the substances that are essential to life.

Apart from greenstuff and weeds with semimature seeds, the well-prepared breeder also has the appropriate soft or rearing food at his disposal. This is once again the ordinary hard food which is allowed to germinate or, alternatively, real soft food in the form of hard-boiled egg, soaked bread and rolls, or commercial ready-made soft food.

HARD-BOILED EGG that has been finely chopped is readily accepted by some species, whereas others need to have it served mixed with ground rusks or fine white bread crumbs. Egg food, pure or in the form of a mixture, must be served fresh daily. The quantity supplied should never be more than the birds will eat within four or five hours. Egg that has gone bad has a toxic effect and is very dangerous, particularly to the young.

HARD WHITE BREAD is another good soft food. The hard bread (not brown or whole meal bread) is soaked in water for a short period, squeezed well, and broken up into smaller particles by hand. One has to make sure that the white bread is not moldy before one soaks it in water. The bread can be given on its own or with vitamin supplements added.

READY-MIXED COMMERCIAL RAISING FOOD is available from pet dealers. Since it must be moistened, which reduces its ability to remain fresh, this food should always be prepared in small quantities. The composition of the food is usually given on the packets.

GERMINATED FOOD requires some trouble and care in its preparation. It should be fed to the birds when the husks burst open, i.e., when the seedling is ready to break through. This is usually the case after about 50–60 hours. It is, therefore, necessary to have seeds at three different developmental stages available at all times. The seeds are washed and put into a big sieve or water container, making sure the water is covering them. The water is drained off the next day; the seeds are then rinsed inside the sieve under a strong water jet and put into fresh water again over night. The water should be of room temperature (80°C), if possible. The next day the seeds are rinsed again and then spread out in a thin layer between two thick cloths. On the day after, the seeds are ready and can be fed to the birds. On warmer days, the water may need to be changed more often to prevent fermentation. Germinated food spoils rapidly; if not absolutely fresh, it ferments or grows moldy and does the young birds no good at all.

In principle, any kind of hard food normally fed to the birds is suitable as a base for germinated food. However, very oily seeds such as hemp should not be used. Very well suited, on the other hand, are the different varieties of millet, canary seed, and oats.

Animal food

Whether parakeets in the wild consume animal food has so far not been established with certainty. Some ornithologists confirm that they do, while others only assume so. In addition, there is probably a great deal of variation between the different species. What is known for certain, however, is that animal food (live food) does not play a crucial role in the nutrition and rearing of parakeets, although it is popular with some species.

The fancier will primarily be feeding mealworms to his pets. If accepted, these should not, however, be supplied in excessive quantities. A maximum of ten mealworms per bird per day is sufficient. Ant eggs, i.e., the pupae of the black ant (the red wood ant is a protected species!), fresh or dried, are equally suitable, as are the dried shrimps that are used in the breeding of domestic hens. All other forms of live food, essential for soft food eaters, can be dispensed with where parakeets are concerned.

Vitamins, minerals, and trace elements

Thanks to the nutritional research that has been done in the last few decades, we now know quite a bit about the foundations of nutrition. We have learned that without vitamins, there is no diet than can enable a bird to survive for a prolonged period. The natural fare eaten by birds in the wild supplies these substances automatically.

Birds kept in captivity, if receiving the food described earlier, should not come to suffer from vitamin deficiency. Nevertheless, it is advisable to administer a few drops of a commercial vitamin preparation during the breeding season and the molt. There are a number of multivitamin preparations on the market which contain all the important vitamins; these can be added to the soft food or water

without any difficulty. Alternatively, they can be sprinkled onto the carrots or apples.

Some minerals and trace elements are absolutely vital. In addition, the birds must have calcium available to them all year round. A good calcium preparation for animals should also contain minerals such as soda, phosphorus, manganese, magnesium, iodine, iron, copper, cobalt, and potash. It is a good idea to use a separate container which, while readily accessible to the bird, cannot be contaminated by other food. Small wooden boxes on the wall of the indoor shelter have proved successful. Crushed eggshells can, of course, also be given to the birds, but they should be boiled before use in case they harbor any pathogenic organisms. Old mortar (without cement), sea shells, and cuttlefish bone are also suitable. To prevent egg binding, cod liver oil should be administered during the laying period. It contains plenty of vitamin D, which promotes the absorption of calcium inside the bird's body.

A good river or sea sand enables the bird to ingest small stones which are necessary for digestive purposes. Additional minerals are consumed at the same time. Most commercial sands consist purely of ground quartz and are not only useless but positively dangerous because of the sharp splinters they contain.

Australian Parakeets: Paradise Parakeet, *Psephotus pulcherrimus,* female (A) and male (B). Blue-bonnet Parakeet, *Psephotus haematogaster,* female (C) and male (D). Painting by Graeme Stevenson.

Prent Stevenson

A tame, hand-reared Golden Conure, *Aratinga guarouba*. Assessing the physical condition of a parakeet such as this one is no difficult task. Photo by Isabelle Francais.

Diseases

Inspection of birds prior to purchase and during acclimatization

By exercising care when purchasing and acclimatizing birds, one can do a certain amount towards the prevention of diseases. For this reason, particularly cautious bird fanciers do not obtain any birds by mail order but always select them personally from the dealer or breeder. Potential buyers observe the animals, without disturbing them, by coming close. This enables one to identify sickly birds by their dull eyes and the slightly ruffled plumage. When the observer approaches such birds quickly smooth their feathers and give the appearance of being lively and healthy; only animals that are seriously ill remain conspicuous. If individual animals cannot be observed closely, the animals one is interested in can be put into a smaller cage and observed once more from some distance away.

This superficial examination alone is not sufficient. A more thorough checkup is required to establish a bird's exact state of health. By picking up a bird with one's hand one can, with a little experience, draw conclusions as to its nutritional state from its weight. Palpation of the breast musculature (which must not have become so sunken that the ridge of the breastbone can be felt like the back of knife) provides the final answer. It would not be wise to acquire animals that are too severely emaciated. A reddened cloaca and dirt in the plumage surrounding it indicate a disease of the digestive system. One should make sure that no claws or toes are missing. While such deficiencies do not make a bird any less active, the reduced steadiness may cause complications during copulation. It goes without saying that the beak also needs to be examined for any abnormalities. Absent feathers in newly imported parakeets are due to trapping and transport and, therefore, are generally without significance. In animals bred in captivity they point towards the early stages of feather plucking or to growth abnormalities of the feathers. A dangerous source of infection, most particularly an infestation of worms, stems from inadequately cleaned and disinfected transport containers. Unfortunately this is a danger that is all too often overlooked.

Even if newly acquired birds give the outward impression of being healthy, they may still be carriers of hidden diseases. The fact that an importer may have put them through quarantine is still no guarantee of perfect health. For this reason newly purchased birds must never be allowed to come into contact with other birds immediately, but kept in cages of their own for at least a few days and preferably for four weeks, until the second fecal analysis, for further observation. If the first examination and the second one about four weeks later give negative results, the birds can be transferred to their permanent accommodation. In both cases the feces are subjected to parasitological and bacteriological analysis.

Signs of disease

A hygienic environment and a balanced diet ensure that the parakeets remain in good condition and are the best preventive measures against diseases. Nevertheless one is never entirely safe from an outbreak of disease among the stock since the total exclusion of infectious agents is impossible. Due to the intensive metabolism of these animals, bird diseases usually run a very rapid course. A thorough daily check of every animal is particularly important since it makes it possible to spot diseases in the early stages. Quick action when the first symptoms appear tends to be crucial for successful treatment.

Sick birds are quieter than the healthy members of their species, giving a lethargic impression; shy birds suddenly grow confiding. The regulation of the temperature is disturbed, for which reason the bird raises the feathers in an attempt to increase the layer of air that surrounds the body. The head is retracted or hidden among the plumage; as a result the body surface that gives off heat is diminished. In the early stages of the illness or where the latter runs a mild course, the bird behaves normally as soon as it feels it is being watched. With daily observation of the animals, any such abnormalities will be spotted if the birds are left undisturbed.

In animals that are seriously ill the eyes appear small and dull; sometimes they may look sunken. Due to a discharging secretion the nostrils may be damp or encrusted. When the respiration is disturbed, the beak is open. The feathers in the proximity of the beak and cloaca may be sticking together. The food intake is often reduced whereas conspicuous quantities of water are being drunk, which makes the administration of water soluble medicines easier. Such food as has been ingested may build up inside the crop.

The feces of healthy animals are well-formed. The white components consist of uric acid, while those of a dark color are the end product of digestion. Pulpy, let alone runny and yellowish, feces point towards a general disturbance in the digestive tract. If blood can be seen in the feces, a severe enteritis is present.

It is virtually impossible to tell what disease is involved from these symptoms. A loss of activity and raised feathers are very general signs of disease. But diarrhea, difficulty in breathing, and a nasal discharge can also have a variety of causes.

Examination of dead birds

Instead of being submitted to a veterinary institute for examination, all too often parakeets that have died are simply thrown into the dustbin. To have the bird examined, wrap it in newspaper (never in plastic bags!) when the dead animal is cool, and put loosely into a large cardboard box. It is then sent to the place of examination by the quickest possible method. Do not freeze dead animals! A short report on observed pathological symptoms and the keeping and feeding conditions should be enclosed. The result of the examination can yield important hints with regard to the remaining stock.

Veterinary surgeon and first aid

Only few veterinary surgeons specialize in bird diseases. For this reason a suitable specialist should be located before a disease occurs. Information can be obtained from clinics for diseases of fowl, zoological gardens, and bird fancier associations. The veterinary specialist will also be able to give advice on the contents of a small first aid kit. The latter should always include an antibiotic eye ointment, broad spectrum antibiotics, wound ointment, wound powder, hemostyptic fluid, animal charcoal, boric acid solution, chamomile tea, liquid paraffin, cotton wool buds, vitamin preparations, disinfectants, an infrared radiator, pipettes, a crop syringe, as well as scissors or clippers suitable for trimming beaks and claws.

Organic diseases

GOUT Due to inadequate excretion the blood level of uric acid rises, resulting in deposits in the skin, in joints and on internal organs. Conspicuous deposits on the joints lead to swellings and ultimately burst open, discharging a light gray crumbly substance. Affected birds are in considerable pain and consequently their ability to move is restricted. A cure is not possible. To prevent the disease from occurring in other birds kept under the same conditions, the protein content of the food should be reduced, the provision of vitamin A improved, and good opportunities for exercise made available.

THYROID ENLARGEMENT This occurs primarily in Budgerigars. The cause is thought to be a lack of iodine in the drinking water. The enlarged thyroid gland presses on the

The Red-fronted Parakeet, *Cyanoramphus novaezelandiae*. Thanks to New Zealand aviculturists, it has been possible to reintroduce some of these parakeets into the wild in recent years.

The requirements of Yellow-fronted Parakeets, *Cyanoramphus auriceps,* can be met in captivity; thus this species has come to have the reputation of being easy to keep and to breed.

gullet, windpipe, and blood vessels. The consequences are a buildup of food inside the crop, vomiting, inflammation of the crop, as well as severe respiratory difficulties. Affected animals often hang from the wire mesh by the upper mandible, presumably because in this position the neck is extended slightly and breathing becomes easier. Due to the increased excitability of such birds, the danger of death from shock during netting is very great. Being more active, parakeets kept in aviaries drink more than cage-birds do and consequently consume more iodine as well. Hence they rarely, if ever, suffer from this condition. All treatment is aimed at the provision of iodine. Affected parakeets have a few dissolved crystals of potassium iodide added to their drinking water for several days. Some tincture of iodine may be painted onto the skin of the wings and is then absorbed through the skin. If the bird has not already grown too weak, treatment usually effects a sudden improvement. The traces of iodine that are present in various commercial food mixtures help to prevent the condition.

TUMORS Benign fatty tumors can under certain circumstances be removed surgically. Cancerous tumors are not curable. These diseases affect mainly Budgerigars.

Infectious diseases

ENTERITIS One of the most common pathological conditions. The causes are poor quality food, a change of diet, colds, parasitic infestation, bacterial infections, or the ingestion of poisons. Apart from the general signs of disease, there is diarrhea and an increased intake of water combined with a reduced appetite. Affected birds are given chamomile tea to drink. In addition they receive food that is easy to digest and high in energy (e.g. millet sprays, boiled rice, rolled oats, biscuits, invalid food, animal charcoal). In the case of infections, antibiotics should be administered as instructed by the veterinary surgeon. A constant high temperature of about 35°C should be maintained in the environment.

PSITTACOSIS Psittacosis (which occurs in parrots) and ornithosis (which occurs in birds) are caused by different strains of the same causal agent—a bacterium and not a virus. Affected birds eat less, are lethargic, and take little interest in their surroundings. Other symptoms which do not, however, permit a definite diagnosis are raised feathers, diarrhea, respiratory difficulties, conjunctivitis with running eyes, and a nasal discharge. An examination of blood and fecal samples clarifies what condition the bird is suffering. To obtain fecal specimens, plastic sheets are put under the roosting places at night. The fresh feces (chilled in the summer) must be taken to the place of examination by the quickest possible method. The disease is contracted primarily by the aspiration of dried-up, dust-like infected feces and also from nasal and eye secretions. Further, it is transmitted by mites and bird lice. Hence the special importance of accommodating the birds in hygienic conditions. Once contracted, the disease may run a rapid and severe course. Affected animals present with the symptoms described above, shivering, rapid emaciation; and, with signs of paralysis and fits, die of circulatory and cardiac failure. Alternatively, they may live without showing any obvious signs of the disease, in which case they will be permanently excreting the causal agents in their feces and so become particularly dangerous vectors of the disease. If there is external stress such as transport, a change of diet, or inadequate nutrition, then the birds will quickly succumb to the disease especially if they are young.

In West Germany it was found that about 60% of human infections could be traced back to parrots. These infections are in fact more dangerous than a transmission of the disease by domestic fowl or wild birds. Human beings contract the disease by inhaling feces which contain the causal agent, or by close contact with the birds. The symptoms in man resemble those of flu, and they may develop into a specific type of pneumonia. In every case where the disease is suspect, the possibility of an infection with psittacosis should be drawn to the doctor's attention just to be on the safe side. The best prevention is a strict adherence to the quarantine regulations for newly imported birds and a quarantine for all new acquisitions. Animals affected by the disease are given long-term treatment with chlortetracycline which is administered via the food. To counteract upsets of the intestinal flora, vitamin concentrations (notably vitamins of the B complex, C and K) must be added to the drinking water.

INFECTIONS WITH COLI BACTERIA These intestinal bacteria are present in large numbers in all birds and mammals. In certain circumstances they can cause disease. Primarily young animals and weakened animals are at risk. An outbreak usually occurs during or after transports. The casual agents are excreted via the feces and taken into the body mainly with contaminated water and food, or through the inhalation of dry, dust-like fecal matter. Affected animals have an elevated temperature, show little interest in food, and suffer from diarrhea, passing paste-like feces. They sit about with drooping wings and are lethargic and disinterested. If eggshells are contaminated with the bacteria, the causal agents penetrate the shell and infect the embryo, causing it to die or causing mortality of the young birds just a few days after hatching. Keeping the birds in absolutely hygienic conditions prevents the outbreak of this disease. Affected animals are treated with tetracyclines or chloramphenicol.

SALMONELLOSIS (PARATYPHOID) Bacteria of the *Salmonella* group occur all over the world and can cause diseases in a wide variety of animal species. While stocks of large parakeets are less often affected by this infection, the most important preventive measures should nevertheless be applied. A transmission can occur via infected food, notably protein concentrates, via the droppings of mice and rats, as well as through flies. Stocks of domestic ducks and domestic hens are often reservoirs for *Salmonella* sp. Wild birds, particularly town pigeons, are another common source of danger to aviary birds where this infection is concerned. If a weakened bird takes up the causal agents, the latter multiply unchecked and rapidly produce death from toxemia. Affected birds fluff up their feathers, appear to feel cold, are lethargic, have drooping wings, and sometimes show signs of paralysis. Diarrhea with watery, smeary, whitish or greenish feces is common. Here an accurate diagnosis is only possible after the feces have been examined. Treatment consists of the administration of tetracyclines or chloramphenicol. Because of the possibility of the disease being transmitted to man, it is absolutely vital for the bird keeper to be scrupulously clean. The hands must be disinfected and the clothes changed after diseased birds have been attended.

FUNGAL INFECTIONS Fungal spores are present in the air virtually everywhere. Favorable conditions for their development are found in a dark, damp, and warm environment, most particularly on decaying vegetable matter. Damp food (e.g., germinated food), litter, and nesting material provide good culture media. The opportunity for a rapid spread exists mostly in enclosed rooms. Through hygiene in the enclosures and the simplest of cleaning measures, the spreading of fungal disease can easily be prevented. Fortunately the risk of infection is only slight where large parakeets are concerned. Affected animals suffer from respiratory difficulties; they breathe more rapidly, open the beak widely, but without there being a rattle in the throat. While doses of vitamin A and B can do something towards helping the bird to fight the disease, the treatment of affected birds is seldom successful. Antimycotics should be administered in the form of aerosols.

Internal parasites
Among these are coccidians (which belong to the class *Sporozoa*) and intestinal worms. Before any treatment is given, an exact determination of the parasites is necessary. Fresh feces, about half a cubic centimeter in a small plastic container, are submitted to the Institute for Parasitology of a veterinary school. This specimen should be accompanied by a letter requesting a parasitological examination. Since there may not necessarily be eggs in the feces even in a case of worm infestation, a further

fecal specimen must be examined about four weeks later if the result of the initial examination is negative.

COCCIDIANS Most wild birds harbor these *Sporozoa* which parasitize the cells of the intestinal mucosa. The resistant forms that have been excreted only become infective after having undergone a complex development. In a damp environment and at a temperature of 30°C this development is completed very rapidly. While frost inhibits their development, the resistant forms survive even temperatures of -20°C. The parasites are ingested with the soil as well as with contaminated water and food. Inside the bird's body they proceed to multiply extremely rapidly; as a result they quickly accumulate on the ground in the aviaries, less so in cages that are cleaned at regular intervals. Affected birds are weak, fluff up their feathers, eat very little, and suffer from diarrhea with the feces usually being frothy, bloodstained and of a greenish or brownish color. Coccidiosis is a typical disease of young animals. Any infected young birds that survive may harbor the coccidians for the rest of their lives and excrete the resistant forms without showing any signs of disease. The prevention of coccidiosis is scrupulous cleanliness. Affected animals are treated with sulfonamides (administered via the food or drinking water). Ample provision of vitamin A and K is important. An effective disinfection of contaminated aviaries is difficult to achieve because of the resistance of the oocysts. It is best to remove the top 15 cm or so of the soil and replace with fresh soil.

TAPEWORMS These parasites are sometimes harbored by newly imported birds. Affected birds can be treated with Dromcit, Yomesan, etc. The development of tapeworms is dependent on specific intermediate hosts which do not occur in some countries. Consequently there is little likelihood that the infection will spread.

MAW WORMS According to research carried out in Leipzig, the round maw worms, which are several centimeters long, occur in over 40% of large parakeets. The worms

themselves are rarely excreted but the feces contain masses of the resistant eggs (several thousand per g of feces). Before these become infective they need to undergo a development which is dependent on dampness and warmth. The area around water containers in aviaries is a good culture medium. The eggs are ingested with soil and through contaminated food and water. When the larvae have hatched they continue their development among the villi of the small intestine. Once sexually mature the worms live free inside the intestine, where every female can produce thousands of eggs per day. Acute stages of the disease are usually detected in young birds. In older animals a certain balance is possible between the bird and its intestinal parasites. Unfavorable external circumstances can, however, lead to a breakdown of this balance and the affected bird will become ill. Even if the parakeets are only mildly infested and apparently in good condition, the worms still deprive them of nutrients. Furthermore, the parasites give off toxins which also have an adverse effect on the host. Metabolic disturbances and enteritis are then the consequence of such worm infestation. In cases of very severe infestation, the intestinal lumen may become completely blocked, making it impossible for any further food to pass through. In aviaries which are severely infested, this can become the cause of heavy losses. Initial manifestations of the disease are molting problems (e.g., the molt continuing over too long a period) and developmental disturbances in immature birds. Subsequent pathological signs are emaciation, diarrhea, and obvious weakness. Good results are achieved by treatment with benzimidazol preparations such as Panacur, Rintal, Mebenduzol, which paralyze the worms so that they are excreted within just a few hours. The developmental stages are not always affected; therefore it is necessary to repeat the treatment four to six weeks later. The most effective method of treatment is the administration, as per veterinary instructions, of carefully dosed anthelminthic by means of a crop syringe. The destruction of the worm eggs in the aviaries, on the other hand, is more difficult since disinfectants such as Dekaptasol are only of use in the case of solid floors. Where the ground consists of soil or sand, the top layers of these should be removed since a steam jet appliance or gas burner are not at everyone's disposal.

HAIR WORMS The hair worms (*Capillaria*) are so thin that they are barely visible to the naked eye. They attach themselves to the intestinal mucosa (with the anterior end), which explains their resistance to the usual anthelminthics. Injury to the intestinal mucous membranes results in bleeding and thus an increased risk of infection. Infestation with hair worms leads to diarrhea, emaciation, and anemia, and in immature birds to growth disturbances. The development of the worms is promoted by a lack of vitamin A. The eggs are excreted in the feces. For their subsequent development they need a high environmental humidity; some species even require an intermediate host, usually consisting of earthworms. Good results are achieved by treated affected birds with the tetramisol preparation Nilverm, whereby it is important that a dosage of two milliliter per one kilogram of body weight is strictly adhered to. In animals that have become very weak the treatment can result in death. A drug that is better tolerated is levamisol (administered at half the concentration), contained for example in Citarin (Bayer).

External parasites

RED BIRD MITE This mite parasitizes sleeping and incubating birds as well as nestlings. Mites saturated with the blood they have sucked can be identified as dark-red, spherical creatures of about half a millimeter in diameter. During the day they hide in crevices and holes inside the cages, in the grooves of perching rods, and in nest boxes. An infestation weakens the birds and makes them restless. A heavy infestation with these mites leads to anemia, ultimately resulting in death. That these parasites may also be the vectors of pathogenic organisms makes them still more dangerous. In an effort to control the infestation all sorts of hiding places are treated, in the closer proximity of the cages as well, prior to which the birds should be removed. Treatment may, for instance, consist of hanging up a Vapona strip inside the cage if the latter can be sealed off with plastic. Bird mites survive frost and months of starvation. This means that the aviaries are by no means free from mites after the winter and have to be checked very thoroughly before being restocked.

MANGE MITE This mite, which burrows into the skin and horny layers, occurs particularly among Budgerigar populations, more rarely in Cockatiels as well. Affected parts of the body react with gray proliferations which can be seen above all in the corners of the beak, on the ceres, in the immediate vicinity of the eyes, more rarely on the cloaca and on the legs. For treatment, Odylen represents the drug of choice.

BIRD LICE Most species live on feather particles, epidermal scales, and glandular secretions. The parasites complete their whole life-cycle on the bird's body. The egg parcels are attached to the feathers. On closer inspection of the birds, the brownish bird lice are readily identifiable with the naked eye. They are flattened and 1–2 mm long. The feather areas on which the parasites have fed are also conspicuous; in cases of severe infestation the shaft is frequently the only thing that remains. Affected birds are restless, biting themselves constantly. Weakened birds or those with deformities of the beak are unable to look after their plumage properly, and they are the ones on which the parasites are present in particularly large numbers. The consequence is emaciation and, in immature birds developmental disturbances. Treatment is given in the form of an aerosol insecticide, but bear in mind that the insecticide might also be harmful to the bird.

Other disorders

DISEASES OF THE RESPIRATORY ORGANS Chills manifest themselves by a discharge from the nostrils, sneezing, and frequently by inflammation of the eyes as well. Heat therapy is helpful, in severe cases antibiotics. Inflamed eyes are treated with an antibiotic eye ointment. Where there are difficulties in breathing (a pumping respiration with the beak open) the bird may be suffering from pneumonia or bronchitis, which are conditions that are frequently present in cases of infectious diseases. Difficulties in breathing can also occur where the respiratory organs are perfectly intact but the internal oxygen transport and oxygen exchange are disturbed (in metabolic diseases and diseases of the heart, circulatory system, and the liver).

CROP BINDING If food which has gone bad is ingested or the muscles have grown flaccid, it can happen that the food inside the crop is not passed on. In such cases it is advisable to withhold food (for half a day if the birds are of Budgerigar size, for a whole day where larger species are concerned) and subsequently provide a special diet (enteritis) and chamomile tea. If this treatment remains unsuccessful, one has to try and soften the contents of the crop by means of a crop syringe. If this fails, surgery is used as a last resort.

EGG BINDING This condition is more common in Budgerigars than in larger species. Cold and faulty nutrition (a shortage of minerals and vitamins; too nutritious a diet resulting in obesity) or an inflammation of the oviduct are the possible causes. The birds stop eating and defecating, and the affected females give the impression of being utterly exhausted (weakness, a fluffed up plumage, a high respiratory rate). That egg binding is the cause can readily be established by palpating the egg in the abdominal region. A few drops of liquid paraffin (at body temperature) are inserted into the cloaca by means of a pipette, and the sick bird is kept warm inside a padded cardboard box (hot water bottle, electric blanket). If necessary, the egg can be removed surgically by a veterinary specialist.

AVITAMINOSES The main causes of diseases resulting from vitamin deficiency are errors in feeding food of the wrong composition and the use of food stuffs that are too old.

Eye diseases, poor healing of wounds, infertility, and developmental disturbances in young birds are due to vitamin A deficiency. A difficult molt, poor appetite, disturbances of movement, and fit-like states point towards a lack of vitamin B. Vitamin D deficiency leads to disturbances of skeletal growth in young birds (rickets); conspicuous consequences are deformation of the legs and wings. Vitamin D preparations are always administered in conjunction with a mineral mixture (above all calcium and phosphorus). The need for these substances is particularly great in Australian parakeets (e.g., Australian King Parakeet, Crimson Rosella, Superb Parakeet, Red-winged Parakeet). Particularly where these species are concerned, additional minerals and vitamin D should be added to the nesting food. A vitamin B deficiency results in reduced fertility. All these manifestations of vitamin deficiency should be prevented by regular supplementation of the diet with cod liver oil, dried yeast, wheat germ, germinated seeds, and greenstuff. Other than in exceptional circumstances, the administration of additional vitamins then becomes unnecessary.

Molting problems
Delays in the molting process and stunted growth of new feathers are caused by inadequate keeping conditions (unsuitable environmental temperatures, sudden changes in temperature, too low a humidity, the absence of bathing facilities) and faulty nutrition. Effective counter measures are an increase in the protein content of the food, the provision of vitamin A and of minerals, bathing facilities or increased humidity, and access to the open air in the summer (activation of the metabolism by means of exercise, exposure to unfiltered sunlight). Molting due to fright is not an illness but a sensible defense mechanism in birds attacked by predators. If a bird suddenly finds itself attacked, it reacts by shedding tail feathers and contour feathers. This applies above all to nervous species, particularly where the latter are attacked in the night when roosting.

FRENCH MOLT This is a disturbance of feather growth in immature birds. Just before or immediately after fledging, the latter lose primaries, tail feathers, and sometimes contour feathers as well. The feathers break off at a constricted point of the shaft. The birds thus become unable to fly and sit about on the ground as "runners." Although there usually is a complete regeneration of the feathers, such animals should never be used for breeding. The condition is particularly common among Budgerigar populations (it was first observed in birds from French mass cultures, hence the term "French molt"). Occasionally it also occurs in breeding stocks of Cockatiels and *Agapornis* species. Among the causes mentioned are unbiological keeping conditions, notably an inadequate provision of protein for immature birds. A disturbance of the thyroid metabolism may also be implicated.

Feather plucking, feather eating.
Apart from the plucking out or biting off of a bird's own feathers, observed mostly in large parrots kept on their own, there is another phenomenon affecting some *Agapornis* species. Here the parent birds virtually "graze" on the plumage of their nestlings. Birds maltreated in this way show a retarded development and sometimes take months to fledge. More often than not, the hen is the culprit. She should be removed and the young raised by the remaining parent. It goes without saying that such animals are unsuitable for further breeding. Treatment of the "pluckers" is seldom successful. Nevertheless one should try to find an explanation for this behavior; the animal should be examined for parasites and for skin diseases, and one should check whether the food contains protein, minerals, and vitamins in adequate amounts. "Plucking" can also be precipitated by an unsuitable temperature, too low a humidity, poor light conditions, or the absence of bathing facilities. An organic cause is sometimes kidney damage. The main reason for the maltreatment of a bird's own plumage would appear to be boredom, the absence of a partner, as well as social stress where the birds are being kept in overcrowded enclosures. Treatment

has been attempted with tranquilizers (e.g., 2% Solusediv) or small doses of sodium chloride (a pinch per half liter of water); in the latter case salt-free water should also be available to the animals at all times, with fresh twigs supplied as occupational therapy. Bitter principle preparations in the form of sprays do not get to the root of the problem and therefore do not give satisfactory results. Various vitamin/mineral preparations in liquid form are useful in the treatment of growth disturbances of the plumage, but hardly in the treatment of "pluckers."

EXCESSIVELY LONG CLAWS, BEAK MALFORMATIONS
Perching rods that are too thin lead to insufficient wear and tear of the claws. Excessively long beaks are due to inadequate usage of the beak, vitamin A deficiency, and infestation with mange mites (responds to treatment with Odylen, etc.). Nail or claw clippers are used for trimming the claws; for the finer correction of the beak a file is required. Any bleeding (most commonly occurring on the short hind toe) is arrested with coagulating agents. The animals must not be put on their backs during this treatment.

Injuries and frostbite

INJURIES OF THE SKIN AND FRACTURES Injuries of the skin usually heal without any complications. In cases of persistent bleeding, coagulating agents (e.g., Stryphnon) should be used. Wounds are treated with an antibiotic powder.

Fractures can be expected to heal within three weeks. The immobilizing of broken extremities is a problem in parrots, as they tend to remove bandages and splints with the beak. Adequate immobilization in broken wings is often achieved by tying the tips of the pinions of one wing to those of the other with thin wire. Where the site of the fracture necessitates for the wing to be immobilized by being strapped to the body, the animal needs to wear a collar. In compound fractures of the leg, especially when the nerves and blood vessels are injured as well, amputation should be considered. When climbing, the lost leg will be compensated for by the increased use of the beak.

DISLOCATIONS Usually affecting toe joints, as a result of parakeets getting trapped in the wire due to excessively long claws. The chances of a cure are not very good.

FROSTBITE Careless keeping in outdoor aviaries in the winter frequently leads to frostbite in the legs. Particularly when startled by cats, owls, or mice the birds hang in the wire mesh for a prolonged period, losing too much of their body heat to the metal. Frostbite has to be treated with appropriate ointments that stimulate the circulation and have a healing effect on the damaged tissue. Frost damage can be prevented by the provision of roosting boxes for the birds, by shutting up the indoor shelter at night, and by refraining from supplying drinking water when the temperatures are below freezing.

The Turquoise Grass Parakeet, *Neophema pulchella*, has proved to be a reliable breeder; it is likely that this parakeet is more numerous in captivity than it is in the wild. Photo by Dr. Herbert R. Axelrod.

Breeding

The term breeding can be defined in very different ways. In aviculture we are generally concerned with purely propagative breeding or species preservation. It is only when we come to domesticated forms, among which nowadays rank the Canary and the Budgerigar, that this changes. Here specific selective breeding is practiced, with the aim of attaining certain colors or standardized forms, shapes, figures or particular songs.

The breeding of large parakeets and parrots is intended purely for propagation; however, this does not mean propagation at any price. Wherever possible, the species concerned should be preserved in its natural form, pure bred and healthy. Hybridization, with regard to large parakeets and parrots, was therefore practiced only in the early stages of ornithological research by scientists and ornithologists with the view of establishing evolutionary relationships and arranging the species accordingly. Today this task has been completed, which means hybridization has now become pointless and unnecessary.

Selection of the breeding pairs

Generally speaking, good breeding pairs which produce offspring at regular intervals are the well-guarded treasures of large parakeet breeders and are seldom parted with. There are, however, species of parakeets that cause fewer problems and breed more readily. These beginner's birds, as they are called, also tend to be less expensive. Anyone embarking on the breeding of large parakeets should already have gained avicultural experience elsewhere, for instance with Budgerigars, the Cockatiel, or the small *Agapornis fischeri* or *personata*. Only then should he try his hand at breeding Rosellas. Here *Platycercus eximius ceciliae* (subspecies of the Eastern Rosella) and the Western Rosella or, among the Asian species, the Plum-headed Parakeet and the Rose-ringed Parakeet are the least problematical—they breed relatively readily. The rarer and more expensive species should be avoided until one has become sufficiently experienced.

Buying a "breeding pair" is not recommended. One would need to know both the breeder and the breeding pair extremely well. Only if the birds have actually been witnessed breeding can there be positive proof of getting a proper breeding pair, and even then there is no guarantee that this pair will breed as well in the new environment as it had in the old.

Similar problems are encountered when one tries to match two old birds with each other. Large parakeets are individualists who do not always accept a new partnership, particularly if they already had another partner with whom they bred for years. It is best, therefore, to buy immature birds in the fall; to avoid any kind of inbreeding, they should be of different parents. Young birds that have been kept together from the beginning are more likely to form an attachment when they have assumed their adult coloration or attained sexual maturity.

In this conjunction, the aviculturist would be advised wherever possible to obtain several specimens of the rarer species. This is likely to cause a space problem. If space allows a mere ten aviaries at one's disposal, 12 species cannot be kept. In that case it is better to confine oneself to four or five species and to keep at least two pairs of the rarer species. If the birds concerned are immature ones, these can in any case be kept together in a flock during the juvenile stage, prior to the onset of sexual maturity. A practiced eye will be able to observe signs of sympathy between the sexes, and often these become good breeding pairs later on. Occasionally this will enable one to differentiate the sexes at an early stage, which is not easy with some species, when the birds are still in their juvenile plumage. When several specimens are being kept, one can still exchange the partners in the spring or replace any partner that has died. If only one pair of these rarer species is owned, it would hardly be possible to find a replacement just before the breeding season and a whole year would be lost.

Acclimatization of the pairs

Generally speaking, it is best to transfer large parakeets to their new home in the afternoon. The birds should have the opportunity to locate and consume food and water and then calmly choose their new roosting place. They should be disturbed as little as possible at this stage. One should merely observe from a safe distance whether everything is going smoothly with the new partner. Not all large parakeets hit it off instantly, not even birds of opposite sex. Old birds in particular can pose a problem, and for this reason a new partner should be put in with an already well-established parakeet only with utmost caution. Driven by its territorial instincts—shared by many species of birds, hens as well as cocks—the acclimatized bird will try immediately to impress its superiority on the newcomer. This can lead to serious injuries or to shock in the new bird, which may later have difficulty in making contact or may refuse partnership altogether. For this reason, old birds should always be put into a new aviary together, at the same time, and kept under observation during the first few hours. Where serious fighting ensues (minor squabbles can be disregarded), the birds should be separated at once and accommodated in two adjacent aviaries; this enables the two birds to make contact without danger. If only one bird is aggressive, this bird should be removed for several days while the other is left in the aviary. When the two birds are together again, the one that was weaker originally has the territorial advantage it has since gained and the partnership is established. However, if there is still no peace days later, the only remedy is a general exchange of partners. It goes without saying that the acclimatization should take place in the fall if at all possible, or early in the spring before the onset of the breeding season at the very latest. Once the breeding period has begun, peace and quiet must prevail in the aviaries.

Nesting facilities

With the exception of the Monk Parakeet, large parakeets nest in hollows and in the wild favor the natural hollows in old trees. Individual pairs also nest in hollows in the ground or in rock crevices, but this fact can be disregarded here. Nest building in the true sense of the word does not take place. Rather, a cavity must be present which can be used as a breeding site. In some cases this cavity is made slightly bigger by gnawing at the wood. As a rule however, it is taken over exactly as it is found.

An entrance hole in the upper half and a nesting hollow at the bottom are essential. The hollow is an absolute must, for if the bottom were flat the eggs would roll to the side, grow cold and die. Whether we use square wooden boxes or hollow tree trunks, a nesting hollow must be present.

The size of the nest box largely depends on the size of the species concerned. For *Neophema* species, for instance, a box with a height of 30 cm, a diameter of 18 cm, and an entrance hole of 4–5 cm is sufficient. For large species such as the Australian King Parakeet or the Port Lincoln Parakeet, the box should be at least 80 cm high, 35 cm broad, and have an entrance hole of 8–10 cm. The size of the nest box is not the only crucial factor with regard to successful breeding. Since with a square wooden box the interior space is usually too large, on cool days the young brood does not sit close enough together and the heat loss is too great. For this reason one should never use wood that is too thin; choose thick planks. Planed wooden boards should not be employed either—at least they must not be planed on the inside—the adult bird needs to be able to get a good grip with its claws. Because of this, a few crosspieces are fitted below the entrance hole, making it easier for the birds to climb in and out. Many aviculturists prefer long nest boxes. These have the advantage of forcing the bird to climb, which means it does not jump straight from the entrance hole on to the clutch, damaging it in the process. Every box must have a detachable top, not just to facilitate checks but also for reasons of cleaning, which is absolutely essential after each breeding period. Large boxes would be improved by a small control flap in one of the side walls.

Breeders often debate what type of box is the better one: a natural tree trunk or a homemade wooden box. The breeding results, which are after all what really matter, can be equally good or bad with either. The natural tree trunk probably has the advantage because its internal temperature is more constant and corresponds to conditions in the wild. Some birds prefer the natural tree trunk while others accept the wooden box just as readily. Often the site is a more important criterion than the type of box concerned. The kind of box a bird has grown up in influences it to a certain extent, the bird instinctively preferring a similar box. The natural tree trunk is considerably heavier, not easily detached, and more difficult to clean: all factors which speak against it. Where there is sufficient space available, one should hang up two different boxes and later remove the one that is not being used; then the pair can decide for themselves. Equally important is the correct positioning of the nest box. Wherever possible, the entrance hole should be facing south or southeasterly, never west or, worse still, north. The nest box should be located in the most quiet part of the aviary. Neighboring pairs should be out of sight so that they cannot disturb the pair. Where an enclosed indoor shelter is available, one nest box should be hung up indoors and another one out. The outdoor box must not be directly exposed to wind and weather. It is always a good idea to provide a roof for the box and to find a corner that is sheltered from the wind. It is also important to make sure that the box is securely fixed to the wall. It would be a great pity if, after a successful start, a brood were to be destroyed as a result of the box dropping down to the ground.

The nesting hollow can be lined with a little sawdust (oak, if possible) or pulverized rotted wood, which can be found inside hollow tree trunks. Not too much,

else the eggs will be covered! Peat dust is unsuitable as it gets too dry.

Courtship and breeding

Early in the spring the older cocks already start trying to impress the hens. They fly alongside the hen, display themselves, and utter tender call notes at times. If the sun is shining, this early precourtship behavior can be seen quite frequently. In bad weather it instantly wears off again. While this is all very promising, it should not tempt the breeder to hang up the nest boxes at this early stage. Those parakeets derived from generations of birds bred in captivity will be encouraged to start breeding as soon as the nest boxes appear and, during periods of bad weather, will not be able to successfully raise the brood. In heated indoor aviaries matters are different, of course, but even then one still has problems with the greenstuff that is essential for rearing the young and which is not available so early in the year. The nest boxes can be hung during the second half of March; by that time the birds' breeding drive will have become stronger. The cock's courtship behavior will be seen more and more often, and he now also starts feeding the hen from the crop. This indicates that the pair are ready for breeding. Now the aviculturist should start to administer soft food in small doses, just as he will when the young are being raised. The quantity of food given should only be as much as will be eaten during the day. Germinated food and greenstuff are also important. During this period the keeper has the best chance to find out what kind of soft food the pair prefer. This means one can supply the usual and correct rearing food as soon as the young have hatched. During the period of courtship and egg laying the aviculturist can do a lot towards making the breeding attempt a successful one. Greenstuff, germinated food, and soft food are essential. Care is needed with regard to supplying such highly nutritious foods as oats and hemp. Ideally, they should not be used at all, or only given to pairs in whom the breeding drive is not yet strong enough so that they will start breeding. Obviously, throughout the breeding period the birds should only be disturbed when absolutely necessary. This is most certainly not the time for spring cleaning the aviaries—there was enough time for that earlier on. One's curiosity should be contained. A brief look inside the box is permissible only when the female has left it voluntarily to search for food and does not feel disturbed by it.

In most parakeets the incubation period extends over 20 to 22 days. Determining the exact date of hatching is difficult since the hen does not start sitting properly until just before or just after the last egg has been laid. However, the only important reason for knowing the date is that the aviculturist must on no account disturb the hen while the chicks are hatching. The provision of soft and greenfood is continued in any case at this stage, ensuring that there is food for the parents to give to their young.

The size of the clutch can vary considerably and be anywhere between three and ten eggs. As a rule, however, four to five eggs are produced, occasionally fewer where the large species are concerned.

Development up to the time of fledging

That the young have hatched is not difficult to establish. The thin chirping noises made by the young can be heard outside the box. Now the cock becomes much more active as well. He feeds his hen from the crop with increasing frequency. The quantities of soft food supplied by the keeper should be increased gradually, making sure, however, that not too much is left uneaten and fermenting; this would be very harmful for the young. The same applies to germinated food. Greenstuff complete with seed heads is ideal; this should be provided fresh every day, twice a day if possible. The development of the young proceeds very rapidly during the first few days. From the fourth to fifth day onwards the hen already leaves the box for slightly longer periods from time to time. This gives one an opportunity to check on the young and to establish whether their crops are well filled. If close ringing is desired, this is best carried out between the sixth and ninth

day, even slightly earlier where smaller species are concerned. Close ringing is not advisable with regard to problem birds, i.e., species that are rare or difficult to propagate. In all other cases, close ringing is highly recommended, however, since it makes it possible at all times to tell where a bird comes from and exactly how old it is. Few breeding pairs are troubled by the rings.

If the raising period runs a normal course and the parents are indeed a good breeding pair, then there are no problems. All the breeder has to do is to procure the rearing food; everything else is done by the adult birds. Most species leave the nest box between the 25th and 30th day, but the larger species may not do so until the 35th to 40th day. A problem does not arise until one notices that the young are not receiving enough food from the adult birds. This can be established, during occasional checks, if the crops are found to be empty, or from the increased volume and persistence of the begging sound emitted by the young birds. Then the aviculturist has to come to the rescue. One of the causes may be that the adult birds are ready to breed again; this is indicated by the cock starting once more to court and drive the hen. The food may also be responsible, or there may be other causes. Sometimes it helps to remove the cock from the aviary for a day. The latter is accommodated separately and given nothing but water. Sometimes this brings him back to his senses and reminds him of his paternal duties. There is, however, also a possibility that there is too great a number of young birds and the parents are unable to cope. If the birds are valuable or rare, some of the young can be transferred to breeding pairs of related species who have young of roughly the same age. With regard to the different Rosellas, for instance, this poses few if any problems. Where this possibility does not exist one has to use a feeding syringe to supply the young birds with additional food. The complete removal of the young from their parents should only be considered as a last resort, i.e., where it can be seen that the parents do not feed the young at all and they can only be saved by being reared artificially. Although hand reared young birds have the pleasant characteristic of becoming hand tame, there is also the danger of human imprinting; such birds are often useless for breeding later on. It is, therefore, always advisable to hold back initially and just help out, in the hope that the adult birds will resume their parental duties after a day or two, as they often do.

From fledging to first molt

The moment of fledging is approaching as soon as the young birds stick their heads through the access hole and let themselves be fed in that position. Now begins the time during which all onlookers should be kept away from the aviary, with the aviculturist moving about only with extreme caution. Newly fledged birds are easily startled, and if anything frightens them they will usually fly straight ahead in a panic. Clumsy fliers as yet, they are unable to brake and collide dangerously with the wire or the wall. Strange people, dogs, cats, or a low flying jet may all be the cause of such panicking. A bird that has had a crash landing and is lying on the ground should be left where it is in hopes that it will recover. Being picked up and placed on the perching rod might be traumatic enough to finish it off.

Fledging, for the immature bird, means entering a new world in which it has to learn to find its way about. Both parents help their young to overcome this stage of panic. Eventually, the young bird grips the perch confidently and no longer misses it when trying to land. It has also learned to judge the dimensions of its flying space and has stopped flying up into the air at the slightest instigation. Another critical period is entered when the parents gradually cease to feed the young. Some species will start picking up food as early as four to five days after fledging, others not until eight to ten days have elapsed. This does not mean, however, that they are ready to feed themselves independently. Juveniles are fed by the adults for at least four weeks, and only in the four weeks following this period does the feeding gradually taper off, depending on the species. Smaller species, such as the Grass

Parakeets (*Neophema*), often have a second brood overlapping with the first, and the cock continues to feed the first young until the second brood has hatched. Large species such as the Australian King Parakeets often feed their young on and off for over eight weeks. As a rule of thumb one can say that immature birds are generally independent after eight weeks and can be separated from the adult birds at that stage. It is a good idea, however, to leave them with their parents longer, particularly if the parents do not start a second brood. Theoretically, juveniles can spend the whole winter with the adults or stay with them until the onset of sexual maturity. At that time the adult cock may attack a young one. If it does, the birds must be separated. Until the first molt, which usually takes place in the fall, there should be little to worry about.

In healthy juveniles the molt passes almost unnoticed, except in those species where the young start to assume the adult coloration. This usually applies to the smaller species, which are then ready for breeding in the spring. The larger species do not usually change their colors until the following fall and hence do not get the adult plumage until they are 1 ½ years old. In the Australian King Parakeet, for example, it actually takes a year longer.

The first molt is a critical period for every bird to undergo. A healthy bird, free from parasites, with food at its disposal which has a high vitamin content and trace elements in the form of calcium preparations, living out-of-doors or in an outdoor aviary and hence receiving natural sunlight as well, will get through this molt without difficulties. Immature birds from an indoor aviary, on the other hand, without a single ray of sunshine, without any natural soil, wholly dependent on what they get from humans, can turn into problem birds at this stage. This can also happen if the adult birds did not consume sufficient nutrients during the feeding period and the young suffered from nutritional deficiencies as a result. Early intervention is possible by adding a vitamin preparation to the soft food, from time to time, during the feeding period and by administering at least one dose of Vigantol; this is absolutely essential for the growth of the skeleton. Greenstuff is very important during the molt and the most natural basis for a good vitamin supply.

However, if a young bird has been unlucky and is experiencing difficulties with the molt, there are special products on the market which can be added to the drinking water or vitamin drops that can be inserted into the beak. While direct administration into the beak is the surest method, it does entail additional stress for the young bird during daily snares. Good results have been achieved with Multibionta, a combined vitamin preparation.

Cases where molting has come to a sudden halt can be spotted immediately. Such birds are listless, the plumage is no longer smooth, and there are a great many bloody quills which often do not break through. The bird loses some of the old feathers and there is an insufficient growth of new ones. This may be so severe as to render the bird incapable of flying.

To pass as healthy, the birds need to have a complete, smooth plumage, give the impression of being lively and interested, and be confiding without being tame. These are the young birds one should choose when making one's purchase, but not until they have completed the molt.

Hand rearing

This is a subject which is surrounded by a great deal of controversy in specialists' circles. There is no doubt that one can list as many arguments for as against artificial rearing. Natural rearing by the two parent birds is without a doubt the best method. That is not being disputed. If the parent fails in this task, should the aviculturist intervene by artificially feeding and rearing the young? There is no definitive answer to this question. If the birds concerned belong to rare species, one should make the attempt if for no other reason than to preserve the species. There is, however, no guarantee that the hand reared parakeet will be suitable for breeding later on, since it may lose natural contact with other members of the species and have its human foster parent imprinted

on it (Immelmann). This can happen but is not invariably the case. In addition to that, a hand reared young bird usually turns out to have inherited the adverse breeding characteristics of the parents. The advantage of a hand reared parakeet is its tameness. If one wants a really hand tame bird that is to be kept on its own and perhaps taught to speak as well, then artificial rearing is recommended. In other words, before deciding for or against artificial rearing, all avenues should be investigated. If the young bird belongs to a rare species whose propagation in captivity has a great value; there are no suitable foster parents available; and we have tried to bridge a disturbance in the adult birds by supplementally feeding their young and still the adults are not performing their parental duties, then we are left with no alternative. Successful artificial rearing requires the correct composition of food adapted to the age of one's charge. During the first few days of the bird's life use a baby food in powder form, turn it into a pap (not liquid!) by moistening it with carrot juice, and administer it with a small spoon, wooden rod, etc.. A better method is to use a small cake decorating nozzle for which one has made a wooden mouthpiece of the appropriate size. When the mouthpiece is changed, be sure that the color remains the same. Red has proved successful since the majority of parakeet beaks are reddish in color. If at a later stage a different opening becomes necessary and a white mouthpiece is used, the young may refuse food. This may seem inexplicable at first, but the sole cause of this is the color.

Once the first few days are over and have been successful, and the young are accustomed to the icing nozzle, subsequent rearing does not present any great problems. Throughout the rearing period, a few drops of a multivitamin preparation should be added to the food at least every third day. Further, one should not forget to administer a pinch or two of calcium and twice during the rearing period a large dose of Vigantol. A small daily addition of a cod liver oil preparation does no harm either. "Little but often" is the rule with regard to all these necessary supplements.

The food itself should become "coarser" as time goes by. The basic substance is mixed with white bread crumbs or ground millet, grated carrots, finely chopped chickweed, and every so often hard-boiled egg. Once the young birds have grown their first feather quills, the ground millet or canary seed can be a little coarser but has to be soaked in water for several hours so that the young bird is able to digest it. At a later stage, pre-germinated seeds can be mixed into the food. In principle, all the food supplied to adult birds during the breeding season is given to the young as well, but in a suitably processed form which resembles the pap the adult bird passes to the young. Very important are the feeding times. Initially, when newly hatched, the young should be fed at two-hour intervals. As they grow older this period is gradually extended to three hours, then to four hours. In the early stages of fledging it is sufficient just to feed the young birds in the morning, at noon, and at night. When the young start feeding themselves, the midday feeding is omitted and then the morning meal. The evening feeding can only be eliminated when the birds have become truly independent and no longer beg. So that they can learn to eat independently, the first food offered to them should consist of the same feeding pap they have been receiving and of the various foods which one would also be supplying to the adult birds during rearing.

Buying, selling, dispatching

As a rule, large parakeets are not cheap, and for many a novice, although for experienced fanciers as well, the purchase of a particular pair can mean a considerable financial strain. As with all business transactions, therefore, one should allow oneself to be governed by a minimum of commercial principles and customs.

Trust is good and appropriate, but there are black sheep among aviculturists as well. When getting in touch with breeders not yet known, this should be borne in mind.

Thus, when buying birds, it is particularly advisable to collect them in person. This will allow a visual assessment of the bird in its normal environment. If one decides in favor of the purchase, the risk for the seller comes to an end once the bird is inside the transport box. Payment brings the transaction to a conclusion. Anyone selling birds himself should only accept a check if he knows the buyer or if the check is covered by a banker's card. Cash remains the most popular method of payment. Where sales or purchases by mail order are concerned, the following rules should be adhered to.

Dispatch only by express rail with the request that the addressee is notified by telephone immediately on arrival of the consignment. If this is not possible, the purchaser must be informed beforehand, in writing, as to when the bird will be dispatched and when it is due to arrive; every unnecessary hour inside the transport container means stress for the bird. The buyer should be able to assume that live arrival is guaranteed. The seller can obtain confirmation of the scheduled dispatch at the railway station and take out an insurance against the transport risk. On collecting the bird, the buyer must check that the latter has arrived in good condition. The buyer's right to return the bird and have his money refunded does not entail any risk for the seller if the birds he has to offer are in perfect condition. The buyer should, therefore, exercise it where necessary and return the bird, but not until after the animal has been allowed a few days' rest in the aviary. Payment is made in advance or on receipt by check or postal order. One important point for both parties to note is that all agreements become legally binding when all the details of the transaction have been set down in writing. Verbal agreements are invariably difficult to prove. Hence one should always make a point of opting for the written form.

In the exceptional case of a bird being dead on arrival or dying shortly afterwards, it is highly advisable to take a photograph and to submit the bird to an institute of veterinary medicine for examination without delay. The result of the autopsy will establish with certainty whether death was due to external factors or whether it was the result of some disease, thereby clarifying one vital issue from the outset. If the bird is already dead when it arrives at the railway station, one can refuse to accept it. This only makes sense, however, where one has not paid for it in advance. Otherwise one requests official, written confirmation and then has the bird examined as described above.

Every sale and purchase of a bird inevitably entails an element of risk for both parties, the seller as well as the buyer. It is essential, therefore, that both parties conduct the transaction with honesty and decency.

Import and quarantine regulations

Although large parakeet fanciers rarely import their birds directly from these animals' countries of origin, they do frequently obtain them from abroad, i.e., from breeders in the neighboring countries. To prevent, as much as possible, the introduction and spreading, above all, of psittacosis, and the highly contagious atypical fowl-pest (Newcastle disease), the import of all parrot-like birds is subject to certain requirements. The most important points of the conditions laid down by the veterinary authorities of the German Federal Republic shall be mentioned here.

GERMAN FEDERAL REPUBLIC: For the import and transit of parrots of whatever species, a license needs to be obtained from the veterinary police. The license is issued via the local offices of the Ministry of Agriculture. Exempt from this regulation are parrots carried by performing artists for the latter's professional use. Private persons, after submission of the relevant official certificate giving the identity of the animals (foot rings), are allowed to re-import up to three parrots which have been temporarily exported in the tourist traffic.

Import licenses are granted when the country of origin is free from infectious disease. The consignment needs to be accompanied by a certificate of health issued by an official veterinary officer. Only certain custom authorities deal with parrot transports. They must be notified of the consignment at least 24 hours prior to its arrival. Immediately after clearance, the animals must be taken to their destination, where they are to be kept in quarantine for a minimum of eight weeks. In accordance with detailed instructions by the official veterinary officer, they are to be treated with antibiotics over a period of 30 to 45 days. Before treatment commences the birds must be ringed and entered in a book that must be presented on request. Final clearance of the consignment is possible only after relevant examinations have determined that the birds are free from the causal agents of psittacosis.

AUSTRIA: Import licenses are issued by the Federal Ministry of Health and Environmental Protection. The consignment must be accompanied by a certificate of origin and a health certificate. Persons importing or passing through the country with a maximum of two parrots do not require an import license but only the two certificates mentioned above. This regulation is very often used by students from the developing countries as a means of boosting their income by importing parrots. The certificates must be in German, English, or French and are valid for two weeks from the date of issuance. The customs veterinary officer must be notified of the impending arrival of the consignment in good time. On arrival of the consignment the appropriate veterinary officer has to be notified.

Quarantine extends over a period of at least four weeks, generally, however, spanning 40 days. During this time the parrots must be housed separately from all other animals. Before the birds can be released from quarantine, they have to be examined and, above all declared free from notifiable infectious diseases.

Genera and species

Night Parakeet (*Geopsittacus*)

The large head and the short tail give this parakeet a plump appearance. Because of these characteristics, as well as the green coloration of the plumage with the dark transverse undulations, the bird bears at least an external resemblance to the New Zealand Kakapo. The Night Parakeet is in fact regarded as a link between the Kakapo and the *Platycercini*. The claws are shorter and less strongly curved than in other parrots, the characteristic of a ground dwelling form. No sexual dimorphism. One species.

The terrestrial habits of the Night Parakeet, *Geopsittacus occidentalis,* are a principal factor in its decline.

Night Parakeet

Geopsittacus occidentalis (Gould)

Characteristics: 23 cm long. Of a dull green color with dark brown, black and yellow speckles. The underside of the body is yellowish; its beak of a dark horn color, tip and upper mandible slightly lighter. Iris is black, according to Gould, and legs are brown. Juveniles are duller in coloration and show some yellow on the neck and nape.

Range: Presently found in a few areas in the interior of Western Australia, in the northern parts of South Australia, and in the northern regions.

Habitat: Dry, rocky landscapes where porcupine grass is growing.

Habits: Extremely rare; in the 20th century only a single specimen has been trapped by ornithologists. Since the localities in which the Night Parakeet has been found lie in virtually uninhabited areas, there is hope that the Night Parakeet has not yet become extinct. Active during the night; even water

places are visited by night, whereby the birds glide to the ground in a hovering flight. Periods of extreme drought induce the Night Parakeet to migrate over long distances. *Spinifex* or porcupine grass is vital to its survival. The seeds of these grasses form its staple diet. The nest, found just a few centimeters above the ground, is built in the center of a grass fascicle. A narrow tunnel leads to the nesting chamber, in which 4-5 eggs are laid. Thus far, these parakeets have been encountered either singly or in pairs. Like other Australian ground animals, the Night Parakeet is endangered particularly by dingos, foxes introduced by man, feral cats, and by brush fires.

Keeping: In 1867 and 1873 respectively, one Night Parakeet survived at London Zoo for a short period. The animal kept there in 1867 spent the day perched on a grass cushion and did not become active until the evening, when it bounded about, moving mainly by a series of leaps. Apart from millet and canary seed, it was especially partial to greenstuff. Unfortunately, this Night Parakeet died of pneumonia.

Ground Parakeet (*Pezoporus*)

Apart from the longer tail and the slightly livelier green, it is fairly similar in appearance to the Night Parakeet. Similarities to the genus *Cyanoramphus* have, however, also been noted. Wings rounded. Claws long and only slightly curved. No sexual dimorphism. One species.

Ground Parakeet
Pezoporus wallicus (Kerr)
Two subspecies.
Characteristics: 30 cm long. Green, with

The plumage of the Ground Parakeet, *Pezoporus wallicus,* serves to camouflage it in its habitat. Photo by G. Chapman.

black striations on the crown. Underside greenish-yellow with black transverse bands. Back and wings are yellow with black speckles. Red bar on the forehead. Beak brownish, iris dark yellow, legs are brown. The red bar on the forehead is absent in juveniles.

Range: Coastal regions of southern Queensland, New South Wales, Victoria, South Australia, and (although very rare) southwest Australia. In Tasmania, regularly occurring in areas further from the coast as well.

Habitat: Flat coastal areas, treeless swamps, moorland, grazing land. The habitat of this species is characterized by a dense growth of tall and hard grasses.

Habits: The densely growing grass permits the Ground Parakeet to lead a clandestine existence. The natural tunnels formed by the grasses enable the birds to run quickly. They fly up only when disturbed, landing in the grass about 30 m away. This behavior is reminiscent of quails and other small game birds. Due to the parakeet's hidden way of life, it has only been observed in its natural environment on a very limited number of occasions. The author of this chapter, who was on a fairly long excursion in the southwest of Tasmania, did not catch sight of a Ground Parakeet—the only proof of the occurrence of these birds was furnished by a feather that had been found. These parakeets are said to be inactive until evening. Then their call-notes can be heard. The seeds of grasses, rushes, reeds, herbs, and acacias serve as food. Breeding season: September to December. 3–4 eggs, generally laid into a nest (15 cm in diameter, 5 cm deep), though sometimes straight into a shallow depression in the ground. The Australian ornithologist, Forshaw, once came across a nest with four young and was able to make some observations. The young were fed shortly before dusk, whereby the adult bird landed about 6 m from the nest and gained access by a tunnel. After 3 ½ weeks—by which time the young were almost fully feathered, except that the tail was only a few centimeters long—they hid in the grass tussocks in the proximity of the nest. As with the Night Parakeet, the greatest threat to this species are various mammals introduced by man and brush

fires. The strong odor of the bird causes the Ground Parakeet to be easily tracked down by dogs.

Keeping: At London Zoo in 1865. Of three parakeets that lived at Adelaide Zoo for a prolonged period, the last one died in 1949. The birds soon grew confiding. They neither climbed nor perched on branches. The Ground Parakeets kept by an Australian bird fancier only grew active after sunset. They then fed and bathed, the latter even in the middle of the night.

Diet: Sunflower seeds, canary seed, millet, alfalfa, thistle seeds, greenstuff.

Breeding in captivity: First bred in 1948, in Sydney. Incubation period 20 days, nestling period three weeks. First downy feathers dark-gray. The four young birds that hatched had to be hand reared after a while. They died at the age of seven weeks.

Parakeets of the genus *Cyanoramphus*

All species are green. Markings in other colors on the head and on both sides of the rump. The beak is gray. Tail longer than the wings. Cocks slightly larger than the hens. White wing bar present in females and juveniles, in males either very faint or completely absent. This bar is usually quite distinct in females of the *Cyanoramphus* species or in young males who do not yet show the adult coloration and consists of a row of white spots on the underside of the flight feathers.

Frequently seen on the ground—scraping, typically like domestic hens. Equally characteristic for these parakeets is the ability to climb about, even on vertical wire netting, without the aid of the beak. In the wild, since no support from the beak is required, they climb through dense thicket with particular speed.

These birds are well worth keeping, as they neither destroy wooden constructions nor make a nuisance of themselves by being noisy. Although some of these species are native to cooler zones, they should at least be protected from frost during the winter. Apart from eating the usual seed mixtures, they are especially partial to greenstuff (chickweed, dandelion). A variety of seeds can be left to germinate in shallow boxes (seed trays). Wherever possible, these should not be placed underneath perching branches, so that contamination of the seed by droppings is avoided. Sod that has been spread out for the birds allows them the opportunity to peck out small insects, snails, worms, and minerals. They also nibble at the grass roots, however. The need for a diet that is rich in protein can be met year round by means of commercial raising mixtures and soft food. When there are young to be raised, the birds should be supplied with boiled chicken eggs; in addition, mealworms are also gratefully accepted. Fruit is turned down by some animals, but it seems to depend on how it is offered. My animals ate the apples, cherries, and berries that had been fastened to the branches in the aviary, but were less interested if they came across them in the feeding dish. Clean bathing facilities must be provided.

Both of the more obtainable species are unusually prolific. A pair of Red-fronted Parakeets raised 33 young birds within one year. Birds not even six months old incubated and reared the hatched young very successfully. This early maturity is otherwise at best seen in Budgerigars. However, the aviculturist who does not want to exploit his birds as breeding machines (which frequently results in apparently inexplicable cases of sudden death) does not allow them to breed until they have completed the first year of life. After the second brood the animals should be allowed to have a break. Although they like to roost inside the boxes, these should now be removed. Since cool weather often leads to egg binding, the nest boxes (about 23 x 23 x 30 cm, diameter of the access hole 7 cm) should not be hung up until April.

The male investigates the nest boxes that have been offered and tries to get the female interested in them. The 5–9 eggs are laid at intervals of one day or more. Incubation period 19 days, nestling period 6–7 weeks. The first down feathers are white, later ones are gray. Fledged young birds resemble the parents, apart from the shorter tail and the beak which is horn colored at first. By the size of the head, beak, and body it is already possible to differentiate the sexes at this stage. The female starts the next brood before the young birds have become independent. The male looks after his fledged offspring by himself but soon becomes aggressive towards the young males.

Four living species.

Antipodes Green Parakeet
Cyanoramphus unicolor (Lear)
Characteristics: 30 cm long. Uniformly green without any markings. Beak stronger than in the remaining species, bluish-gray. Iris orange, legs gray-brown.
Range: Antipodes Islands (about 800 km southeast of the southern island of New Zealand). Due to the limited expanse of the islands (the main island being no more than 8 km long and 5 km broad), this species seems to have a smaller range of distribution than all other parrots.
Habitat: Treeless islands with a dense growth of grass. Likes to frequent the cliffs along the shore.
Habits: Antipodes Green Parakeets are not nervous and allow the rare human visitors to the islands to come within two meters of them. They are encountered in pairs or in small groups of up to five individuals. Their favorite food consists of the leaves of a meadow grass. In addition, the birds feed on grass seeds and berries and the remains of dead penguins. The subspecies of the Red-fronted Parakeet (*Cyanoramphus novazelandiae hochstetteri*), which lives on the same island but nearer the center, does not appear to be interested in dead birds. The Antipodes Green Parakeets breed in hollows among the peat-like dead plant particles on the ground. Their young have already fledged by February. The Red-fronted Parakeets breed a little later.
Keeping: First kept at London Zoo in 1831. Said to have been at Berlin Zoo in 1904. In 1930, the Duke of Bedford described the strikingly dense plumage of his Antipodes Green Parakeet. While not being entirely tame, it was not an anxious bird either. It was particularly active in misty and frosty weather.
Diet: Sunflower seeds, canary seed, rape, linseed, apples. When rearing young, in need of particularly big supplies of greenstuff and carrots. Since in their

Cyanoramphus parakeets are successful avicultural subjects.
Depicted here are the Yellow-fronted Parakeet, *C. auriceps,* and
the Antipodes Green Parakeet, *C. unicolor.*

natural habitat the food plants of these parakeets are constantly being sprayed with seawater, these parakeets should have rock salt at their disposal.

Breeding: In recent times this species was kept at the zoos in Wellington and Auckland, as well as at the Mount Bruce bird sanctuary in Wellington. According to observations made so far, the parent birds only become able to raise their young without difficulties by the time they are three years old. One year old females already lay eggs but do not incubate, and the eggs invariably are broken. In the second year they incubate properly, but the young birds are not adequately cared for and are often bitten. The incubation period would appear to span 26 days.

Red-fronted Parakeet

Cyanoramphus novaezelandiae (Sparrman) nine subspecies, two of which have already become extinct.

Characteristics: 29 cm long. Green with a lighter underside. Forehead, crown, and a splotch behind the eyes are red, with a red spot on either side of the rump. Flight feathers are dark blue. Beak blue-gray, iris ruby red, legs gray-brown. Females have a smaller head and beak, the red splotch behind the eyes is paler and less extensive. Juveniles show less red on the head. The beak is horn colored, the iris pale brown.

Range: New Zealand and various neighboring islands.

Habitat: The individual subspecies have adapted to widely differing biotopes. In New Zealand the Red-fronted Parakeets usually live in forests and are found there predominantly in the treetops. On the islands there are hardly any trees, only dwarfed shrubs that offer food and hiding places to the parakeets. The Red-fronted Parakeets from the Macquarie Islands (an extinct subspecies *Cyanoramphus novaezelandiae erythrotis*) were ground dwelling.

Habits: In pairs or in small groups. The animals living in forest terrain are perfectly camouflaged and difficult to detect. The destruction of forests, and periodically persecution by farmers, are diminishing the parakeet populations on the two large New Zealand islands severely.

Food consists of grasses and grass seeds, berries, blossoms, leaves, the flower heads of *Lycopodium* species. The Red-fronted Parakeets from the Antipodes (*C.n. hochstetteri*) walk about among the penguins in search of edibles and extract delicious egg remains from the broken shells. When *C.n. erythrotis* was still common on the coast of the Macquarie Islands, in the late 1800's, this subspecies was seen searching for crabs and other small animals. Seamen and seal hunters killed the majority of the parakeets. The rest are likely to have fallen prey to stray cats. Main breeding period October to December. Five to nine eggs, incubation from the second egg onwards. Depending on habitat, nesting in hollow trees, rock crevices, hollows in the ground, or in dense grass tussocks.

Keeping: At London Zoo in 1864. There were frequent imports of these parakeets prior to World War I. Because no breeding stocks were built up in those days, they gradually disappeared again. In 1963, after staying in New Zealand to do research, the author was granted a special license by the Nature Conservancy for the export of Red-fronted and Yellow-fronted Parakeets for research purposes. Both species were bred in captivity at the Institute for Behavioral Research on the Wilhelminenberg in Vienna. Shortly afterwards a few pairs from New Zealand also reached Germany. Thanks to the rapid and prolific reproduction of both species, they now exist in safe numbers outside New Zealand.

Diet: In addition to the usual seeds, wheat and oats are eaten. A favorite is germinated food which the birds like to search for on the ground.

Breeding: First bred in captivity in Zagreb in 1872. Propagated in nest boxes or natural tree hollows which have to be lined with a mixture of sawdust and peat fibers. Incubation often begins from the third egg onwards. Incubation period 20 days, nestling period 30 days. Fledged young are fed by the parents for a few more weeks. The alarming decline in the numbers of wild specimens resulted in a systematic propagation in New Zealand from 1958, in an effort to preserve the species. Within six years the number of Red-fronted Parakeets kept in aviaries rose from 103 to about 2500. After 1970, Red-fronted Parakeets bred in

The wild populations of the Red-fronted Parakeet, *Cyanoramphus novaezelandiae,* are widely threatened, so it is encouraging that it has been the subject of several conservation programs. Photo courtesy of Vogelpark Walsrode.

captivity were successfully reintroduced in various regions. Perhaps one day animals from our stocks will also prove of importance to such undertakings. Whatever happens, aviculturists should refrain from the pointless hybridization of this species with the Yellow-fronted Parakeet and concentrate on the preservation of pure breeding strains.

Behavior: Courting males run up and down in front of their females, uttering a call-note, with the pupils contracting.

Yellow-fronted Parakeet

Cyanoramphus auriceps (Kuhl)
Two subspecies.

Characteristics: 23 cm long. Green with lighter underparts. Top of the head orange-yellow, red stripe on the forehead, a red spot on either side of the rump. Beak blue-gray, iris orange-red, legs gray-brown. In the females the yellow on the head is less extensive, the red stripe on the forehead is narrower. In juveniles the yellow and red on the head are less extensive and duller, the beak is horn colored, the iris brownish.

Range: New Zealand and on several of the islands off the coast of New Zealand.

Habitat: Shrubby terrain and forests at altitudes of between 800 and 1000 m. For nesting, the Southern Beech (*Nothofagus solanderi*) is of significance. The Yellow-fronted Parakeet avoids open and populated country. The subspecies *C.a. forbesi* from the Chatham Islands is only found on one of the islands now and there it only occurs in very small numbers.

Habits: Predominantly keeping to the treetops. Occasionally seen in association with Red-fronted Parakeets. Nesting in hollow branches or tree trunks. Breeding from July to April, though mainly from October to December. 5–9 eggs.

Keeping: First kept at London Zoo in 1865. While peaceful towards parakeets of smaller species, they disturbed other birds a great deal during the breeding season. It is, therefore, preferable to keep the pairs in isolation.

Diet: Although in the wild Yellow-fronted Parakeets are seen on the ground less often than Red-fronted Parakeets, in the aviary they search the ground for soaked and germinated seeds. For this reason, the possibility of these birds contracting worms should be prevented through appropriate measures of hygiene.

Breeding: First bred in captivity in 1872, in Zagreb. Incubation period 19 days, nestling period 5 weeks. Fledged young birds are fed by the parents for another 3 weeks or more. For a while the young return to the nest box to roost. Hence, another nest box should be provided for the second brood. That the Yellow-fronted Parakeet can be crossed with the Red-fronted Parakeet has already been demonstrated on many occasions. Hybrids should not be used for further breeding. Only pure breeding can ensure that the Red-fronted Parakeet and the Yellow-fronted Parakeet will continue to exist.

Orange-fronted Parakeet

Cyanoramphus malherbi (Souance)

Characteristics: 20 cm long. Green with lighter underside. Crown pale yellow, stripe on the forehead and lores orange-red, likewise the spots on both sides of the rump. Looks like a slightly smaller and duller edition of the Yellow-fronted Parakeet. Beak blue-gray, iris orange-red, legs brown.

Range: The southern island of New Zealand. The rarest *Cyanoramphus* species.

Habitat: Forests and low vegetation in the mountains.

Habits: Virtually unresearched. After no Orange- fronted Parakeets had been observed for 30 years they were seen once more in the Nelson Lake National Park in 1965.

Keeping: Imported into England during the second half of the 19th century.

Breeding: First bred in captivity in France in 1883. In New Zealand attempts are

Of the *Cyanoramphus* parakeets, the Yellow-fronted, *C. auriceps,* appears to be the most arboreal in its habits. Photo courtesy of San Diego Zoo.

presently being made to prevent this species from becoming extinct by systematic propagation in captivity. Similarly as with the Kakapo (*Strigops habroptilus*), the great difficulty lies in procuring the required animals.

Horned Parakeets
(*Eunymphicus*)

Similar to the genus *Cyanoramphus* and closely related to the latter. Characteristic are a few elongated feathers in the region of the crown. Tail long and broad.

One species.

Horned Parakeet *Eunymphicus cornutus* (Gmelin)

Two subspecies.

Characteristics: 33 cm long. Green with lighter underside. Back of the head, aural region, and rump yellowish, top of the head red. Region of the eye, lores, and lower cheeks blackish. On the crown there are two almost erect narrow feathers, 5–6 cm in length (black with broadened red ends). The subspecies *E.c. uvaeensis* has six such feathers, dark green with red tips. Beak red, iris orange-red, legs dark gray. In the females, the crest is half as long as in the males. Juveniles have horn colored beaks, a dark iris, and the facial markings are duller and less extensive.

Range: New Caledonia, Island of Uvea. In 1925 an attempt was made to introduce the Horned Parakeet to the Island of Lifu. However, the birds flew back to where they had originated. A similar attempt was made in 1965; the outcome of this is as yet unknown.

Habitat: Damp spruce forests. Progressive deforestation poses a threat to this species. That its nests are easily accessible has nearly proven fatal to the subspecies *E.c. uvaeensis*; since 1959 trapping of this race has been prohibited by law.

Habits: In pairs or in groups of four to ten animals. The birds are fairly confiding and allow one to get quite close. They feed on spruce seed, berries, the nectar of flowers, fruits (e.g., those of the melon tree, *Carica papaya*). Breeding season October to December. Two to four eggs.

Only two young are raised as a rule. The nest is located in hollow trees, occasionally in depressions on the ground among the roots of trees.

Keeping: At London Zoo in 1882. Imports of Horned Parakeets have always been rare. In 1969 ten animals reached Germany; at present a few are being kept in France. In their movements they are similar to *Cyanoramphus* species: they frequently scrape on the ground, and their low voice can constantly be heard. They also grow quickly confiding. Once acclimatized, Horned Parakeets are supposed to be fairly resistant to cold, but a bird fancier lucky enough to ever get hold of this rare species should avoid experiments and let the birds spend the winter in heated accommodation.

Diet: Sunflower seeds, canary seed, oats. All seeds to be offered in a germinated condition if at all possible. Hemp should be avoided. Soaked white bread, biscuit, rolled oats, fruit, berries (rosehips, rowanberries), mealworms, ant pupae.

Breeding: First bred in captivity in Milan, in 1889 (five eggs, all five young hatched after 18 days). A pair belonging to a German aviculturist raised a young male in 1971. According to the experience of a French aviculturist who succeeded in raising a Horned Parakeet in 1979, the incubation period extends over 21–23 days. During the first 10 days of life the young bird was fed almost exclusively on mealworms, but subsequently it was supplied with grain, fruit, grass seeds, and biscuit as well. According to another report, the parent animals used germinated food and soft white bread for rearing their young. Egg food was left untouched. First down feathers are gray, first juvenile molt occurs

Above: The Horned Parakeet, *Eunymphicus cornutus,* is only one of many parakeets for which suitable habitat is constantly diminishing.

Below: As Budgerigars were bred in captivity, blue varieties soon occurred and were propagated.

after 3 months, sexually mature after one year. The two subspecies were crossed with each other. Hybridization with the Red-fronted Parakeet.

Behavior: The male feeds the female outside the breeding season as well. Part of the social behavior is bowing to the partner, whereby the feathers of the crest fall into disarray and are thrown forward. Courting males move the head up and down several times, with the feathers on the head remaining raised. The female responds by making plaintive noises. After bending and stretching the neck several times and regurgitating some food, the male feeds his partner. The pupil contracts to the rhythm of the broken song.

Budgerigar *(Melopsittacus)*

Although, strictly speaking, the term "large parakeets" does not include the Budgerigar, some basic information on this member of the Platycercini shall be supplied here for reasons of completeness. The smallest of the Platycercini, which despite its isolated position, has certain characteristics in common with Grass Parakeets *(Neophema)*, and the Ground Parakeet *(Pezoporus)*. The differential characteristic of the Budgerigar is the swollen looking cere.

One species.

Budgerigar
Melopsittacus undulatus (Shaw)
Characteristics: 18 cm long, domesticated birds slightly larger. Green. Forehead, lores, and lower cheeks yellow, the latter with three round black patches. Back of the head, nape, back, and wing coverts with black and yellow transverse bars. Ceres blue in the male, whitish brown to brown in the female. Beak olive gray, iris gray-white, legs gray-blue. Juveniles slightly duller in coloration, ceres bluish white to pink, iris dark. Color mutations occasionally occur in wild birds as well.

In the wild form of the Budgerigar, *Melopsittacus undulatus,* the principal colors are yellow and green.

Parent Budgerigars with their five nestlings. As the eggs hatch in the order in which they were laid, the youngsters exhibit differences in development. Photo by Harry V. Lacey.

Range: In the Australian interior. Introduced in Florida.

Habitat: Grassy terrain with a scant growth of trees, open country. Deforestation has resulted in the expansion of this habitat. Locally, artificial water places have brought improved living conditions. The parakeets nest in areas with good food resources; during extreme droughts they relocate.

Habits: Probably the most common species of bird in Australia. A nomadic way of life. During periods of drought millions of Budgerigars sometimes congregate at water places. As experiments have shown, if fed exclusively on dry seeds these birds can survive without water for over a month. They feed predominantly on the seeds of grasses and herbs. The animals are active in the morning and in the later afternoon; during the day they hide away on trees, in the shade of the leaves. Breeding season in the south from August to January, in the north from June to September. The birds may, however, also breed at any other time of the year if there have been rainfalls followed by favorable feeding conditions. Nesting inside hollow trees or hollow wooden posts. The 4–8 eggs are deposited on the soft decayed wood at the bottom. Incubation period 18 days, nestling period 30 days. Often several pairs breed in the same tree. Young birds are able to reproduce at 3 months of age, thus the species can multiply rapidly when conditions are favorable. The adaptability to unfavorable conditions is an essential prerequisite for the Budgerigar's suitability as a pet.

Keeping: First imported into England in 1840. Provided a dry shelter is available to them, Budgerigars can be allowed to spend the winter in unheated accommodation once they have been acclimatized. They must have adequate flying space. Cage birds must also be allowed to fly about in the house periodically.

Diet: Various kinds of millet, oats, canary seed, half-ripe seeds, soaked white bread, fresh twigs. To avoid disturbances of the thyroid gland, cage birds in particular (who drink very little as a rule) should receive food to which iodine has been added.

Breeding: First bred in captivity in 1846, in Paris. Despite the early sexual maturity of the parakeets, no animals under one year of age should be used for breeding. Furthermore, only two successive broods should be permitted. Nest boxes about 15 x 25 x 15 cm, diameter of the entrance hole 5 cm, bottom of box to have a depression. Newly hatched Budgerigars are completely naked, the first down feathers to sprout after 5 days. At first all the feeding is done by the female alone, she in turn receiving food from the male. Fledged young birds are independent at 2 weeks of age. Budgerigars have proved invaluable as foster parents for Parrotlets, Lovebirds, and various smaller members of the Platycercini.

Bourke's Parakeet (*Neopsephotus*)

No closer family relationships to other species, no reports of hybridization either. Plumage without green, body of a thickset build. One species.

Bourke's Parakeet

Neopsephotus bourkii (Gould)

Characteristics: 20 cm long. Upper parts olive brown. Forehead, superciliary stripe, outer upper tail coverts, vent, and under tail coverts pale blue. Feathers on the throat and breast brownish with a pink margin. Abdomen pale pink. White bar on wings absent in males with adult plumage, faint in young males, conspicuous in females of all age groups. Beak light gray, iris brown, legs gray-brown. Females without blue stripe on forehead and duller in coloration. Juveniles slightly duller in color than the females. Isabel, yellow, and blue mutations. In flight, the feathers of the wings produce a whistling sound.

Range: Interior regions of Australia from southwestern Queensland to eastern Western Australia. Due to the irregular

Bourke's Parakeets, *Neosephotus bourkii,* tend to become most active toward evening.

migrations, the exact boundaries of distribution are not known.

Habitat: Steppe with acacia scrub. In color, Bourke's Parakeet blends well with the reddish sand.

Habits: Seen in small family units or in pairs, after prolonged droughts in big flights. From the late 30s onwards this species was regarded as extinct. Today, however, these parakeets are very common, particularly in the Mulga steppes in southwestern Australia. It is possible that the food plants of the parakeets were destroyed due to overgrazing by sheep. After a reduction in the number of sheep following a prolonged drought, the vegetation recovered and the population of Bourke's Parakeets increased again. The birds roost in the shade of trees and shrubs during the day and do not become active until about two hours before sunset. Water places are not visited until after sunset. The parakeets are calm and confiding in the wild; sometimes they even come into the gardens. Food is gathered on the ground and consists of the seeds of grasses and herbs, acacia seeds that have dropped to the ground, and sprouting blades of grass. Breeding season August to December. The nests are located in hollow trees at a height of 1–3 m. Four to five eggs. Incubation period is 18 days, nestling period 4 weeks. Complete juvenile molt at the age of 4–5 months. The male guards the breeding territory and feeds the female, who only leaves the nest once a day to defecate and drink.

Keeping: 1867, at London Zoo. These pleasant aviary birds neither scream nor gnaw, leave plants unharmed and are even peaceable towards waxbills. Bourke's Parakeets thrive even in small aviaries.

Being fond of warmth and dryness, they have to be protected from damp weather. In the winter they require a heated shelter. The outdoor aviary should be equipped with a shrub that provides shade. Bathing is engaged in above all in the rain or under the jet of a shower. It is only towards the evening, when most other species are already asleep, that these parakeets start to become active.

Diet: Various kinds of millet, woodland bird mixtures with little niger, few sunflower seeds, no hemp, germinated and unripe seeds, some apple, charcoal, fresh twigs, greenstuff. For raising, lots of different seeds (germinated and unripe), stale white bread soaked in water, biscuit, chopped hard-boiled egg.

Breeding: First bred in captivity in Belgium in 1877. Nest box 45 x 15 x 15 cm, diameter of access hole 6 cm, bottom of box to be lined with a layer of sawdust. Propagation is easy and succeeds even in small wire cages. Up to three broods in succession. These parakeets are already able to reproduce themselves during the first year. The female leaves her nest several times a day and lets herself be fed by the male who perches nearby. If the nest is being examined she sits tight and even lets one push her out of the way. The nest box needs to be cleaned before the young fledge. If this is not done, inflammations of the eyes may result due to encrustation with feces. After fledging the young birds are very nervous. To avoid injuries resulting from

Captive propagation of Bourke's Parakeet has been sufficiently extensive that color mutations have appeared. To the left is a Pied specimen (photo by Chelman & Petrulla); the two below are the variety known as the Rosy Bourke's (photo by Terry Dunham).

A pair of Bourke's Parakeets: the facing bird is the male, while the female is seen from the rear. Photo courtesy of Vogelpark Walsrode.

flying into the wire, the latter should be covered with reed-matting or brushwood. The young are fed for approximately another 10 days. Bourke's Parakeets have proved useful as foster parents for Grass Parakeets and Mulga Parakeets.

Behavior: Although the pairs form a close attachment, there is no social preening. Courting males move round the female, leap up into the air and bow a few times, afterwards stretching out to their full height. The wings are raised, revealing the blue flanks beneath. There have been reports of polygamous males.

Parakeets of the genus *(Psephotus)*

Stronger in build than the Grass Parakeets, a long tail arranged in steps. Look like a transitional form between Grass Parakeets and Rosellas. Powerful fliers of great endurance but moving with less agility on the ground and among branches. The pairs form a closer bond than is known with other Australian parakeets. Social preening exists in the Red-rumped, Mulga, and Blue-bonnet Parakeet. With the exception of the Blue-bonnet Parakeet, the sexes in all species show a distinct difference in coloration. A white bar on the wings is present in females and juveniles. All members of the genus *Psephotus* inhabit open terrain. Some species nest not only in hollow trees but also in sandbanks and termite hills. Of all species, only the Red-rumped Parakeet—which, in its native range, has learnt to take advantage of human settlements—can be kept in a cage.

Five species.

Red-rumped Parakeet
Psephotus haematonotus (Gould)
Two subspecies
Characteristics: 28 cm long. Bluish green. Nape, breast, upper tail coverts light green.

Rump red, abdomen yellow, under tail coverts gray-white. Greenish yellow patch on the anterior wing coverts. Primary coverts and shoulder blue. Beak black, iris brown, legs gray. The hens are a grayish olive green and have a gray beak. The red patch on the rump is absent. Immature birds resemble the female; young males often already have red feathers on the rump. The species owes its name to the melodious call note. Blue and yellow mutations.

Range: Southwestern Queensland, New South Wales, Victoria, southeastern South Australia.

Habitat: Loosely wooded grassy plains, agricultural land. Deforestation has led to an expansion of the range of distribution. At altitudes of up to 1250 m. Usually in the vicinity of water. In drier regions this species is replaced by the Mulga and Blue-bonnet Parakeet.

Habits: Common, has learned to exploit civilization. Red-rumped Parakeets frequently nest in the roof constructions of farmhouses and feed in the yard along with the domestic hens. Very often encountered by the roadside. Feeds and flies in association with Eastern Rosellas. Even in the wild the two species may interbreed. In some areas Starlings and Sparrows turned out to compete for nesting sites. Since these parakeets do not do any damage to wheat fields and are therefore popular with the farmers as well, people hang up nest boxes for them. The parakeets feed on grass seeds, the seeds of various oraches, millet, various flaxes, the seeds of weeds, poppies, and chickweed. Charcoal and grains of sand are ingested routinely. Outside the breeding season the animals gather in large flocks which split up into small groups at night, going off to roost in the trees. Breeding season from August (early spring) to December, sometimes already in May (depending on rainfall). Nesting not only in hollow trees but also in old sparrow's nests or inside the breeding chambers of Bee Eaters. Whether a nest is accepted depends on the hen, however. Four to seven eggs. Incubation period 17–20 days, from the second egg onwards. The eggs are laid at 48-hour intervals at onset, later at intervals of up to a week. During the early stages of

The Red-rumped Parakeet, *Psephotus haematonotus,* a popular species in its Australian homeland, has learned to exploit   cultivated areas.

incubating the male stays in close proximity to the nest. In the event of a disturbance the male utters a warning call and both animals fly off. A few days later the male once again attaches himself to a flock but returns to the nest every hour to feed the female in a nearby tree. Only the immediate vicinity of the nest is defended against members of the same species. Nesting period 30 days. The hen roosts inside the nest until the last of the young has fledged. First complete molt at the age of 3 months. The young birds pair off the following June.

Keeping: Probably in 1857 at London Zoo. A pleasant voice, persistent. Outside the breeding season it gets along well with members of its own species and with other parakeets. If an animal becomes ill, it may get attacked by its healthy partner. Red-rumped Parakeets can be left in the outdoor aviary even in the winter, but they must have access to a dry shelter free from drafts. An aviary length of at least 2 m. As the birds like to move about on the ground, germinating seeds should be provided for them there. Necessary measures must be taken to prevent worm infestation. Bathing facilities should be made available. Red-rumped Parakeets have also been successfully kept in free flight conditions.

Diet: Sunflower seeds, millet, canary seed, groast, grass seeds, woodland bird mix, greenstuff (chickweed, plantain, milk thistle, dandelion, lettuce, spinach), corn on the cob, apples, carrots, white bread soaked in milk.

Breeding in captivity: Nest box 25 x 25 x 35 cm, diameter of access hole 7 cm. First bred in captivity in 1857 in London. Matching of pairs virtually always successful. One-year-old birds are already able to breed. Cool temperatures often result in egg binding, hence the nest boxes should not be offered until April. Incubation from the second egg onwards. The brooding hen is fed by her partner outside the nest. Examinations of the nest are tolerated, often the sitting hen even allows herself to be pushed off her eggs. During rearing, half-ripe seeds and ample greenstuff must be supplied to the birds or the parents may desert the brood. The birds remain with their parents, in loose association, for a long time. Where a second brood has been started, however,

the cock attacks his male offspring. Newly fledged young birds are very shy. They become independent after one week but get fed for another 3 weeks or so. Good foster parents. Hybridization with all the other members of the genus, with Eastern Rosella, Pale-headed Rosella, Western Rosella, Yellow Rosella, Mallee Ringneck Parakeet, Red-capped Parakeet.

Behavior: The pairs stay together all year round. Social preening, feeding of the female by the male outside the breeding season as well. More frequent feeding when the birds start breeding. Courting males call loudly, nod the head, show a trembling of the slightly dropping wings, and fan the tail feathers. The defense of the breeding territory commences with singing and repeated tail shaking. This leads to close combat with the beaks.

Mulga Parakeet, Many-colored Parakeet
Psephotus varius (Clark)
Characteristics: 27 cm long. Bluish green. Forehead yellow, red patch on crown, belly and thighs yellow with orange-red. Primary coverts, wing margin, under wing coverts blue. Middle wing coverts yellow. The coloration of the males varies greatly, particularly where the expanse of red is concerned, which in turn has led to a division into geographical races. The division into races has since been abandoned again. Beak dark gray, iris brown, legs brown-gray. Females more brownish olive green, the middle wing coverts red (clearly distinguishing them from female Red-rumped Parakeets), beak of a brownish gray color. Juveniles resemble the hen, some young males are, however, already of a more intense green on the neck and breast when still in the nest, having red feathers on the belly and yellow wing coverts.

Range: The interior of the southern half of Australia.

Habitat: Grassland with a sparse growth of trees, dry scrubland. Generally speaking, the Mulga Parakeet inhabits drier terrain than the Red-rumped Parakeet, although it can happen that both species occur in the same locality. Expanding of the habitat due to deforestation. In the west, due to the

Mulga, or Many-colored, Parakeets, *Psephotus varius,* are inclined to form strong pair bonds with their mates.

absence of competition from the Red-rumped Parakeet, also found in townships.
Habits: Examinations of the crop contents have yielded a great deal of information on the natural diet. The following were found to be present: Half-ripe and fully ripened grass seeds, the seeds of oraches, *Cerastium* species, acacias, seeds and fruits of garden plants, mistletoe berries, the larvae of gall-wasps, as well as sand, small pebbles, and charcoal. Virtually all the food is gathered on the ground. As opposed to the Red-rumped Parakeet, this species does not form larger flocks even outside the breeding season. Occasionally seen in association with the Port Lincoln Parakeet. Breeding season July to December or, depending on rainfall, at other times of the year as well. Nesting inside hollow trees on a layer of rotten wood. Four to six eggs, incubated from the second egg onwards. Only the female sits on the young, but they are fed by both parents. While there are eggs or young in the nest the male remains in close proximity. The young fledge at 5 weeks of age. They live with their parents, in a family group, until there is another brood.
Keeping: At London Zoo in 1861. Mulga Parakeets are quieter and more tolerant than Red-rumped Parakeets. Appropriate protection from cold and wet is essential. Otherwise to be cared for as per Red-rumped Parakeets. This species is particularly susceptible to worm infestation.
Diet: Like that of the Red-rumped Parakeet, but fewer sunflower seeds. Millet sprays are a special favorite. Mulga Parakeets need a lot of greenstuff, germinated seeds, as well as the half-ripe seed heads of grasses and cereals. Egg food and soft food containing insects with grated carrots serve as rearing food, as does white bread soaked in milk. Since the birds ingest charcoal in their natural environment, this should also be made available to aviary birds.
Breeding: First bred in captivity in 1876, in France. Nest box about 20 x 20 x 35 cm, diameter of access hole 7 cm. A 3 cm deep layer of decomposing wood at the bottom. The animals should be offered the same nest box for subsequent broods. To avoid unnecessary excitement when the animals are breeding, no related species should be housed in the adjacent enclosures. The birds get into the breeding mood early in the spring. In a room heated to 15°C the breeding process can be expected to run a normal course. Where such premises are not available the nest boxes should not be offered until April. The female only sits on her young for a week; in cool outdoor temperatures the latter are at risk from the cold. Egg binding occurs less often than in Red-rumped Parakeets. Three to six eggs, incubation period 20 days, nestling period about 35 days. In contrast with young Red-rumped Parakeets, the newly fledged young are calm and quickly grow confiding. Hybridization with Red-rumped Parakeets, Blue-bonnet Parakeets, Paradise Parakeets, and Hooded Parakeets. Animals resulting from hybridization with the Golden-shouldered Parakeet resemble the Paradise Parakeet.
Behavior: The paired partners stick close together. If separated, their call notes can be heard for many days. This close bond should never be severed, if at all possible. The courting male perches on a branch, extending the neck and moving the head in a vertical direction. The wings are slightly raised, the fanned tail is moved from side to side. Soft, chattering sounds can be heard at the same time.

Paradise Parakeet

Psephotus pulcherrimus (Gould)
Characteristics: 27 cm long. Top of head, nape, back, wings and brown. Stripe on forehead, belly, under tail coverts, thighs, and middle wing coverts scarlet red. Head, sides of neck, throat, and breast bluish green. Eye region yellow, rump and upper tail coverts blue. Beak gray, iris dark brown, legs gray-brown. Female duller in coloration, almost without red, stripe on forehead yellowish green. Juveniles like the females. In the young males the green color on the head and breast is more intense.
Range: Queensland and the extreme north of New South Wales. Possibly already extinct, certainly very rare. At most, isolated populations in mountain regions far from human settlements.

Habitat: Savannahs with few trees but with termite hills.

Habits: Around the middle of the previous century this parakeet was still common in Queensland, but by the turn of the century it was already considered extinct. The pairs stay together throughout the year. Seeds of herbs and grasses form the bulk of the diet. The breeding period coincides with the rainy season. The 3–5 eggs are usually laid inside breeding chambers in termite hills. Often the parakeets make use of the deserted breeding chambers of Kingfishers. A tunnel measuring about 30 cm in length leads to the nesting chamber, which may be as much as 45 cm in diameter. Sometimes the birds nest on steep sandbanks inside the breeding chambers of Bee Eaters.

Keeping: Imported into Europe on several occasions in the previous century. Paradise Parakeets were regarded as problem birds who had great difficulties in adapting to the changed diet and often died within a few weeks. Birds that had been successfully acclimatized are, however, said to have been hardier.

Diet: Millet, canary seed, some oats and hemp, chickweed, meadow grass.

Breeding: First bred in captivity in 1878, in Belgium. Later also bred elsewhere on several occasions. Incubation period 3 weeks, nestling period 5 weeks.

Golden-shouldered Parakeet

Psephotus chrysopterygius (Gould)

Two subspecies, of which above all the Hooded Parakeet (*Psephotus chrysopterygius dissimilis*) is being kept.

Characteristics: 26 cm long. Back and shoulder feathers brownish gray. Underparts and rump turquoise. Top of the head black-brown, stripe on forehead and the eye region pale yellow. Median wing coverts golden yellow. Lower abdomen, vent, under wing coverts, and thighs light red. In the subspecies *P. c. dissimilis* (Hooded Parakeet) the black of the top of the head extends to as far as the nape.

In the wild, the Golden-shouldered Parakeet, *Psephotus chrysopterygius,* will often choose to nest inside termite mounds.

Forehead and eye region are also black. The red on the underside is more delicate, the yellow on the wing coverts more extensive. Beak gray-brown, iris dark brown, legs gray-brown. Females duller in coloration, anterior or neck and the breast are yellowish green.

Range: Nominate form in northern Queensland, Hooded Parakeet in the Northern Territory.

Habitat: Has a preference for dry, open forest and savannah landscapes with plenty of termite hills.

Habits: Trapping has led to a slight reduction in the numbers of both subspecies. Outside the breeding season these rather confiding parakeets live in small groups. They feed on grass seeds, nectar, pollen, leaf buds, and insects. Usually they search for their food on the ground. They prefer to be active in the morning and at night, roosting in the shade of the trees during the day. In the morning, with the utmost caution, they visit the water

The sexes of the Golden-shouldered Parakeet, *Psephotus chrysopterygius,* are easy to distinguish, as the hens are markedly duller. These are the nominate form, *P. c. chrysopterygius.* Photo courtesy of San Diego Zoo.

places. Breeding season May to January, but always after droughts. Generally nesting in termite hills, the Hooded Parakeet also nests in hollow trees. All around the termite hills, on black soil, grows an abundance of grass with green seed heads (the favorite raising food) after the floods. During the drought the hills are so hard that even a parakeet would find digging impossible. Access tunnel about 30 cm long; 4–6 eggs are laid on to the bottom of the breeding chamber. Incubation period 20 days, nestling period 5 weeks. First molt at 4 months. By the time they are 16 months old the males have assumed the adult coloration, but they are already able to reproduce themselves before then. The female only sits tight for one week and is then generally seen in the proximity of the nest. The reason for this is connected with the heat storage inside termite hills. (Interesting to note is the symbiotic relationship, so far observed only in respect to the nominate form, with a small butterfly, *Neossiosynoeca scatophaga*, whose caterpillars feed on the feces of the young parakeets inside the nest. They keep the nesting chamber absolutely clean and even clean up the legs of the nestlings. What has remained a mystery so far is the synchronization, since the parakeets and the butterflies have to lay their eggs at approximately the same time. Inside the nesting chambers of Rosellas a closely related species of butterfly has been found. A similar symbiosis was described in respect to the Brown-throated Conure, *Aratinga pertinax*.)

Keeping: The nominate form was first imported into England in 1897. Outdoor aviaries must be adequately protected from rain and wind. Mist and wet weather are not tolerated. A heated indoor shelter is vital. Bathing facilities need to be provided. Birds should be able to gather their food on the ground (necessary hygienic measures are essential). Because of their aggressiveness, these parakeets have to be kept in pairs. Even among themselves, squabbling may ensue if both partners of a pair do not get into the breeding mood at the same time. A male in the care of an Australian bird fancier lived to the age of 30.

Diet: Millet sprays, seeding weeds, niger, sunflower seeds, soft food. Milky white seeds, still unripe, are particularly favored. For reasons of hygiene, germinated seeds are best offered in shallow dishes placed on the ground. During the breeding season greenstuff and biscuit are taken in larger amounts than at other times.

Breeding: The Golden-shouldered Parakeet was first bred in captivity in 1956, in Australia. In Germany it was propagated for the first time in 1966. The Hooded Parakeet was first bred in captivity in 1911, in England. In Germany the first successful breeding attempt was made in 1964. It took a long time for the parakeets to adjust to the northern hemisphere's seasonal rhythm. For this reason winter broods were common at first. All sorts of nest boxes are accepted, only new ones are not very popular. De Grahl devised the method of partially blocking the entrance hole with a piece of bark. This means the parakeets are forced to widen the access hole themselves, by gnawing, which increases their interest in the artificial nest. Successful breeding results were achieved with nest boxes of about 15 x 15 x 25 cm. Three to nine eggs, egg laying every other day, incubation period 20 days, nestling period about 30 days. The female already stopped warming the young Golden-shouldered Parakeets after one week. It is, therefore, essential for the breeding room to be heated appropriately. A particularly critical stage is reached by about the 10th and 11th day when the feather quills start to sprout. As reported by de Grahl, the sex differences are at their most distinct in young birds of 25 days of age. The male animals show a more intense coloration on the lower belly. The young birds, which only seldom beg, are fed by both parents. One-year-old animals can already be used for breeding.

Behavior: The courting male flies round the female a few times and then perches on the branch beside her. On the ground the male walks behind the female with a series of exaggerated leaps. The feathers on the breast are blown up, and those on the forehead are raised to form a small crest. The wings are drawn up, and with the head lowered the bird nods in rapid succession. The tail feathers are shaken sideways.

A subspecies of the Golden-shouldered Parakeet, the form *Psephotus chrysopterygius dissimilis* is often called the Hooded Parakeet. Photo courtesy of San Diego Zoo.

89

Two forms of the Blue-bonnet Parakeet, *Psephotus haematogaster:* the nominate subspecies, *haematogaster,* has yellow under tail coverts, while the other bird belongs to the subspecies *haematorrhous.*

Blue-bonnet Parakeet

Psephotus haematogaster (Gould)

Four subspecies.

Characteristics: 29 cm long. Upper parts, head, throat, and breast gray olive brown. Face, shoulders, wing margin, and outer wing coverts blue; inner wing coverts olive yellow, underparts pale yellow, central region of belly red. Under tail coverts yellow (*P.h. haematogaster*). *P.h. haematorrhous*: under tail coverts red. *P.h. pallescens*: paler in color. *P.h. narethae*: smaller, more intensely colored. Beak pale blue, iris dark brown, legs gray-brown. Female slightly smaller, beak thinner, less red. A white wing bar is present in females and juveniles.

Range: P.h. haematogaster: Western and southern New South Wales, northwestern Victoria, southeastern South Australia. *P.h. haematorrhous*: southern Queensland, northern New South Wales. *P.h. pallescens*: interior of South Australia. *P.h. narethae*: southwestern Australia.

Habitat: Dry savannahs with scattered trees (sandalwood, *Casaurina* sp., cypresses).

Habits: Quite often seen by the roadside, near farms and drinking troughs for cattle. The pairs stay together throughout the year; after breeding, family groups of 8–10 birds are formed. The parakeets only gather together in larger flocks during a drought. Food is usually collected from the ground and consists of grass seeds, the seeds of herbs (special favorites are one orache and a number of the goosefoot group), fruits, berries, blossoms, and nectar. Sand and charcoal are also taken up. Preferred nesting sites, chosen by both partners, are the hollows in low, dead trees. Breeding season from July to December; further inland the birds also breed outside this period after abundant rainfalls. Four to seven eggs. The eggs are laid at intervals of 2 days and are incubated from the second egg onwards; incubation period 22 days, nestling period 5 weeks, complete juvenile molt at the age of 3–4 months. In the event of danger, the hen does not leave the nest until the last moment.

Keeping: London, in 1862. Newly trapped birds, now rarely reaching Europe, are delicate. Acclimatized Blue-bonnet Parakeets tolerate temperate climates fairly well. These parakeets tend to pick fights outside the breeding season, which means they have to be kept in pairs all the year round. Even then, incidents are possible. The author kept a pair which had been imported directly from Australia. They got on well in quarantine, but a few days after they had been moved into an aviary the male kicked up a row with his partner.

Diet: As per preceding species. Apples, chopped carrots, and berries are accepted. Seeding weeds in a semi-ripened condition serve as rearing food. *P.h. narethae* did not touch soft food.

Breeding: The pairs are not easy to match where Blue-bonnet Parakeets are concerned. Mutual preening carried out at frequent intervals is an indication that the partners get on with each other. The first eggs may be laid as early as March. Consequently the nesting hollow, preferably a natural tree trunk of about 20 cm in diameter and 50 cm in height, should be located in the indoor compartment. Some aviculturists recommend nest boxes with a tube-like extension of the access hole. *P.h. haematogaster* was first bred in captivity in 1878, in Belgium. *P.h. narethae* was propagated for the first time in 1941 in Australia; after 1971 it was also bred in Germany. Hybridization with Red-rumped Parakeet, Mulga Parakeet, Pale-headed Rosella, and a subspecies of the Eastern Rosella (*Platycercus eximius ceciliae*).

Behavior: A striking characteristic is the play behavior reminiscent of that seen in lories. The birds play with twigs and stones and roll around on the ground with the partner like playing cats. When excited, the birds raise the feathers on the forehead and make jerking movements with the head. Courting males stretch out to their full height; the head, with the raised feathers giving it the effect of a color signal, is moved up and down while the neck is extended. The slightly raised wings vibrate and the fanned tail is moved rapidly in a sideways direction.

Parakeets of the genus *Barnardius*

Some taxonomists treated the two species as one and added them on to the genus *Platycercus* (Rosellas). There are certain distinct differences, however, which justify a separate classification. All parakeets of the genus *Barnardius* have special skeletal characteristics of the skull and a yellow ring round the nape; in addition, they do not show the typical squamations on the back that all species of Rosellas have in common. The sexes are not so easily differentiated by the size of the beak. As opposed to Rosellas, they do not congregate in large flocks but live in pairs or in small family groups.

Barnardius species have powerful beaks and long, narrow tails. There are no differences in color between the two sexes. They are hardy birds and manage with a frost-proof shelter in the winter. Wooden

One of the subspecies of the Port Lincoln Parakeet, *Barnardius zonarius semitorquatus,* is also known as the Twenty-eight Parakeet. These parakeets are still very common, thanks to their adaptability.

constructions are chewed, thin wire may be destroyed. Peaceable towards smaller species. Diet as per Eastern Rosella, but preferring more greenstuff. Area of nest box about 35 x 35 cm, minimum height 70 cm, diameter of entrance hole 9 cm. The two species frequently interbreed; hybridization with various *Platycercus* species is also common.

Two species.

Port Lincoln Parakeet
Barnardius zonarius (Shaw)
Five subspecies, among them the Twenty-eight Parakeet (*B.z. semitorquatus*).
Characteristics: 38 cm long. Green. Top of the head brown-black. On the forehead a few individual red feathers. Lower cheeks with a blue edge anteriorly. A yellow band round the nape. Upper breast dark green with a bluish shine. Upper part and sides of belly yellow. Under wing coverts blue. These characteristics apply to the nominate form. *B.z. semitorquatus* is distinguished from the latter by the red stripe on the forehead, dark blue patches on the cheeks, and the green color of the belly. Beak gray-white, iris brown, legs gray-brown. Females can sometimes be identified by the slightly smaller, rounded head. Juveniles are duller in color, the beaks are flesh colored. Adult plumage at 12–14 months. In most adult animals the white bar on the wings is absent; in young females it is present.
Range: Central and west Australia to the west of the 138th degree of longitude. *B.z. semitorquatus* is confined to the coastal regions of southwestern Australia.
Habitat: A wide variety of habitats, from dense forests to desert regions where a few water places can still be found. This adaptability has also led this species to exploit civilization; hence it has become common in townships, in areas where cereal is being grown, and on fruit plantations.
Habits: Despite persecution, the most common species of parakeet in west and southwestern Australia. Resident, but prolonged droughts may cause it to migrate. Enjoying improved living conditions due to artificial water places. Even after sunset these parakeets are still active; on bright moonlit nights their call notes can be heard

all night long. Food is frequently gathered on the ground; therefore, the birds walk considerable distances. They feed on various seeds and fruits, the buds of leaves and flowers, the nectar of eucalyptus blossoms, and on wheat. From the capsules of the eucalyptus trees they extract the semi-mature seeds, but they also eat the fleshy green parts of the nuts. Nesting in hollow branches and tree trunks at a great height. Breeding season August to February, further inland after rainfalls. Two broods if conditions are favorable. Four to seven eggs. While the female is incubating the male is on guard nearby. Early in the morning and shortly before sunset both of them fly off together in search of food.

Keeping: *B.z. semitorquatus* at London Zoo in 1962, *Barnardius zonarius* a year later. Peaceable towards other species until the breeding season begins. Quickly acclimatize and are not afraid of their keeper. Enjoy bathing.

Diet: Aviary birds were noted to require animal protein; they look for earthworms and feed them to their young. On one occasion they were even observed to sample a small dead bird. Mealworms are not always accepted. During the breeding season they not only need soft food but plenty of different greenstuff. Potatoes, carrots, and tomatoes are also accepted.

Breeding: *Barnardius zonarius* was first bred in captivity in France in 1878, *B.z. semitorquatus* in 1881 in Belgium. Long nesting chambers, put up diagonally or provided with climbing facilities on the inside, are accepted most readily; the female is the one who makes the selection. Egg laying may start as early as March. Four to five eggs, egg laying every other day, incubation from the third egg onwards, incubation period 21 days. Newly hatched young of the genus *Barnardius* are covered in gray down feathers. They fledge at the age of 5 weeks and are then fed by the father for another 3 weeks. The onset of the molt usually prevents a second brood. In 1928 an English bird fancier bred a blue specimen of this species. The two subspecies mentioned have been crossed with each other. There has also been hybridization with Mallee Ringneck Parakeet, Barraband's Parakeet, Pale-

headed Rosella, Crimson Rosella, Yellow Rosella, and the Eastern Rosella.

Behavior: Courtship takes place either on the ground or, more frequently, on the branches. The wings are slightly raised, with the tail spread out and moving rapidly from side to side; the male bows to his partner. After a quick regurgitating of the food, the female is fed.

Mallee Ringneck Parakeet
Barnardius barnardi (Vigors and Horsfield)

Three subspecies, among them the Cloncurry Parakeet (*B.b. macgillivrayi*).

Characteristics: 33 cm long. Green. Bluish patches on the cheeks. Underside turquoise green, abdominal region yellow. Back blackish blue. A red stripe on the forehead, a yellow band on the nape. In the Cloncurry Parakeet the cheeks are of a more intense blue, and the red stripe on the forehead is absent. Beak whitish gray, iris dark brown,

The Malee Ringneck Parakeet, *Barnardius barnardi,* is becoming increasingly rare in its native Australia as a result of human expansion.

The subspecies of the Port Lincoln Parakeet also known as the Twenty-eight Parakeet, *Barnardius zonarius semitorquatus,* occurs only in a restricted area of West Australia. Photo by F. Lewitzka.

legs gray. Female sometimes duller in coloration, head smaller and slightly narrower than in the male. An exact differentiation is very difficult, however. In the females and immature young the white bar on the wings is usually present. In young birds the adult coloration is complete by the time they are 12–14 months old.

Range: Inner Australia, east of the 138th degree of longitude: northern Queensland, New South Wales, South Australia, northwestern Victoria. The Cloncurry Parakeet is distributed over northwestern Queensland and the adjoining parts of the Northern Territory.

Habitat: Inhabits the so-called mallee scrub (a thicket formation of dwarf eucalyptus), open dry forests, savannahs, and the trees that grow by the riversides. Densely populated areas are avoided. Hence this species, as opposed to the Twenty-eight Parakeet, became rarer with the spread of human settlements.

Habits: Flies to the watering places in the morning, hiding in the shade of the leaves during the day, not reappearing until the evening. Food is frequently searched for on the ground. According to analyses of the crop contents, the birds consume grass seeds, the seeds of plants belonging to the

Barnardius barnardi macgillivrayi, a subspecies of the Mallee Ringneck Parakeet sometimes called the Conclurry Parakeet. Photo courtesy of Vogelpark Walsrode.

nightshade group, of oraches, acacias, one naturalized tobacco plant, and various kinds of melons. In addition, they feed on the seeds, flower buds, and nectar of eucalyptus trees. Breeding from August and September onwards, in the north after rainfalls. Four to six eggs, incubation period 20 days, nestling period 5 weeks. Often having a second brood. The favored nesting site consists of the hollows of dead trees. While the female is sitting in the nest, the male perches on a tree nearby and warns her of any disturbances. The female briefly leaves the nesting hollow in the morning and at dusk.

Keeping: At the London Zoo in 1853. Firm aviary constructions are essential since the parakeets gnaw through wood and weak wire. No related species should be kept in the adjacent compartments. Animals bred in Europe can withstand the winter; an unheated shelter is sufficient. The Cloncurry Parakeet came to England in 1939. In Germany this subspecies has been represented since 1965.

Diet: The birds are partial to germinated seeds picked up on the ground. Half-ripened seed heads, various kinds of fruit, walnuts, and plenty of greenstuff are taken in addition to the usual seed mixtures. Soaked rusk, egg biscuit, baby food, soft food, chopped egg, and fresh ant pupae, but most particularly dandelion heads, have proved suitable as rearing foods. Occasionally, worms are dug up and even bones are gnawed.

Breeding: First bred in captivity in France in 1884. The animals become suitable for breeding at 2 years of age. Many different nesting facilities are accepted, from the simple nest box of the dimensions 30 x 30 x 40 cm to natural tree trunks of over 1 m in height. Diameter of the entrance hole about 9 cm. A layer of earth and peat fibers should cover the bottom. After weeks of having been fed by her partner the female starts to lay eggs at the end of March. The eggs are produced at 2-day intervals. The incubating hen only leaves the nest for a short period in the morning and afternoon respectively. The fledged young birds are fed predominantly by the male and are independent after two weeks. Sexing the young is easiest at the time of fledging.

Head and beak are noticeably smaller in the female. The Cloncurry Parakeet was first bred in captivity in 1939 in Australia. First successful German propagation in 1969. Color mutations have been cultivated so far; only once was a yellow Mallee Ringneck Parakeet spotted in the birds' natural environment. Hybridization with *B. zonarius, B.z. semitorquatus*, Crimson Rosella, Pale-headed Rosella, Green Rosella, Eastern Rosella, Yellow Rosella, and Red-rumped Parakeet.

Behavior: Courtship begins with the male flying rapidly to and fro, calling constantly. There is no severe driving of the female. Here, too, the courting male assumes a square body shape by raising the wings. Throughout the mating display the male utters chattering call notes, and the fanned tail is moved quickly in a sideways direction.

A Port Lincoln Parakeet, *Barnardius zonarius,* investigating a tree cavity. Photo by L. Robinson.

Cockatiel, *Nymphicus hollandicus,* exhibiting the Pied mutation.

Cockatiel *Nymphicus*

The Cockatiel continues to be an object of controversy where zoological taxonomists are concerned. Although similar to the Broad-tails in body shape, the pointed crest, string-like ceres around the root of the beak, patches on the cheeks, and the fact that the male helps with the incubating are characteristics observed in the Cockatoos. Hence this form could either be a Cockatoo with the shape of a Parakeet or a Parakeet with the characteristics of Cockatoos.

One species.

Cockatiel

Nymphicus hollandicus (Kerr)
Characteristics: 32 cm long. Gray, underside paler and slightly brownish. Forehead, cheeks, crest, and throat yellow. Ear coverts a rusty red. Beak gray, iris dark brown, legs gray. In the female head and crest are gray, with only a slight tinge of yellow. Ear

With wild-colored Cockatiels, *Nymphicus hollandicus,* it is easy to distinguish the more dully colored females from the males.

coverts interspersed with gray feathers. Underside of tail gray, with yellow transverse bands. Juveniles similar in appearance, but sometimes the males already show more intense colors when still in the nest.

Range: The heart of Australia, accidental migrant in Tasmania.

Habitat: With the exception of dense forests occurring practically everywhere. Always in the proximity of water, often by the sides of country roads.

Habits: Common, not nervous. Often encountered in association with Red-rumped Parakeets. Outside the breeding season in small groups of 10–50 animals, gathering in huge numbers at the watering places during droughts. Droughts and food shortage cause the animals to migrate. In favorable conditions they raise several successive broods in the same locality. Food is looked for on the ground. The seeds of grasses and herbs as well as fruits and berries are consumed, millet fields are visited.

Above: Among Lutino Cockatiels some are more yellow, others more white.

Below: A male Cockatiel in flight. The white wing patches have a signaling function.

Many bird fanciers hold the opinion that no parakeet makes a better pet than a Cockatiel. Photo by Dr. Herbert R. Axelrod.

Breeding: Breeding season in the south from August to December, in the north at the end of the rainy season. In central Australia the birds may breed at any time of the year after rainfalls. The nests are often no more than a few meters above the ground, usually inside the hollows of dead eucalyptus trees. As noted by the author on one occasion in New South Wales, Red-rumped Parakeets and Budgerigars may be breeding in the immediate vicinity at the same time. Four to seven eggs, an incubation period of 21 days, a nestling period of 30 days. The male incubates from morning to late afternoon. It has been observed that incubating birds returned to the eggs with the plumage still damp from bathing.

Left: Cockatiels kept singly quite often become very trusting toward the people around them. Photo by Dr. Herbert R. Axelrod.

Below: Since Cockatiels, like many other parakeet species, exhibit a need to gnaw, wooden materials should be made available.

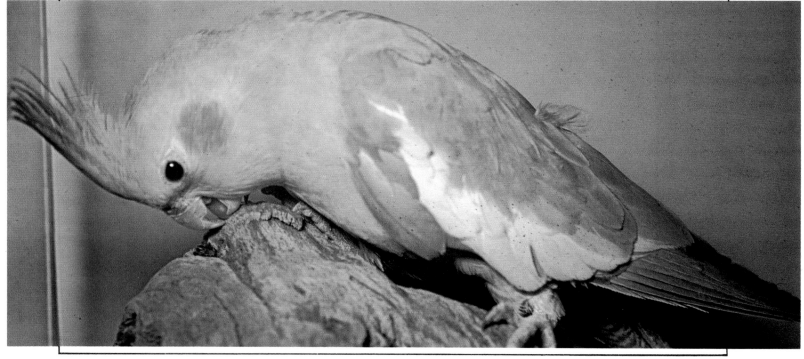

The wild-colored, or normal, adult male Cockatiel shows the full palette of colors possible in the species. All the current color varieties amount to subtractions of these colors in location or intensity. Photo by B. Kahl.

Keeping: Probably imported into Europe around 1845. Aviaries of the dimensions 2 x 3 x 2 m are sufficient. Not only is it possible to keep several pairs together, but the parakeets can also be associated with waxbills. Cockatiels do not do much gnawing, hence wooden constructions and thin wire suffice. Tame animals can be kept in a cage inside the house, provided they get the opportunity to exercise their wings every day. These birds react to disturbances and unexpected happenings with a loud fright behavior which can disturb even the neighbors. It certainly gets all the other birds in the aviary worked up. Nervous breeding birds should not, therefore, be accommodated too near the Cockatiels. Maximum age 25 years.

Diet: Canary seed, different millets, oats, just a few sunflower seeds, some hemp and niger, apples, carrots, germinated seeds, plenty of greenstuff. For rearing, soft food with hard-boiled egg, white bread soaked in milk.

Breeding: First bred around 1850 in Germany. Nest box 25 x 30 x 20 cm, diameter of entrance hole 8 cm, a perching rod to land on, a layer of sawdust on the bottom. Cockatiels allowed free flight inside the bird house even breed in half-open drawers. Only animals with a completely adult plumage can be used for breeding. Several successive broods, but only two successive broods should be permitted. Depending on the weather, the nest boxes may be hung up in March or April. Egg laying at 2-day intervals. The male incubates during the day; during the night both partners are in the nest. Incubation starts from the second or third egg onwards. Incubation period 19–21 days. If one of the partners dies, the brood is abandoned. First down yellow, first complete molt at the age of 4 months, adult plumage at 9 months. As soon as the young have hatched, the bottom layer of nesting material must be replaced from time to time to diminish the dirt accumulation. The young birds can be ringed at the age of 10 days. Cockatiels have proved useful as foster parents for various Rosellas. In recent years a number of color mutations (cinnamon, silver, pearled, pied, white black-eyed, albinos, and lutinos) have become increasingly popular.

Facing page: The appearance of this Cockatiel results from the presence of Pearl and Cinnamon factors. Photo by Michael Gilroy.

Below: Head study of a young Cockatiel hen. Photo by Dr. Herbert R. Axelrod.

Behavior: If disturbed in the nest, both young and adult birds sway from side to side and hiss. In large aviaries the males' wheeling courtship flight can be observed. In a manner similar to some Cockatoos, the courting birds hang head downward, the wings spread out, from a branch or from the entrance of the nesting hollow. On a branch the wooing male trips round his partner, warbling constantly, the wings raised high.

The Swift Parakeet, *Lathamus discolor,* cannot be kept successfully unless its dietary requirements are satisfied. Photo by A. J. Mobbs.

Swift Parakeet *(Lathamus)*

This species was frequently referred to as Swift Lory. The similarities with this group of parrots are, however, confined to certain adaptations of the beak and tongue, for feeding on pollen and nectar, which are not as extensive as in the Lories. The jerky movements of the Lories are absent, as are social preening and the close physical contact when roosting. As regards beak structure, arrangement of the feather flags, structure of the skull and pelvis, as well as the course of the arteries, it is a Rosella-type bird we have got here. This relationship is also indicated by the round-the-back way of scratching. One species.

Swift Parakeet

Lathamus discolor (White)
Characteristics: 24 cm long. Green, lighter and more yellowish on the underside. Crown blue; forehead, throat, under wing coverts red. Lores yellow. Shoulder brown-red. Under tail coverts light red. Beak horn colored, iris pale yellow, legs brownish. In females the color of the face is duller. Juveniles are duller in color and show less red on the face and on the under tail coverts. Iris brownish. Adult plumage at 6 months. A white wing bar is present in young birds; in adults it is not complete.
Range: Frequently nesting on Tasmania and several larger islands in the Bass Strait, winter visitor in southeastern Australia.
Habitat: Originally savannah woodland, today also in gardens and city parks. This parakeet is dependent on flowering trees and, therefore, finds the food situation in

parks particularly favorable.

Habits: Small groups, sometimes also larger flocks, which search for food among the high branches of flowering trees and fly at great heights, occasionally in association with Lories. Always conspicuous by their loud calls and, when feeding, not unduly alarmed by the approach of a human observer. Rarely seen to perch quietly, almost ceaselessly climbing about among the leaves. Only coming down to the ground in order to drink or to pick up seeds that have fallen down. The diet consists of nectar, insects (e.g., aphids), fruits, berries, greenstuff, and a variety of seeds. Fruit plantations are also visited. The nests are located at heights of 7–20 m in the hollows of eucalyptus trees. Often several pairs breed in the same tree. Two to five eggs, incubation period 20 days. While the male is seen in the nest periodically, there is no conclusive evidence that it actually does any of the incubating. In January the Swift Parakeets start to leave Tasmania (probably travelling by night); by the end of May they have all disappeared. In August they make their way back.

Keeping: At the London Zoo in 1863. Sufficient flying space must be provided. Before the birds are put in, above all the wire wall at the end of a long aviary must be covered with loose reed-matting or with branches to prevent the birds from flying into it. If moved into the aviary at the same time, several pairs can be kept together. Outside the breeding season peaceable towards other birds as well. Swift Parakeets do not gnaw, quickly grow confiding, and do not disturb anyone by screaming. They need to be protected from frost. Only rarely seen on the ground. In adaptation to their habits in the wild, the food should be offered on a high table or a shelf on the wall.

Diet: Lots of fruit, flowering twigs (as often as possible), berries, soft food, ant pupae, perhaps mealworms, a pap consisting of infant food and honey, white bread soaked in milk, greenstuff, canary seed, millet sprays, groats, half-ripened cereal, fresh corn on the cob, softened or germinated sunflower seeds, niger, and hemp are accepted. Although the parakeets get used to seeds very quickly, too much of this "unnatural" food tends to cause obesity and death.

Breeding: First bred in captivity in 1882, in France. In Germany from 1967 onwards. Nest box about 17 x 17 x 35 cm. Diameter of entrance hole 7 cm. Cover the bottom with a layer of rotting wood or a mixture of sawdust and peat fibers. Hang the box as high as possible. The male chooses the nest; he perches outside the access hole and flaps his wings. The approaching female is not allowed in until a few days later. First brood in April, sometimes a second one in June. Checks on the nest are tolerated. First down feathers of the young birds gray-white. During the first two weeks of life they are fed by the female, then by both parents. Fledging at 35–40 days, independent 2–3 weeks later. One-year-old birds can be used for breeding.

King Parakeets *(Alisterus)*

Like the next three genera, these birds belong to the Loriini. The characteristic shared by all members of this group is the smooth, wax-like surface of the beak. At least the upper mandibles of the males are red in most species. Tail feathers longer than the wings. In two species the sexes differ in coloration. All King Parakeets are readily identifiable by their intensely red, green, and blue plumage.

A similar coloration is found only in *Prosopeia tabuensis splendens*, a subspecies of the Red Shining Parakeet.

King Parakeets and the Red-winged Parakeets, discussed subsequently, should only be accommodated in aviaries with a length of at least 4 m. Even more suitable, of course, are enclosures that are longer still. If the birds do not get adequate flying space, they tend to become obese. In both groups, relentless persecution of the female by the male is not uncommon. One can ensure the female is able to escape by clipping a few of the male's flight feathers.

Three species.

In the king parakeets, the feathers of the tail are longer than those of the wing. This is the Amboina King Parakeet, *Alisterus amboinensis.* Photo by Dr. Herbert R. Axelrod.

King Parakeet

Alisterus scapularis (Lichtenstein)
Two subspecies.
Characteristics: With a length of 43 cm the largest Australian parakeet. Back and wings dark green, shoulders light green. Head, neck, and underside scarlet. Rump and a stripe on the nape dark blue. Tail greenish black. Upper mandible red with a black tip, lower mandible black. Iris yellow, legs gray. Females green with a red belly and a blue rump. Beak blackish. Juveniles of the same coloration as the hens. Beak light brown, iris brown. After a few months the upper mandibles in the females grow dark, in the males they turn red. After the first molt at the age of 14–18 months those areas of the plumage that later assume a red color grow red and green. The birds attain their complete adult coloration during the third year of life.
Range: Coastal regions of Queensland, New South Wales, and Victoria.
Habitat: Tropical rain forests at altitudes of up to
1600 m, eucalyptus forests, and dense scrubland in wet areas. Locally decreasing due to the cutting down of eucalyptus trees

or their replacement with Scots pines and other exotic trees.

Outside the breeding season also seen in parks, gardens, and on farms where they often come to the feeding places of the domestic hens.
Habits: Common. Pairs or family groups, young birds not yet showing the adult coloration. Flock together in groups of about 30 in the fall. Adult King Parakeets normally stay in one locality, only the birds that nest in mountain forests in the southern part of the range move down into the valleys. Food is looked for on trees and on the ground. The diet consists of berries, fruit, leaf buds, nectar, various seeds, wheat, and fresh corn. It is very likely that this species spreads the seeds of the mistletoe, rather like the Waxwing. Nesting in hollow trees, usually in dense forests. Entrance hole high up, the actual nest often near ground level. Breeding season September to January. Three to six eggs, incubation period 20 days, nestling period about 35 days. The male does not go far from the breeding tree and feeds his partner several times a day. The fledged young stay with their parents in a family group for some time.
Keeping: 1859 at London Zoo. Around 1870 frequently on the market at low prices. Newly imported Australian King Parakeets are delicate and require careful acclimatizaiton. Once acclimatized, however, the animals are hardy and long-lived. One Australian King Parakeet was kept for 30 years and bred right up to the end of its life. No related species must be housed in adjacent aviaries. Australian King Parakeets can be associated with unrelated species. Not sensitive to cold, an unheated shelter suffices. Australian King Parakeets do not gnaw, the aviaries may even be planted.
Diet: Sunflower seeds, wheat, oats, canary seed, some hemp, fresh corn on the cob, peanuts, apples, carrots, berries, rose hips, chickweed and other greenstuff. On the aviary floor the birds look for germinating seeds. For rearing, white bread soaked in milk, egg food, and plenty of vitamins and minerals, as the young birds are prone to rickets.
Breeding: First bred in captivity in 1880, in Germany. A large aviary is essential to

The Australian King Parakeet, *Alisterus scapularis,* is a sexually dimorphic species. The specimen shown here is a male. Photo by Irene & Michael Morcombe.

successful breeding. Nest boxes or natural tree trunks (internal diameter 33 cm, diameter of entrance hole 10 cm) must be affixed high in the outdoor aviary. Nest boxes are more readily accepted if camouflaged with bark. Females that are ready for mating invite the male to feed them. If the latter does not respond, another male should be introduced. Females are suitable for breeding at two years of age, males at the age of 3–4 years. The animals usually start breeding in May. The fledged young are fed for an additional 3–4 weeks, although still begging for food later on. Hybridization with Green-winged King Parakeet, Red-winged Parakeet, Superb's Parakeet, Red-rumped Parakeet, Crimson Rosella.

Behavior: In courting males the feathers on the head are erect while the remaining plumage remains smooth. Jerkily and whilst nodding the head he unfolds his wings. The calls that are being uttered at the same time are similar to the clucking of a domestic hen. Contractions of the pupils make the iris light up. Females in the breeding mood also raise the feathers on the head, keep the remaining plumage smooth, and invite the male to feed them. Contractions of the pupils can be observed.

Green-winged King Parakeet
Alisterus chloropterus (Ramsay)
Three subspecies.
Characteristics: 36 cm long. Head and underside crimson. Wings green with a light yellow-green patch on the shoulder. Lower back and rump blue, mantle black. The blue stripe on the nape is broader than in the Australian King Parakeet. Beak dark gray, upper mandible having an orange base. Iris orange, legs dark gray. Females having a green head, a green hind neck with red feather margins, a red belly, blue under tail coverts with reddish edges. Juveniles resemble the females but do not have any red on the throat and breast. Under tail coverts lacking the red edges. Beak brownish black with a lighter tip. Iris brown.

Range: Northwestern, central and eastern New Guinea.
Habitat: Very warm regions with a high humidity. Forests at altitudes of up to 1700 m.
Habits: Feeding on seeds, berries, fruits, nuts, buds, blossoms, and possibly insects. One male in the breeding mood was seen in July.
Keeping: 1909 at London Zoo. Today this species is said not to be represented in England at all, while a few pairs are being kept on the Continent. In view of the climatic conditions in the natural environment it is important above all to ensure the prevention of colds and chills during acclimatization.
Diet: Like that of the Australian King Parakeet. During the period of acclimatization freshly cooked or soaked corn, soaked sunflower seeds.
Breeding: First bred in England in 1945 when one pair, after nine years in captivity, raised a single young bird.

Amboina King Parakeet *Alisterus amboinensis* (Linne)
six subspecies.
Characteristics: 37 cm long. Head, neck, and underside crimson. Shoulder, back, rump, and upper tail coverts blue. Under tail coverts black with red feather margins. Tail black-blue, black below. Wings green, under wing coverts blue. No light patch on wings. Upper mandible red with a black tip. Iris orange, legs dark gray. The female is identical in coloration; the head is said to be smaller and rounder than that of the male. Juveniles generally having a green back. Beak orange-yellow, later turning brownish black. Iris brown. Orbital ring white.
Range: Various Indonesian islands (Amboina, Ceram, Halmahera, Buru, Sula, Peleng), northwestern New Guinea.
Habitat: Forest regions on plains and in the mountains (up to 1400 m).
Habits: Solitary or in pairs. Feeding high among the branches without becoming conspicuous by calling. The food consists of seeds, fruits, berries, buds, and acorns.
Keeping: Very rarely kept in the past, since 1971 imported more frequently, particularly the nominate form. As with the preceding

species, it is essential to provide warmth and a higher humidity, particularly during the period of acclimatization. Experience has shown that these parakeets are easier to acclimatize if kept in groups. Get on well with finches and small parakeets.

Diet: As per Australian King Parakeet and Green- winged King Parakeet. One pair raised its young on sunflower seeds, hemp, stone pine nuts, soaked millet, apples, and large quantities of greenstuff.

Breeding: First bred in captivity in 1940, in England. This was the subspecies *A. a. dorsalis* from New Guinea. Three eggs, incubating from the second egg onwards, incubation period 21 days, the young fledge at about 7 weeks. The nest boxes that were used had the dimensions 45 x 15 x 120 cm as well as 30 x 30 x 180 cm. Newly hatched young birds are coverd in fluffly white down feathers. Already four weeks after fledging the iris changes from its original brown color to orange.

Red-winged Parakeets (*Aprosmictus*)

Closely related to the Australian King Parakeet but slightly smaller, with a shorter tail.

Two species.

Red-winged Parakeet

Aprosmictus erythropterus (Gmelin)
Two subspecies.

Characteristics: 33 cm long. Bright green. Upper back and shoulders black. Wing coverts scarlet. Median portion of back and region of hump blue. Beak coral red, iris orange-red, legs dark gray. Females of a duller green, the red on the wing coverts less extensive. Iris light brown, beak lighter than in the males and more brownish in color. Juveniles similar to the females, the beaks of very young animals are yellowish, iris dark brown. Differentiation of the sexes normally not possible until 18 months when

Female Red-winged Parakeet, *Aprosmictus erythropterus*. This parakeet occurs in Australia and New Guinea. Photo by Dr. Herbert R. Axelrod.

The male Red-winged Parakeet, *Aprosmictus erythropterus,* is easily distinguished from the female by the more extensive red wing patches. Photo by G. Ebben.

the males show their first black feathers on the back. Also appearing at this stage is a further row of red feathers on the wing coverts. A report exists of a young male already possessing the fully-developed plumage of an adult bird after as little as one year. As a rule the adult plumage is not complete until after the second molt in the third year of life. Sometimes parakeet fanciers attempt to sex their animals prematurely by pulling out a few of the feathers on the back. If the regenerated feathers are black, the bird concerned is a male. This method is not always successful.
Range: Northern Queensland, central New South Wales to northeastern South Australia. The slightly smaller subspecies *A. e. coccineopterus* is distributed over Northern Territory and the southern part of New Guinea.
Habitat: Open eucalyptus forest, scrubland, mangrove regions. Dense forests are avoided.
Habits: Common, shy. In pairs, or outside the breeding season in groups of up to 20. An even greater number of parakeets may assemble among the branches of flowering trees. Where the range of distribution overlaps with that of the Australian King Parakeet mixed flocks occur. Among

sandarach cypresses the Red-winged Parakeets are seen together with Pale-headed Rosellas and Mallee Ringneck Parakeets. Usually the parakeets keep to the treetops, only coming down to the ground to drink or to pick up seeds that have dropped. The diet consists of seeds, fruits (also from plantations), berries (including mistletoe berries), buds, and insects. Usually nesting in the hollows of eucalyptus trees in the proximity of water. Breeding season in the south from September to December, in the north from April to July. Three to six eggs, incubation period 3 weeks, nestling period 5 weeks. The fledged young remain with their parents for a considerable time. In order to feed or to be fed by the male, the incubating female leaves the nest in the morning and early in the afternoon. The breeding hollows are frequently very deep. In one case the distance between the entrance hole and the actual nest base was as much as 9 m.
Keeping: 1861, at London Zoo. Acclimatized birds are quiet, they neither scream much nor do a lot of gnawing. Newly imported specimens are often nervous, have a tendency towards feather plucking and to

Red-winged Parakeets, *Aprosmictus erythropterus,* do not attain mature coloration until they are eighteen months old.

sudden molt due to shock. It can happen that the parakeets, which remain shy for a long time, refuse to go inside the indoor shelter at night. Spacious aviaries with attached indoor shelter. Like the Australian King Parakeet, this species—particularly animals that have been raised in captivity—tolerates winter temperatures. Bathing facilities must be available. Immature birds of up to 12 months can be kept in association with other species. Later the birds have to be kept in pairs. The adjacent aviaries must not be occupied by related species.

Diet: Sunflower seeds, canary seed, various kinds of millet, wheat, hemp. All these seeds also in a germinated condition. Groats, apples, carrots, berries, plenty of greenstuff. During the breeding season egg food, soft food, chopped hard-boiled egg, a few mealworms, soaked white bread.

Breeding: Bred in captivity for the first time in 1881, in France. High nest boxes with an internal diameter of 30 cm and a length of 1–2 m have proved suitable. Diameter of entrance hole 10 cm. Provision for climbing should be made on the inside wall. In March the male starts to drive his partner. If he becomes too aggressive, a few of the primaries should be clipped. In outdoor aviaries the nest boxes must not be put up until April, in case there is another cold spell. Egg laying at intervals of 2 days. The male comes inside the nest several times a day in order to feed the female. Later he helps to feed the young at the same time. If the male abandons his responsibilities, the female will manage to rear the brood on her own. First down plumage white and dense, second down (after ten days) gray. By the time the young are 2 weeks old the female leaves the nest more frequently. Until they fledge she still warms them during the night, however. The fledged young are independent after about 4 weeks. A second brood is rare, although there will be a second clutch if the first one does not survive. Male sexually mature in the third year, female in the second year. Hybridization with Timor Red-winged Parakeet, Amboina King Parakeet, Regent Parakeet.

Behavior: Courting males fly around the female a few times and then land near her.

The wings are made to droop, revealing the blue color on the back. With the feathers lying close to the body and the pupils contracted a further approach is made, eventually resulting in feeding; the female begs with a soft cawing noise. Copulation takes place mostly early in the morning and at dusk.

Timor Red-winged Parakeet
Aprosmictus jonquillaceus (Vieillot)
Two subspecies.
Characteristics: 35 cm long. Head, underside, and upper tail coverts bright yellow-green. Upper region of back dark green with blue feather margins, lower back blue. Only outer and anterior wing coverts red, remainder yellow-green. Beak reddish at the base, tip yellowish. Iris orange, legs dark gray. In the female, the blue margins are absent from the feathers of the upper back. Juveniles of the same coloration as the female, iris light brown. After the first molt the wing coverts of the young males are yellowish with a few red feathers.
Range: Timor Island (at altitudes of up to 2600 m), Wetar Island.
Keeping: Imported on various occasions since 1970.
Breeding: First bred in captivity in 1974, in Germany. Hybridization with Red-winged Parakeet.

Parakeets of the genus *Prosopeia*

The largest species of parakeets. Slender; long, rounded tail; rounded wings. In need of warmth and a high humidity, therefore, hardly suitable for being kept in the European climate, certainly not in outdoor aviaries.

Two species.

The Red Shining Parakeet, *Prosopeia tabuensis,* is indigenous to the Fiji Islands. This specimen is a female. Photo courtesy of San Diego Zoo.

The male Red Shining Parakeet, *Prosopeia tabuensis,* exhibits a brighter shade of red than the female. Photo courtesy of San Diego Zoo.

Red Shining Parakeet
Prosopeia tabuensis (Gmelin)
Five subspecies.
Characteristics: 46 cm long. Head and underside red. Face reddish black. Broad blue band on the nape. Back and wings green. Greater coverts and under tail coverts blue. Beak dark gray, iris yellow-orange, legs dark gray. In the female the head and beak are smaller. In juveniles the underside is said to be green. Beak paler, iris brown.
Range: Fiji Islands.
Habitat: Rain forest, mangrove regions.
Habits: Common, also encountered in villages. Not shy. Looking for food in small groups in the morning and at night, rarely seen during the day. Fruits and berries constitute the preferred foods. Visiting not only fruit plantations but also corn fields. Kept as pets in their native regions. Animals allowed free flight spend the day in the forests and return at night. Nests have been found in August.
Keeping: In 1864 *P. t. splendens* was kept in London. Imported very rarely. Newly imported birds retreat into the darkest corner of the aviary at first. At dusk and in moonlit nights they are active. Later, these parakeets are quiet during the day. Acclimatization is difficult; the birds need hothouse conditions.
Diet: Sunflower seeds, canary seed, millet, oats, hemp, peanuts, berries, apples and other kinds of fruit, greenstuff. At San Diego Zoo, Red Shining Parakeets are fed on milo maize, wheat, millet, stone pine nuts, oranges, papayas, figs, bilberries, lettuce, and bread.
Breeding: A few attempts at crossing subspecies of this species with each other have been successful, but also hybridization of *P. t. splendens* with *P. personata*. Pure breeding of *P. t. splendens* first succeeded in 1976 in Texas, U.S.A. Incubation period 24 days. Color change of the iris from brown to yellow at 6 months.

Masked Shining Parakeet
Prosopeia personata (G. R. Gray)
Characteristics: 47 cm long. Emerald green. Face black. Breast and upper central abdominal region yellowish. Lower abdomen orange in the center. Primaries

The Red Shining Parakeet, *Prosopeia tabuensis,* is a delicate species than can be maintained only under greenhouse conditions.

pale blue on the outside, secondaries green on the outside. Greater coverts and primaries gray-black, iris orange-red, legs gray-black. In the female, head and beak slightly smaller. Juveniles having paler beaks, the iris is brown. One striking characteristic of this species is the penetrating musky odor.
Range: The Fiji Island of Viti Levu.
Habitat: Forests, mangrove swamps, dense scrub on river banks.
Habits: By no means rare but endangered by progessive deforestation. In pairs or small groups. Loud and nervous. Food consists of seeds, berries, the fruits of mangroves, and bananas. Nesting in hollow trees. Two to four eggs.
Keeping: Represented in a menagerie in 1848, in 1862 at London Zoo. Very rarely kept. More recently, after 1970, a single pair was kept at San Diego Zoo and a few Masked Shining Parakeets lived in the aviaries of Dr. Burkard in Zurich.
Diet: Sunflower seeds, oats, soaked corn, peanuts, a variety of fruit.

Breeding: Crossed with *P. t. splendens* in Zurich in 1973.

A male Masked Shining Parakeet, *Prosopeia personata.* Like its congener, the Red Shining Parakeet, this species is very rare in captivity. Photo courtesy of San Diego Zoo.

Parakeets of the genus *Psittacella*

Body of a short, stocky build; thick bill, swollen at the sides. Ceres as in Rosellas. Tail short (about two thirds the length of the wings) and rounded. Sexes differing in color.

Three species.

Brehm's Parrot

Psittacella brehmii (Schlegel)

Six subspecies.

Characteristics: 24 cm long. Body, wings, and tail green, upper parts with black transverse bands. Head olive brown. A yellow stripe on each side of the neck. Under tail coverts red. Beak gray with a light tip, iris red, legs gray. Female slightly smaller without yellow stripes on the neck, breast yellowish with black transverse bands. Juveniles like the female, but breast green and with dull yellow bands.

Range: Northwestern, central, eastern, and southeastern New Guinea.

Habitats: Dense mountain forests at altitudes of between 1700 and 3600 m.

Habits: So far only observed singly or in pairs. Shy. Feed on seeds, fruits, and berries. On one occasion a male in breeding condition was seen in January. Nestlings were found in June.

Keeping: To date, this species appears to have been kept only in New Guinea. But even here the life span was short.

Diet: Sunflower seeds, various kinds of fruit.

Painted Parrot *Psittacella picta* (Rothschild)

Three subspecies.

Characteristics: 19 cm long. Upper parts green, crown reddish brown, sides of head gray-brown. An orange- yellow band on both sides of the neck. Rump and upper tail coverts deep red. Back and rump with black

Brehm's Parrot, *Psittacella brehmii*, is one of three species of a genus that is mostly unknown in aviculture. Photo courtesy of San Diego Zoo.

transverse bands. Chin, throat, upper breast blue. Under tail coverts red, remaining underparts green. Beak bluish gray, iris orange, legs dark gray. Female without yellow bands on the neck, breast and lateral abdomen yellow with black bands.
Range: Southeastern and southern New Guinea.
Habitat: Mountain forests between 2500 and 4000 m.
Habits: Common but difficult to detect. Males in breeding condition were observed in June and August.

Modest Parrot
Psittacella modesta (Schlegel)
Six subspecies.
Characteristics: 14 cm long. Head and neck olive brown. Back uniformly green. Breast of a dirty olive color. Under tail coverts red. Beak bluish gray with a light tip. Iris orange, legs gray. Female yellowish green beneath with dark brownish transverse bands, breast with black brown and red transverse bands that have yellow margins.
Range: Northern half of New Guinea.
Habitat: Mountain forests between 1700 and 2800 m.
Habits: The diet consists of seeds, berries, fruits, greenstuff. Sexually mature males were observed in June. Egg laying was recorded in the month of September.

Grass Parakeets *(Neophema)*

The endearing little Australian Grass Parakeets like to spend their time on the ground. This behavior and their preference for grass seeds explain the name of this group of parakeets. All species are seemingly dainty, being slightly larger than Budgerigars.

In the wild they often climb about on dense shrubs, when they are running about on the ground persistently nibbling at grasses. This should be taken into consideration when it comes to preparing the aviary. Part of the latter may be stocked with plants, since these parakeets do little if any gnawing, and one portion of the ground (which is not subjected to contamination from above) covered with grass sods. To house a single pair an aviary with heat available, measuring about 3 x 1 x 2 m with an attached indoor shelter is needed. Assoication with waxbills is possible, with related species squabbles result even through a wire partition. Four species are being kept and bred on a regular basis outside their native range. The most pleasant attribute of the small parakeets is their melodius twittering which even in small gardens does not disturb the neighbor. These parakeets are unsuitable for a permanent life in the cage. If they do not get enough exercise, they very quickly grow obese. At the very least such birds must not be given any oily seeds. New imports (which seldom reach Europe nowadays) are delicate and need to be acclimatized in a warm room. They must be offered grass seeds, millet, canary seed, poppy seeds, ant pupae, egg food, and greenstuff. Even later they will remain sensitive to cold and damp. In addition to the foods already mentioned, the birds may be given small amounts of hemp, niger, small sunflower seeds, linseed, and groats. Special favorites are millet sprays and panicles. Soaked and germinated seeds, the half-ripened seed heads of millet and grasses, white bread soaked in milk, commercial parakeet rearing food, and greenstuff should be provided, particularly when there are young being reared. Various kinds of fruit as well as carrots round off the menu.

Grass Parakeets are suitable for breeding when they are one year old. During the first breeding year some hens only lay once, in subsequent years there are usually two broods. Nest boxes should be hung in April.

Its dimensions should be approximately 20 x 20 x 30 cm. The diameter of the entrance hole about 6 cm (starling box). Natural tree trunks are preferred nesting grounds. The nest bottom should be covered with a mixture of peat fibers and soil. Four to six eggs are laid as a rule, in exceptional cases up to 10 may be laid. Since a female is only able to cover 7 eggs at the most, the surplus must be removed. Incubation frequently starts after the second or third egg is in the nest, lasting 18–19 days. Newly hatched chicks are first covered in long white down. Until they are 10 days old they are constantly warmed by the hen. Fledging occurs at 4 weeks. To prevent the young birds from flying into dangerous wire surfaces they must be covered with branches, reed-matting, or corrugated plastic in good time. Three weeks after fledging the young are independent. Until the young males show the complete adult coloration they can be left with the parents. It is a sight that makes the heart of every bird fancier leap when in the morning sun a flight of these dainty parakeets comes up to the wire mesh, twittering, and collects the tidbits that are being pushed through. Immediately after the young have fledged the females proceed to lay a second time. It is advisable to provide a second nest box for this.

Six species.

Elegant Grass Parakeet
Neophema elegans (Gould)
Characteristics: 23 cm long. Olive green. A dark blue band on the forehead, above it and running parallel with it a pale blue band which extends to beyond the eyes. Cheeks yellowish. Abdomen yellow with a

The Scarlet-chested Grass Parakeet, *Neophema splendida,* is the smallest of the grass parakeets. These are male and female.

small, orange-red patch. A bright blue area on the outer wing coverts. Under wing coverts dark blue. Tail blue above, yellow below. Beak gray-black, iris brown, legs gray-brown. Females duller in coloration, the band on the forehead is narrow and light blue, the orange-red patch on the belly is absent. The white bar on the wings is only present occasionally, in the males it is absent. Juveniles similar to the females. A blue band on the forehead, if present at all, very faint. Full adult plumage at 4–6 months.

Distribution: Two geographically separate ranges of distribution, southwestern Australia as well as South Australia, New South Wales, and Victoria. Of all the Grass Parakeets this species is the one that is most widely distributed.

Habitat: Open landscapes, but particularly grass terrain where shrubs grow. This species also penetrates into eucalyptus woods, although avoiding really dense forest regions. A marked increase in numbers in Western Australia, which is connected not only with deforestation but also with the increased cultivation of clover.

Habits: Among the shrubs well camouflaged by the color of their plumage. Hence in the event of disturbances they usually only fly off at the last moment and soon come back down again. Only when disturbed a second time do they actually fly off at a great height. The diet consists mainly of the seeds of grasses and weeds, in the areas where clover is being grown predominantly of clover seeds. Breeding season August to November. Nesting inside hollow branches and inside rotten tree stumps.

Keeping: Imported into England in 1859. Provided a frost-proof indoor shelter is at their disposal, Grass Parakeets will be all right in the winter without there being any need for additional precautions.

Diet: Mainly millet and grass seeds. At least during the breeding season the seeds should be offered in a germinated or half-ripened condition.

Breeding: First bred in captivity in 1859 at London Zoo. In 1972 lutinos were cultivated in Belgium. Hybridization with Turquoise Grass Parakeet, Scarlet-chested Grass Parakeet, Blue-winged Grass Parakeet.

In the Elegant Grass Parakeet, *Neophema elegans,* the blue frontal band extends beyond the eye.

Blue-winged Grass Parakeet

Neophema chrysostoma (Kuhl)
Characteristics: 22 cm long. Upper parts olive green. Intense blue of wing coverts more extensive than in the Elegant Grass Parakeet. The blue band on the forehead only extends as far as the eyes. Lores yellow. Throat and breast green-yellow; belly red with an orange colored patch which, according to observations in the wild, is conspicuously bright during the breeding season while subsequently growing fainter and often almost disappearing completely until the molt sets in. Primaries black, under wing coverts blue. Beak bluish gray, iris brown, legs gray-brown. Females duller in coloration, the band on the forehead is less broad, the primaries are more brownish black. Color of juveniles duller still, the band on the forehead is absent. The white bar on the underside of the wings is present at least in young female animals. Beak horn colored.

Full adult plumage at 8–9 months.
Range: Southeastern Australia, Tasmania (where it is the most common species of parakeet), islands in the Bass Strait.
Habitat: No special biotopic adaptation. Blue-winged Grass Parakeets are seen, as often, in inland forests at high altitudes as in meadows near the coast.
Habits: Migrating from Tasmania to the mainland in the late fall. No records, so far, of the birds having bred in New South Wales and Queensland. In the last few years there has been a marked tendency towards wintering in the southern breeding ranges. Feeding on the ground, in the morning and late in the afternoon. In addition to grass seeds, the birds look for seeds and fruit in gardens and fields. Together with Green Rosellas, the Blue-winged Grass Parakeets also visit fruit plantations. The strikingly peaceable sociability remains in evidence even during the breeding season. Up to ten pairs keep fairly close together and where the opportunity exists several pairs breed in the same tree. Mixed breeding colonies with Green Rosellas and Swift Parakeets are repeatedly being observed. Outside the breeding season Blue-winged Grass Parakeets may flock together with Elegant and Orange-bellied Grass Parakeets. The female usually chooses her nesting hollow at a greater height (6–30 m). She cleans the nest and removes the larger pieces of wood. When she is incubating the male supplies her with food outside the hollow. Breeding season October to January.
Keeping: 1874, at Berlin Zoo. The most peaceable species of this genus, can be kept in association with various small birds, including species of parakeets. The bird's quiet nature makes it prone to obesity. This species is not very suitable for cage dwelling. Only in association with members of its own species, as well as with birds of other species in a large aviary, will it receive sufficient exercise and stimulation to stay healthy.
Diet: Oily seeds should only be given in small quantities.
Breeding: First bred in captivity in France,

Blue-winged Grass Parakeet, *Neophema chrysostoma.* In this species the blue frontal band ends at the eye.

in 1879. This species is slightly more difficult to propagate than Scarlet-chested or Turquoise Grass Parakeets. Above all, Blue-winged Grass Parakeets are a little more fastidious when it comes to choosing their partner. They appear to need the stimulation provided by members of their own species. Once a pair has started to breed, however, there will be no further problems.

Behavior: Courting males stretch out to their full height and let their wings droop. The blue color becomes strikingly noticeable as a result. At a later stage the female is fed.

Orange-bellied Grass Parakeet
Neophema chrysogaster (Latham)

Orange-bellied Grass Parakeet, *Neophema chrysogaster*. Photo by F. Lewitzka.

Characteristics: 20 cm long. Upper parts grass green, head, back, and rump darker. Breast yellowish green, belly yellow with large orange-red area. Blue band on forehead bounded at the top by a faint blue stripe running parallel with it. An important characteristic is the greenish lores. Primaries dark blue, middle wing coverts of a paler blue. Median tail feathers green at the base, with a blue edge. Underside of tail yellow. Beak brown-gray, iris brown, legs gray. In the female the band on the forehead is narrower, the upper stripe is absent. Coloration as a whole duller than in the male. Juveniles resemble the female, the orange colored spot on the belly is smaller. White bar on underside of wings. Full adult plumage probably at 8–9 months.

Range: Tasmania, islands in the Bass Strait, southeastern regions of South Australia, New South Wales, Victoria.

Habitat: Seashores, swamps near the coast, landscapes dominated by heather and shrubs. During the breeding season often further inland.

Habits: The rarest species of the genus. In pairs of small groups. Spending the daytime searching for food on the ground or resting under a tuft of grass or a shrub. The active period begins before sunrise and lasts until after dusk has set in. Breeding season November to January. Nesting at low heights in hollow trees. Four to six eggs. The breeding ranges of the Orange-bellied Grass Parakeets otherwise living elsewhere in Tasmania and in Victoria are said to be in southwestern Tasmania.

Keeping: 1873 at London Zoo. After 1970 a few came to Holland and Belgium. Anyone who manages to acquire some of these precious birds should look after them with the greatest care. This means ensuring that the animals are not exposed to extreme weather conditions and preventing a possible infestation with worms by scrupulous cleanliness. As for all species that like to gather their food on the ground, the danger of infection is very real for the Orange- bellied Grass Parakeet. To be on the safe side, fecal specimens should be examined at regular intervals.

Breeding: Possibly first bred in captivity in the 40s in Australia.

Rock Grass Parakeet
Neophema petrophila (Gould)
Characteristics: 21 cm long. Looking like a dark edition of the Turquoise Grass Parakeet, to whom this species is closely related. Of all the Grass Parakeets the dullest in coloration. Olive green, belly and vent yellowish, belly orange in the center. Band on forehead and edges of wings dark blue, lores and eye region pale blue. Beak gray, iris dark brown, legs gray-brown. In the females the pale blue of lores and eye region is less extensive, the band on the forehead is narrower. Juveniles are duller in coloration, the blue on the forehead and in the eye region is not yet present. White bar on underside of wing fully formed. Full adult plumage at about 5 months.
Range: Shores and islands of southwestern and southern Australia.
Habitat: Treeless and shrubless islands, heather and sand dune landscapes. The parakeets never move more than several hundred meters from the shore.
Habits: Usually in pairs, only seldom in groups. Relatively confiding so that one can observe the animals easily. Staple food, along with grass seeds, the seeds of *Mesembryanthemum* which covers vast areas virtually everywhere in the coastal regions. Nesting in rock cavities, often right next to gulls and oyster catchers. Frequently breeding in colonies. Breeding period August to October, 4– 6 eggs. Often two broods.
Keeping: Imported into Europe around 1870. Today no Rock Grass Parakeets are allowed to be kept outside Australia. Because of its unassuming coloration and tendency to become obese, this species was not popular.
Diet: At Adelaide Zoo, Rock Grass Parakeets are fed on canary seed, millet, groats, and the half ripened seed heads of various grasses.
Breeding: First bred in captivity in 1879, in Germany (Dr. Russ). More recently, only propagated in Australia on several occasions. The animals bred among stones, but also in nest boxes. At the zoo in Adelaide boxes of the dimensions 37 x 13 x 15 cm or natural hollows of similar size are hung up in a sloping position.

Turquoise Grass Parakeets, *Neophema pulchella*, are easy to keep and breed.

Turquoise Grass Parakeet
Neophema pulchella (Shaw)
Characteristics: 20 cm long. Olive green. Face, lesser and median wing coverts turquoise blue. Lower wing coverts and outer edge of flight feathers dark blue. Inner wing coverts red ochre. Underside yellow. There is also a variety with an orange colored breast which may have evolved as a result of the constant influence of a higher humidity. Beak black-gray, iris brown, legs dark gray. Females are paler in color, have less blue in the face and no red ochre on the shoulder. White bars on the underside of the wings. Juveniles resemble the females. Young males have slightly more blue in the face and often a few individual red feathers on the shoulders. White wing bars present. Full adult coloration after about six months.
Range: Southeastern Australia. Regarded as extinct from time to time. Today, although rare, not endangered.
Habitat: Woody grassland, woody and hilly terrain, steep rocky valleys.
Habits: Turquoise Grass Parakeets were

Rare in the wild of its native Australia, the Turquoise Grass Parakeet, *Neophema pulchella,* is kept and bred by aviculturists the world over. Photo by Dr. Herbert R. Axelrod.

common right up to the last few years of the previous century. The rapid decline in numbers that set in soon afterwards was due to the destruction of the landscape, although probably also the result of a contagious disease. Today the species is encountered regularly at least in New South Wales. The animals are seen singly, in pairs, and occasionally in groups of up to 30. The water places appear to be visited only once a day, i.e., before sunrise. The birds are particularly wary at that time, whereas they show little fear when feeding on the ground. The basic diet consists of the seeds of grasses and herbs. The species breeds inside the hollow branches of eucalyptus trees at heights of 5–20 m. Sometimes the breeding hollows are up to 1 m deep. Incubation period August to December, but one can still find the occasional clutch as late as in May. The incubating female sits tight on her eggs; the male feeds her in the morning and at night.

Keeping: First imports into Europe around 1850. Due to having been bred in captivity for generations this species has become well acclimatized and is suitable for the beginner. Should be accommodated in aviaries or in the birdroom. The Turquoise Grass Parakeet gets on well with Waxbills and other small birds. It is more likely for the aggressive Zebra Waxbill to disturb the Turquoise Grass Parakeet than the other way round. Less suitable for the cage, unless the birds are allowed to fly about in the room at least once a day. Not as tolerant towards one another, the pairs should be housed separately; the adjacent aviaries should not be stocked with related species.

Breeding: First bred in captivity in Paris in 1855. Four to seven eggs. Generally two broods; a third brood should be prevented. Vertical nest boxes (with landing rod) are more popular than horizontal ones. The bottom should be covered with a thin layer of peat fibers and fine wood shavings. Ready for breeding at the age of one year. In Pinter's experience egg binding and other complications are common in one-year-old females, therefore, he recommends that two-year-old females be used for breeding. The fledged young are independent after about 3 weeks and should be separated from the parents, otherwise the cock may attack his male

progeny. The best rearing foods have turned out to be chickweed with seed heads, half-ripened grass seeds, and green millet panicles. Germinated food and soft food are also accepted. Breeding presents no problems, making it likely that today the Turquoise Grass Parakeets that live in the aviaries of bird fanciers outnumber those in the wild. Yellow mutation. Hybridization with Blue-winged, Elegant, and Scarlet-chested Grass Parakeet.

Behavior: Females have been observed to stick leaves into their plumage on occasion. It is possible that nesting material may be transported in this way, as is done by certain Lovebirds and Hanging Parrots. Courting males "strut about" with retracted feathers, the wings slightly spared.

Scarlet-chested Grass Parakeet
Neophema splendida (Gould)

Characteristics: With a length of about 20 cm, the smallest species of Grass Parakeet. Back green, face and ear coverts blue, throat and upper breast scarlet. Belly and underside of tail yolk yellow. Wing coverts pale blue. Beak blackish, iris brown, legs gray-brown. Females have a green breast, the head is pale blue. The lores are blue (white in the female of the Turquoise Grass Parakeet). Juveniles resemble the hen, but are slightly paler. In young males the head is slightly bluer than in the females; at the age of 2–3 months individual red breast feathers appear. The full adult plumage is only attained in the second year of life. The white bar on the underside of the wings is not present in all young birds.

Range: Western New South Wales, northern South Australia, the interior of Western Australia.

Habitat: Found inland, often at a great distance from the nearest watering place. Dry eucalyptus and acacia scrubland; saltbush and spinifex landscapes, i.e., semiarid terrain.

Habits: Considered extinct at the beginning of the present century. Today rare in the east, but a marked increase in southwestern Australia. Despite the colorful plumage of the males, Scarlet-chested Grass Parakeets are fairly inconspicuous in their natural environment. They almost never call, keep to the undergrowth, and go into hiding

Male Scarlet-chested Parakeet, *Neophema splendida,* in flight. Because of the small size of this species, accommodations that permit ample flight space are more readily provided.

when disturbances occur. Staying in one locality. In Western Australia, however, the parakeets also come into the fields and front gardens. In accordance with the original habitat, the drinking requirements are minimal. Often the parakeets do not visit the water place for days on end, although probably satisfying their needs with dewdrops and chewing plants with a high water content. Breeding season August to December. The nests are usually built inside the hollows of low acacias. Three to five eggs, rarely six.

Keeping: 1871, in London. The parakeets brought to Europe were particularly delicate. Above all they tolerated the damp climate badly and usually died very quickly. An examination carried out by Dr. Frank of Hohenheim University in collaboration with the AZ (German exchange center of bird fanciers and aviculturists) established that infestation with maw-worms and thread-worms was the most common cause of mortality. Once the appropriate counter measures had been taken there were few if any problems. Today this bird has become one of the most common and popular aviary birds, accessible to the less wealthy and no longer presenting any difficulties in keeping and breeding. Obviously these parakeets must be protected from damp and cold; a dry indoor shelther must be made available to them. In view of the origin of the Scarlet-chested Grass Parakeets, warm winter quarters have to be provided. Accommodation in bird rooms (or if necessary, in larger cages) is perfectly appropriate where this drought loving species is concerned. Insufficient opportunity for exercise quickly results in obesity. The aviary should be planted, not just for optical reasons but also to enable the female to take leaves back to the nest. The enclosure should be sunny, since Scarlet-chested Grass Parakeets like to sunbathe with their wings spread out. Dry sand, enabling the birds to take dust baths, should also be made available. If fruit and greenstuff are supplied in adequate quantities, little water is consumed. Scarlet-chested Grass Parakeets are peaceable and can be kept in association with other birds.

Breeding: First bred in captivity in 1932, in Australia; in England, in 1934. Two broods per year are not uncommon. A third brood should be avoided as these young rarely thrive. Checks on the nest hardly bother the incubating female. Popular rearing foods are weeds with half-ripened seeds, half-ripe panic millet, chickweed, dandelion heads, shepherd's purse, germinated millet (particularly spray millet). Appropriate additions of vitamins are especially important, not only during the nestling period but also later on when the young birds go through the critical stage of changing to the adult plumage. If the female starts a second brood the male continues feeding the fledged young on his own. The cock does not invariably attack his offspring later on, but one should always keep the animals under close observation. Blue, yellow, cinnamon, and fawn colored mutations. Hybridization with Blue-winged, Elegant, and Turquoise Grass Parakeet. The hybrids are said to be infertile.

Behavior: Sunbathing position, dust bathing. Females line their breeding hollows with leaves which they carry inserted among the rump feathers. The courting male hops about on the ground in short leaps with fanned tail feathers, encircling the female. Every so often he stops and feeds her.

Red-capped Parakeets, *Purpureicephalus spurius,* were originally woodland birds, but now they may be seen in parks and orchards.

Red-capped Parakeet
(Purpureicephalus)

Closely related to the Rosellas (genus *Platycercus*), but differing in coloration and showing distinct differences in behavior as well. In adaptation to the shelling of eucalyptus seed capsules, the beak is narrow and long.

One species.

Red-capped Parakeet

Purpureicephalus spurius (Kuhl)
Characteristics: 37 cm long. Upper parts green. Crown, down to eye level, red. Cheeks, rump, and upper tail coverts yellow-green. Breast and belly violet-blue. Edges of wings and under wing coverts blue. Under tail coverts, flanks, and thighs red. Tail green above, with a blue luster, pale blue below. Beak dark bluish gray, iris dark brown, legs brown. Females duller in coloration; the red crown has a tinge of green or the red may be entirely replaced by green. More greenish on the flanks and under tail coverts. Wing bar present. Immatures predominantly green, having a rust colored band on the forehead, breast and belly pale vermillion brown. Still

duller in coloration than adult females. In the males only about six white spots can be seen on the underside of the wings, in the females considerably more. Head of male rather more massive. The first red feathers on the head appear in males that are 5 months old. Full adult coloration at 14–16 months.

Range: Southwestern Australia.

Habitat: Originally a woodland bird (eucalyptus), but also found in parks and orchards.

Habits: In pairs or in small groups. Eucalyptus seeds form the bulk of the diet. In addition, pollen, nectar, buds, grass seeds, and insects are eaten and orchards raided. The damage that is done to the latter is considerable because of all the fruit the birds attack in order to get at the core. Despite all the persecution, these parakeets have not become any rarer. Breeding hollows usually at a great height. Five to six eggs, in rare exceptional cases up to 9. Incubation period 20 days, nestling period 5 weeks. It is likely that the fledged young remain with their parents for several months in a family group.

Keeping: First kept at London Zoo, in 1854. In Germany, Red-capped Parakeets have been kept more frequently since about 1960. These agile parakeets should have an aviary of about 5 cm in length at their disposal. For the winter an unheated shelter is sufficient. Sometimes they destroy wooden structures, which can be prevented at least to some extent by a constant supply of fruit tree and willow branches. The preference for a bath is particularly marked. Only a few days after fledging the young birds take a bath; incubating females also bathe at regular intervals, afterwards they return to the eggs and continue to incubate with wet plumage. Red-capped Parakeets interact fairly well with small species of parakeets and other aviary residents. The voice sounds harsh, but is not very loud. Unfortunately these parakeets tend to remain shy. They immediately disappear into the indoor shelter when the aviary is approached.

Diet: Millet, canary seed, oats, peanuts, sunflower seeds, some hemp, seeding weeds, half-ripened wheat, fresh corn on the cob, plenty of fruit (such as apples, currants) and greenstuff.

Breeding: First bred in captivity in 1909, in England. The species breeds reliably; even pairs not yet showing the adult coloration incubate and rear their young without any problems. The nestbox (30 x 30 x 50 cm, diameter of entrance hole 8 cm) should be hung up as high as possible and, to avoid disturbances, be located inside the indoor shelter. During the first few days incubating females react to every disturbance and leave the nest immediately; later they sit tight. Checks on the nest should only be carried out when the pair is not in the proximity of the nest. The female leaves her breeding hollow for a short period each morning and evening. The male feeds her outside the nestbox. The young birds begin taking up food independently 4–5 days after fledging. After two weeks they no longer need to be fed by the parents. Suitable rearing foods have turned out to consist of chickweed, dandelion heads and other greenstuff, sweet fruit, soaked white bread, and commercial raising foods.

Hybridization with Crimson Rosella, Western Rosella, Eastern Rosella, Pale-headed Rosella, and Red-rumped Parakeet.

Behavior: The courtship runs a different course from that of the Rosellas. Constantly calling, the male approaches the female with the red feathers on the head raised, drooping wings (revealing the bright yellow-green plumage of the rump), and a fanned and slightly raised tail.

Rosellas *(Platycercus)*

Parakeets of this genus have the following distinguishing characteristics: four median tail feathers of identical length, outer feathers progressively diminishing in size; a large patch on the cheeks, white, yellow, or blue in color depending on the species; squamations on the back. The latter effect

A pair of Red-capped Parakeets, *Purpureicephalus spurius.* In this species, the differences between the sexes are not particularly obvious. Photo by L. Robinson.

is due to the feathers on the back having a black area in the center which is surrounded by a red, yellow, or green margin. In their Australian home these parakeets inhabit various open landscapes, such as bush and tree steppes, and consequently are good fliers. Outside the breeding season the birds may flock together and migrate over vast distances. The close family relationships of the individual species are proved by the fact that the latter produce fertile hybrids when being crossed with each other; even in the wild the species may interbreed (e.g., Eastern Rosella and Pale-headed Rosella). In the interest of preserving the purity of the species further hybridization experiments should be avoided. All Rosellas are long-lived species which have adapted very well to temperate climate. Apart from the Northern Rosella and the Pale-headed Rosella, these birds can all be wintered without any heating, if an indoor shelter which the animals can be closed into at night and during severe cold spells is provided. All species are lively and good fliers. They are not suited for cage living; in fact, they do not come fully into their own except in an outdoor aviary. It is vital for the enclosure to be equipped with a shallow water bowl that can be used for bathing.

Because of their quarrelsome nature, there is no alternative to keeping the birds in pairs. Adjacent aviaries must not be stocked with other species of this genus; it is best to provide partitions which consist of two layers of wire or of a firm, solid material. While not doing a lot of gnawing, the birds enjoy biting off buds, hence the enclosures cannot be planted. The birds' chewing requirements should be met by supplying fresh twigs.

In their natural environment the birds gather their food predominantly on the ground. The Rosellas have always adapted quickly to new nutritional opportunities inadvertently created by man. They have turned into exploiters of civilization and are described as pests. Thanks to this adaptability, their nutritional needs are relatively easy to meet. The staple food in captivity consists of sunflower seeds, millet, and canary seed. Millet sprays are especially popular. Oats and hemp may be given in moderate quantities during the winter and at the beginning of the reproductive period. Since both these foods tend to cause obesity and are in fact used for the "fattening up" of animals, they should not be served to the parakeets at other times of the year. All the grass seeds and seeding weeds mentioned in the chapter on nutrition are liked by the birds and are absolutely vital during the breeding season and for rearing the young. Also popular are carrots and apples as well as various soft berries. The need for greenstuff is essential while there are young being reared. Other suitable rearing foods consist of soaked white bread with added vitamins, commercial soft food, fresh ant pupae, germinated seeds, and hard-boiled egg.

Differentiation of the sexes by their color is easy only with regard to the Western Rosella. In the other species there are typical, but not so strikingly obvious, male characteristics such as the slightly brighter coloration, the broader head, and the stronger beak. When matching the breeding pairs it is necessary, in the early stages, to keep the animals under close observation, as some males pursue the females with excessive ardor. Where the situation gets out of hand one can clip a few of the male's pinions. During courtship the fanned tail is moved sideways, the shoulders are slightly raised, the head moves jerkily up and down.

Area of the nest box about 25 x 25 cm, height not less than 60 cm, diameter of access hole 8 cm. The bottom should be covered with a layer of rotten wood or peat fibers. The clutches are often large and since one female is able to incubate up to 10 eggs, the birds frequently raise as many as 8–9 young. Newly hatched Rosellas are covered in fluffy white down. For two weeks they are warmed and fed by the female. Then the male, who up to that point has only supplied his partner with food, feeds his progeny for up to about 3 weeks after fledging. A second brood may already be started before the young have left the nest. In this case, a second nest box should be standing ready. Young birds still in the juvenile plumage show a row of white spots on the undersides of 7–8 flight feathers.

The Eastern Rosella, *Platycercus eximius,* benefits from human activity; as more land has come under cultivation, its range has expanded accordingly. Photo by Aaron Norman.

After the molting of the primaries in the first or second year these spots are no longer present in the males. In the females of some species they remain. These spots are simply referred to as "wing bars" in the descriptions of the species. By the age of around 15 months the parakeets have attained the full adult plumage.

One pair can be expected to produce offspring at regular intervals for a period of 20 years. Above all Eastern Rosellas and Crimson Rosellas make good foster parents for birds of difficult species. Even a difference in size does not put them off. A Western Rosella, for example, will feed a considerably bigger Crimson Parakeet it has raised. The fact that their keeping and culture present few if any problems and the color splendor and liveliness of the majority of Rosellas have turned them into popular aviary birds who, with the exception of the Northern Rosella, can be recommended to the beginner.

Eight species.

Green Rosella

Platycercus caledonicus (Gmelin)
Characteristics: With a length of 36 cm, the largest species of the genus. The oldest representation of the Rosellas, the coloration of its plumage resembles the juvenile plumage of the other species. Upper back covered in black-brown feathers with green borders, lower back olive green. Breast and belly golden yellow. Head yellow with red band on forehead and blue cheek patches. Wing coverts blue. Flights and tail greenish black. Beak whitish horn color, iris brown, legs gray-brown. Female usually slightly duller in color, throat generally showing a slight tinge of orange. Head and beak markedly smaller. Compared with male animals, the females look dainty. Immatures are darker than the adults, head and underside are greenish, upper parts dark green. With a blue patch on the cheeks, white wing bars. The first complete molt takes 14–15 months.
Range: Tasmania (particularly in the north), larger islands in the Bass Strait.
Habitat: Semi-open woodland, gardens and parks.
Habits: Despite persecution because of the damage to fruit plantations, the species has remained common. Feeding on grass seeds, fruit, nectar, and insects. Crop examinations have revealed various seeds, green plant particles, insect larvae, charcoal, and sand. The food is gathered on the ground or in the treetops. Of the introduced plants, the berries of hawthorn are liked, as are rose hips. Together with the Eastern Rosellas, Green Rosellas invade the apple plantations in massive flocks. Nesting inside hollow trees at a great height. Six to nine eggs, incubation period 3 weeks, nestling period 5 weeks. The young stay with their parents for about 4–5 weeks and then flock together with birds of their own age. The incubating hen leaves the nest in the morning in order to feed or to allow the male to feed her.
Keeping: 1860, at London Zoo. As this species is exposed to rough weather conditions in its native range, keeping it in the winter presents no problems; an unheated shelter suffices. These parakeets are fairly undemanding in other respects as well. Compared with the rest of the genus, they are less shy and have pleasanter sounding call notes. Despite these advantages Green Rosellas are seldom kept, even in Australia. Due to the export ban imposed on all species of Australian animals, Green Rosellas will only become more widespread in our aviaries when sufficient young birds have been produced by the few breeding stocks kept in Holland and Switzerland.
Breeding: Probably first bred in captivity in 1882, in England. Birds in juvenile plumage are already able to reproduce themselves in their first year. Breeding does not usually begin until May. The nestboxes should be hung in a dark area of the indoor shelter. Two broods are possible. Hybridization with Eastern Rosella, Adelaide Rosella, Mallee Ringneck Parakeet, Port Lincoln Parakeet, Red-rumped Parakeet, Red-capped Parakeet.
Behavior: Courting males droop the wings, the shoulders look square, pectoral plumage and tail coverts are fluffed, the fanned tail is moved sideways. Slight bows are made or the raised head is tilted backwards.

Perhaps because other rosella species are more colorful, aviculturists have tended to neglect the Green Rosella, *Platycercus caledonicus.* Photo courtesy of the San Diego Zoo.

The southern populations of the Crimson Rosella, *Platycercus elegans,* occur at altitudes up to 2,000 m and are exposed to snow and frost in the winter.

Crimson Rosella
Platycercus elegans (Gmelin)
Three subspecies.
Characteristics: 26 cm long. Head and body bright dark red. Cheek patches indigo blue. Feathers of upper back and shoulders black with broad dark red borders (the same red as on the breast), a black spot on the shoulders. Greater wing coverts black with blue borders, lesser wing coverts blue. Median tail feathers dark blue, outer ones light blue with white tips. Beak gray-white, iris brown, legs gray. Head and beak of the female are clearly weaker. In juveniles, those areas of the plumage which are red in adult birds are generally dark green. The blue on the cheeks, wings, and tail is paler than in the adult birds. The white wing bar is present. The color change takes place in stages and is complete at around 14 months, after the molt in the fall. The young of the northern subspecies (*P. e. nigrescens*) already have the red feathers by the time they leave the nest. The young of the larger, more frequently kept nominate form always have a green juvenile plumage in their natural environment. Birds bred in captivity, however, may be leaving the nest completely or partially red. Either the smaller subspecies was crossed in at some stage or the more common cause, poor nutritional conditions and the resultant delayed growth, led to a complete or partial bypassing of the juvenile plumage. This was proved by experiments conducted by the German large parakeet breeder, Preussiger. He ringed the young birds and took some of them out of the nest for an hour at a time so that they received less food. These animals later fledged with red feathers while their well-fed siblings showed the green juvenile plumage. Of great importance, according to these experiences, are the nutritional conditions that prevail in the first two weeks of life.
Range: Southern Queensland, New South Wales, Victoria, Kangaroo Island. Introduced into New Zealand and on Norfolk Island.
Habitat: Dense forest regions. The northern populations live in tropical rain forests. The populations in the Australian peripheral mountains, at altitudes of 2000 m, experience snow and frost in the winter. Forest clearances caused this species to decline in some areas and the Eastern Rosellas to spread still further. Nonetheless the Crimson Rosellas have remained common. They go into fields and orchards; even in city suburbs one always comes across them.
Habits: Living in pairs or in small groups. After fledging, the young remain with their parents in a family association for a few more months and then gather into small flocks with birds of their own age. Food is usually collected from the ground; more rarely, in the trees. A prolonged rest around noon, as enjoyed by other parakeets living in the dry and hot regions of Australia, is not indulged in by this species; the birds search for food almost the whole day long. Grass seeds at varying stages of maturity are the food of preference; further, the seeds of introduced plants (e.g., nightshades, chickweed, sorrel, spurge, thistles, clover, wheat, oats). The favorite fruit consists of apples. A striking number of insects, such as caterpillars or beetle

larvae are eaten. Analyses of crop and stomach contents established the presence of charcoal and sand. Breeding season August to February. The nest is located inside hollow trees at a great height.
Keeping: In 1861, at London Zoo. Minimum length of aviary 5 m, strong wire mesh. Confiding, pleasant voice, very hardy. *P. e. nigrescens* from tropical northern Australia has to be kept inside a heated enclosure in the winter. Because of the strong urge to

Although propagation frequently succeeds, there will always be females that, while laying fertile eggs, do not incubate them. Others peck at their own eggs and eat the contents. If one transfers the eggs from deserted clutches to Eastern Rosellas for incubation, an adverse breeding characteristic (most probably hereditary) is only encouraged to spread. Four to seven eggs are laid as a rule and incubated for about 20 days. The young fledge at 5 weeks

The Crimson Rosella, *Playtcercus elegans,* includes the seeds of evergreens in its diet. Photo by Fritz Prenzel.

gnaw, a constant supply of fresh branches is necessary. These parakeets frequently live to be over 20 years old.
Diet: In addition to the food varieties mentioned above, corn and green peanuts (complete with shells) may be given.
Breeding: First bred in captivity in 1874, in France. Courtship starts in April. The nesting facilities offered should consist of natural hollows, as deep as possible.

and are independent after a further 5 weeks. The nest boxes should be hung in as high a position as possible. A deep box has the advantage of allowing the female to incubate with a minimum of disturbance. Furthermore, the female is obliged to climb up to the clutch after her short periods of rest and consequently the eggs cannot get damaged. Crimson Rosellas normally become sexually mature at 2 years of age, but younger animals have also been known to breed successfully.

Hybridization with Yellow, Adelaide, Eastern and Pale-headed Rosellas, Mallee Ringneck Parakeet, Port Lincoln Parakeet, Twenty-eight Parakeet, and Alexandrine Parakeet.

Behavior: Courting males let the folding wings droop slightly, the fanned tail is moved rapidly to and fro, head and neck are bent backwards, the pectoral plumage is fluffed. Ceaseless chattering noises are made simultaneously. At a subsequent stage the female is fed.

Yellow Rosella

Platycercus flaveolus (Gould)
Characteristics: 34 cm long. Head, breast, and lower back straw yellow. Red band on forehead, blue spots on cheeks. Feathers on the nape, upper back, and wings black with straw yellow margins. Black shoulder spot. Wing coverts blue. Flights and tail feathers greenish black with a bluish hue.

Yellow Rosella, *Platycercus flaveolus*. In the wild this species occasionally interbreeds with the Crimson Rosella.

Underside of tail pale blue. Beak gray white, iris brown, legs dark gray. In females sometimes a tinge of orange-red on the neck and breast, and band on the forehead is fainter. White bar on underside of wings usually present. The most reliable differential characteristic in this case, however, is the difference in the size of head and beak respectively. Fledged young birds have a green back and green wings, head and underside being green-yellow. The red band on the forehead is narrower than in adult birds. White bar on underside of wings present. Color change completed after the first complete molt at the age of about 14 months.

Range: Southern New South Wales, northern regions of Victoria, eastern South Australia.

Habitat: Fringes of open forests on riverbanks.

Habits: Shyer and more dependent on trees than the remaining species. The food consists of the seed capsules of eucalyptus, flower nectar, fruits, various seeds and insects. Breeding season August to January. 4–5 eggs. Nesting hollows at great heights.

Keeping: At London Zoo, in 1867. Because of its unassuming coloration infrequently kept. The building up of breeding strains, in the interest of preserving this Rosella outside its Australian native range, would be a worthwhile project. It should not, however, be attempted to eliminate the shortage of breeding birds by crossing the species with the Adelaide Rosella. Hybrids lose most of the straw yellow color and are instantly recognizable as such.

Keeping: As per Crimson Rosella.

Diet: As per Crimson Rosella.

Breeding: First bred in captivity in 1904, in England. Nesting hollows, natural tree trunk if possible, to be located in a quiet spot inside the indoor shelter. Five to seven eggs, incubation period 22 days. Sometimes there may be two broods in succession. Hybridization with Crimson, Adelaide, Eastern Rosella, Red-rumped Mallee Ringneck, and Twenty-eight Parakeet.

Adelaide Rosella

Platycercus adelaidae (Gould)
Characteristics: 36 cm long. Breast and top of head brick red, nape and sides of head

It is not entirely certain that the form known as the Adelaide Rosella, *Platycercus adelaidae,* should be accorded specific status.

yellowish. Black shoulder spot. Lesser wing coverts, cheeks, and tail blue. Feathers on the back and wings black with broad olive yellow and red margins. Underside, rump, and upper tail coverts of very variable shades of red and yellow. Beak gray-white, iris dark brown, legs gray-brown. Females slightly paler, head and beak smaller. Immatures are pale red on crown, throat, upper breast, thighs, and under tail coverts. The back is olive green, the underside of a pale gray-green. White under wing spots present. Adult plumage at the age of 14–15 months, colors growing more intense in subsequent years.

There is a great deal of variation in color among individual animals; even within a flock one may observe animals of differing coloration. Some ornithologists regard the Adelaide Rosella as a transitional form between the Crimson Rosella and the Yellow Rosella; others are of the opinion that the Adelaide Rosella has in fact originated from hybridization of the Crimson Rosella with the Yellow Rosella, since both these species occur in its range of distribution.
Range: South Australia. A northern and a southern population, separated from one another by a strip of about 70 km in breadth.
Habitat: Wooded areas, but also open savannas. Hence not as dependent on forests as the Crimson Rosella. Gardens and parks on the outskirts of the city of Adelaide.
Habits: On the increase, although in some areas being supplanted by migrant or liberated Eastern Rosellas. Small flocks. Breeding season September to December. Four to seven eggs.
Keeping: In 1863 at London Zoo. A hardy aviary bird that tolerates frost without ill effects. Rarely kept nonetheless.
Breeding: First bred in captivity in 1907 in England. Only one brood since the birds start molting soon after the young have fledged. Has been crossed with various species of the genus, notably the Crimson Rosella. Consequently there is little left of the original coloration which is very variable in any case. Avicultural ambitions should be directed at the propagation of all species and subspecies in as pure a form as possible.

Eastern Rosella *Platycercus eximius* (Shaw)
Three subspecies.
Characteristics: 32 cm long. Head, neck, breast, under tail coverts scarlet red. White cheek patches. Feathers on the back, as well as flight feathers black with yellow borders. Median wing coverts black, under wing coverts and outer coverts blue. Lower back light green. Belly greenish yellow. Flights black with blue outer vanes. Tail dark blue above, outer tail feathers pale blue, white at the tip. Beak gray-white, iris dark brown, legs gray-brown. Females slightly paler, having little brown feathers around the eyes; the cheek patch is off-white and not as clearly defined as in the males. Green nape feathers extend, without any clear demarcation, to the back of the head. A white wing bar is present. Juveniles are slightly paler still, nape and distal part of crown green. White wing bar present. Adult coloration and sexual maturity attained after one year.
P. e. ceciliae is characterized by the darker red, the golden yellow belly, and the golden yellow margins of the feathers on the back.

The subspecies *cecilae* of the Eastern Rosella, *Platycercus eximius,* is characterized by broader yellow edging on the feathers of the back and thus has been called the Golden-mantled Rosella. Photo by Harry V. Lacey.

Although many breeders apply the name of this subspecies to their birds, frequent cross breeding has in fact resulted in the virtual disappearance of truly characteristic representation of this subspecies from our aviaries.

Range: Southeastern Australia, from southern Queensland, New South Wales and Victoria to southeastern South Australia, Tasmania. Introduced into New Zealand.

Habitat: Originally open savannah landscapes. Having learned to exploit expanding civilization, these parakeets are now encountered in fields, townships, and in parks right inside the cities. Clearances have caused, and are continuing to cause, a constant spreading of the Eastern Rosellas.

Habits: Outside the breeding season up to a hundred of these parakeets gather into larger groups, sometimes in association with Red-rumped Parakeets. Violent squabbling breaks out among the males from time to time. According to examinations of the crop contents, the diet is composed of grass seeds, oats, wheat, the seeds of sedges, clover, carnations, chickweed, sorrel, cranesbill, spurge, buttercups, goose-foot, alfalfa, and thistles. The damage they do in the fields is made up for by the browsing on seeding weeds. The damage to apple and pear plantations is offset by the devouring of various insects such as termites, caterpillars, fruit flies, aphids, and springtails. Breeding season September to January, often two broods. If the parents breed only once, the young stay with them for some months. The nest is located in hollow trees at a low height, in wooden posts, empty breeding hollows of the Bee eaters, and sometimes even inside rabbit burrows. Inside the nests one often finds caterpillars of the moth *Nessiosynoeca agnosta* in large numbers which feed on the feces of the young.

Keeping: Kept in Barcelona in 1861. A relatively loud voice. Does not interact well with other birds, consequently it can only be kept in pairs. Resistant to cold.

Breeding: First bred in captivity in 1863, in Barcelona. Courtship begins in early spring. Feeding of the female, which sometimes begs the male for food by making chirping noises. From the time incubation starts the female receives nearly all her food from the male. Four to nine eggs, one egg every 48 hours, incubation from about the third egg onwards. Incubation period 18–20 days. At first the female leaves the nest quite often; towards the end of the incubation period she only does so for brief periods in the mornings and evenings. When the young are two weeks old they are fed by the male. The female now only comes into the nest in cold weather and to spend the night there. At this stage one can examine the nest, the young scream, hiss, and peck at the hand. Breeding presents no problems. Sometimes up to 9 young are raised per brood. British aviculturists annually report a total of around 1000 newly reared Eastern Rosellas. Even 30 year old birds are still capable of breeding. Birds of this species have also proved to be good foster parents. Hybridization with all other species of the genus, as with Superb, Mallee Ringneck, Twenty-eight, Red-capped Parakeet, Blue-bonnet Parakeet, Red-rumped Parakeet, and Cockatiel.

Pale-headed Rosella
Platycercus adscitus (Latham)
Two subspecies.
Characteristics: 30 cm long. *P. a. adscitus*: Head yellow-white. White cheek patch blue at the lower edge. Black feathers on the back with broad yellow borders. Lower back bluish gray, rump yellowish, breast and belly greenish pale blue. Middle wing coverts black, lower wing coverts blue, under tail coverts red. Flight feathers black with dark blue outer vanes. Tail feathers black, with a tinge of blue-green above, outer tail feathers blue with white tips. Beak horn colored, iris dark brown, legs gray-brown. Females identical in coloration, head and beak insignificantly smaller. White wing bars. Juveniles are paler, the greenish head frequently interspersed with some red which disappears again after the molt. Full adult plumage at 15–16 months. Sexual maturity at 12 months. The subspecies *P. a. palliceps* is differentiated by the blue rump and the absent blue edge where the cheek patches are concerned. Characteristic is the

Like the other rosellas, the Eastern Rosella, *Platycercus eximius,* is not suited to being kept in a cage; it does well only in a spacious aviary. Photo by Dr. Herbert R. Axelrod.

In these Pale-headed Rosellas, *Platycercus adscitus,* the female may be told from the male by her somewhat smaller head and beak.

diversity in coloration, due partly to interbreeding with Eastern Rosellas in the south of the range and the interbreeding of the two subspecies along the boundary between their respective ranges of distribution.

Range: Queensland, northern New South Wales. Introduced on Hawaii in 1877, but has not been recorded there since 1928.

Habitat: Eucalyptus savannahs.

Habits: The nesting hollow is usually located at a great height, it may be as deep as 2 m. Breeding season in the south from September to December, in the north at the end of the rainy season (February to June). Three to five eggs. The fledged young stay with their parents in family groups for some months.

Keeping: In 1863, at London Zoo. When it comes to wintering, the tropical origin of these parakeets must not be forgotten. Animals bred in our regions are weather resistant, making it unnecessary for the indoor shelter to be heated during mild winters.

Diet: Food consists of grass seeds and eucalyptus seeds, many fruits and insects. Half-ripened corn is popular, as a result of which this parakeet often does serious damage to the crops.

Breeding: First bred in captivity in 1872, in Belgium. If breeding is to succeed, it is essential to house the birds in an aviary of at least 5 m in length and as far away as possible from other Rosellas. The nest box (natural tree trunks are preferred) should be hung inside the indoor shelter. Usually there is only a single brood. The young fledge at 32 days. Courtship and incubation are similar to those in the Eastern Rosella. Hybridization with Crimson and Eastern Rosella, Western Rosella, Northern Rosella, Mallee Ringneck Parakeet, Port Lincoln Parakeet, Twenty-eight, Red-capped, Red-rumped Parakeet, and Blue-bonnet Parakeet.

Northern Rosella

Platycercus venustus (Kuhl)

Characteristics: 28 cm long. Head black, sometimes interspersed with a trace of red. White cheek patches with blue lower edge. On the nape, upper back, and shoulders are black feathers with pale yellow borders. Lower back and rump pale yellow. Feathers on the breast and belly pale yellow with fine black edges. A black shoulder spot. Wing coverts blue, flights black-brown. Median tail feathers dark blue-green above, outer feathers blue with white tips. Under tail coverts scarlet red. The markings can vary considerably. There is a great deal of variation in the color and expanse of the cheek patches. Beak gray-white, iris dark brown, legs dark gray. Some females slightly duller on the head, head and beak are insignificantly smaller. Juveniles duller all over, in some cases just a few reddish brown feathers are seen on the head and breast. White under wing bar usually present. Change to adult coloration complete at the age of 12–14 months.

Range: Northwestern Australia, Northern Territory, the islands of Melville, Bathurst, and Milingimbi off the coast of northern Australia.

Habitat: Tree savannas, the fringes of open forests near rivers, mangrove terrain.

Habits: Despite the absence of any human

The Northern Rosella, *Platycercus venustus,* is reputed to be the shyest of the rosellas. Photo by Dr. M. M. Vriends.

intervention, these parakeets are becoming rarer all the time. Much shyer than the other species of this genus. Food consists of the seeds of grasses, shrubs, and trees, wild fruits, and probably insects as well. In the morning and at night the birds visit water places; during the hottest hours of the day they keep to the shade of the trees. Nesting high inside hollow branches. Breeding during the rainy season (December to February), but incubating Northern Rosellas have also been observed in the months of June, July, and August.

Keeping: At London Zoo in 1899. Winter temperatures are not tolerated by this species. During the cold season it needs to be kept in a heated aviary which is illuminated for about 12 hours a day (artificial lighting controlled by a timer). If one wants to try and breed the birds, their enclosure must be of sufficient size. If these requirements had always been met, many losses could have been avoided in the past. Anyone planning to keep parakeets from tropical regions has to allow for higher heating and lighting costs when calculating the probable expense.

Diet: Like that of the other Rosellas.
Breeding: First bred in captivity in 1928, in England. An adaptation to temperate seasons rarely occurs; usually the Northern Rosellas get into the breeding mood in the winter months. Matching the breeding pairs is not all that easy owing to the male's unusual aggressiveness towards the female. The aviary must be sufficiently large to allow the female to escape from the male. If necessary, the male's flight feathers should be clipped slightly on one side. When paired the animals form a close attachment and are not easy to rematch later on. Five to seven eggs, incubation period 19–21 days, nestling period 4–5 weeks. Checks on the nest are better avoided. As rearing food ant pupae, egg food, carrots, chickweed, and hemp were accepted. On top of the other difficulties the aviculturist has, with regard to all winter breeding species, is particularly poor fertilization. Early supplementation of the diet with vitamins will help to improve these results somewhat. Hybridization with Eastern, Pale-headed, and Yellow Rosellas.

Western Rosella
Platycercus icterotis (Kuhl)
Two subspecies.
Characteristics: 25 cm long. Head and underside scarlet. Yellow cheek patches. Feathers on upper back and shoulders black with green borders, in some cases red borders. Black shoulder spot. Lower back green. Wing coverts blue, flights black with dark blue outer vanes. Tail greenish blue above, outer tail feathers pale blue with dull white tips. Beak gray, iris dark brown, legs gray-brown. In females the cheek patch is paler and less extensive. Head and upper breast green, interspersed with red. Red band on forehead. Belly pale red with some green. Back the same color as in the male but slightly duller. A white under wing bar is present. Juveniles are predominantly green with a little red on the forehead. Yellow cheek patches and black feathers on the back are absent. White wing bar present. Males have slightly more red on the forehead, the head is larger. At 12 weeks the young birds gradually start to change color; the color change is complete after about a year.
Range: Southwestern Australia.
Habitat: Open landscapes, grassland, cultivated land, trees on rivers and roadsides.
Habits: Like the Eastern Rosella in the east of Australia, this species has learned to exploit civilization. Wheat fields, orchards, and flower gardens are visited and raided. In spite of this, the Western Rosellas are not subjected to a great deal of persecution. Due to forest clearances the habitat of the parakeets has expanded, cereal fields brought advantageous nutritional opportunities. That the Western Rosella has nonetheless failed to become as widespread as the Eastern Rosella is probably due to biological competition from Port Lincoln Parakeet which ousts the smaller relative from nesting and feeding places. Outside the breeding season Western Rosellas live in small groups; they are quieter than the other Rosellas. The diet consists of grass seeds, wheat, leaf buds, fruits, and insect larvae. Breeding period August to December. The nest is located inside the hollow trunks or branches of eucalyptus trees. While the female is incubating the male is always found in the proximity of the nest. The pairs stay together all year round. Feeding of the female can also be observed outside the mating season.
Keeping: 1864, at London Zoo. Western Rosellas can be accommodated in smaller aviaries; they do not gnaw, have pleasant voices, are active all day flying and climbing, and are far more confiding than most other species. Frequently the males, particularly, will take tidbits out of the hand of their keeper. Furthermore, these parakeets intermingle well with woodland birds, waxbills, Australian King Parakeets, Regent Parakeets, and Princess Parakeets. No other Rosella is likely to offer so many advantages. Western Rosellas are usually exposed to winter in unheated indoor shelters. Nevertheless one should always check on them carefully and provide them with heating at the first sign of disturbed well-being. Most important, especially in the winter, is the provision of a diet high in vitamin content.
Diet: Like that of the other species.

Only in the Western Rosella, *Platycercus icterotis,* are the sexes conspicuously different.

Breeding: First bred in captivity in 1908, in England. A special form of behavior, occasionally observed in the Eastern Rosella as well, characterizes a harmonizing breeding pair. The male inclines his head towards the female and for a few seconds presses the forehead and the ridge of the beak against the branch on which he is perching, whereupon the female often responds with the same movement. The pairs stay together throughout the year and feed one another outside the breeding season as well. One-year-old animals are suitable for breeding. Nest box 25 x 25 x 50 cm, diameter of entrance hole 7 cm, bottom layer of decomposing wood. More popular are natural tree trunk hollows of similar size. Three to eight eggs, incubation period 20 days, nestling period 4–5 weeks. After about one month the young birds are independent. A second brood is produced only rarely. Foods that have proved suitable for rearing are seeding grasses, dandelion heads, spinach, rusks soaked in milk, spray millet, fresh ant pupae, and commercial soft food for insectivores. Hybridization with Rosellas of all species, with Red-breasted, Mulga, and Red-capped Parakeets.

Parakeets of the genus *Polytelis*

The most striking characteristics are the greatly extended two median tail feathers. The remaining tail feathers decrease progressively in length from the center outwards. The basic color of the plumage is green, the beak reddish, similar to parakeets of the genus *Psittacula* which also belongs to the tribe of the Loriini. *Polytelis* species also have certain characteristics in common with the Rosellas and by some ornithologists are consequently described as a transitional form of the latter. The sexes differ in coloration. Courtship is characterized by bowing and head swiveling. Inhabiting predominantly the steppe, they are long distance fliers and should, therefore, be housed in an aviary which measures at least 5 m in length, although it need not be very broad. All species are quiet birds and not quarrelsome on the whole. They can be kept in colonies and in association with other birds. Where the aviaries are arranged in a row they are best placed between enclosures with Rosellas, to act as buffers. They do little gnawing, hence may be accommodated in aviaries made of wood.

A suitable basic diet consists of sunflower seeds, stone pine nuts, hemp, peanuts (all foods with a very high fat content should only be given in small quantities), canary seed, millet, oats, wheat, sweet apples, oranges, carrots, various kinds of greenstuff (notably chickweed), dandelion and thistle heads. Half-ripened grass and cereal panicles are regarded as a special treat, as is fresh corn on the cob. The birds like to feed on the ground, which means they find seeds that have softened and begun to germinate in the damp soil of the outdoor aviary. The danger of worm infestation is always a possibility. Fecal specimens should be submitted for examination at regular intervals. At least once a year the top 10 cm of soil should be removed and replaced with fresh soil. As winter quarters, a dry, draft-proof indoor shelter is sufficient. The birds should not roost suspended from the wire netting, as this quickly results in frostbite of the toes. Kept in aviaries, birds of the genus *Polytelis* have an average life span of 15 years.

Although wooden boxes of the dimensions 30 x 30 x 45 cm are accepted for nesting, these parakeets prefer long natural hollows put up at an oblique angle. Bottom layer of damp decomposing wood. Diameter of entrance hole 8 cm.

Three species.

Regent Parakeet, *Polytelis anthropeplus*, male (A) and female (B). Superb Parakeet, *Polytelis swainsonii*, female (C) and male (D). Painting by Graeme Stevenson.

Graeme Stevenson.

Princess Parakeet
Polytelis alexandrae (Gould)

Characteristics: 45 cm long. Top of head sky blue. Chin, throat, and cheeks pink. Breast and belly gray- green, thighs pink. Back olive green, rump violet blue, wing coverts yellow-green. The median tail feathers are particularly elongated. Third primaries with spatula shaped tip (only in males). Tail bluish olive green above, underside black and pink. Beak coral red. Iris orange, legs dark gray. Females having considerably shorter tail feathers, head and rump are blue-gray; all colors, including the bill, are paler than in the male. Juveniles resemble the female; head and rump are green-gray. Full adult coloration after about 15 months. Young males have bigger and slightly flatter heads, and the plumage on the crown is slightly brighter than the remaining feathers. After a few months the males can be identified by a gurgling call and the raising of feathers on the crown.

Range: The Australian interior, from southern Northern Territory to northern South Australia and east Western Australia.

Habitat: Dry steppes and semi-arid terrain where the dry and hard porcupine grasses

Princess Parakeets, *Polytelis alexandrae,* male facing, female seen from the rear.

(*Triodia*) grow. Insular distribution in localities with water places and nesting facilities. A popular perch consists of tall eucalyptus trees on river banks, sometimes also trees of the genus *Casuarina* in sandy areas.

Habits: Small groups of 10–15 birds. Sparsely populated. This may be due to the fact that these parakeets are fairly inconspicuous in the wild. Usually they are seen on the ground, searching for food among grass tussocks. When disturbed they fly off at the very last moment. The bulk of the diet is formed by the seeds of porcupine grasses. If living conditions become unfavorable, the parakeets migrate and for a time may once again settle in localities from which they have been absent for many years. Nesting in the hollows of eucalyptus trees or *Casuarina* species. Often several pairs breed together in colonies. Up to 10 nests have been discovered in a single tree. Breeding season usually between September and January, otherwise after rainfalls, irrespective of the season, and the subsequent flowering of the porcupine grass.

Keeping: 1895, at London Zoo. Although native to the hottest regions of Australia, the species also tolerates low temperatures for short periods. Prolonged frost can lead to damage, hence Princess Parakeets should be kept in frost-proof accommodation in the winter. Intermingles with virtually all aviary birds and quickly grows tame. The enclosure should be equipped with branches of a greater diameter since this parakeet (unlike any of the other species) roosts by perching on stronger branches in a horizontal direction.

Diet: Spray millet and canary seed, half-ripened grass and cereal panicles, as well as the seed heads of dandelion and chickweed, are the favorite foods. Greenstuff is very important, particularly for rearing. Soft food and soaked white bread are also accepted.

Breeding: First bred in captivity in 1899, in Australia. In England, kept in colonies, in 1912. The birds are ready for breeding at the age of two years. One-year-old birds have also been known to breed, but unreliably. If the birds are kept in colonies, one usually achieves better breeding results. All the pairs have to be put into the enclosure at the same time. Two broods are observed only occasionally. The birds prefer their nest boxes or hollow natural tree trunks located high. Four to seven eggs. From the third egg onwards the hen sits tight. Incubation period 20 days. Newly hatched young are covered in long white down. Nestling period 5 weeks. The fledged parakeets are fed primarily by the male. Princess Parakeets can remain suitable for breeding up to the age of 23 years. A blue mutation was developed in 1951, in Australia; lutinos in 1975 in East Germany. Hybridizations with the other two species of the genus, Rose-ringed, Red-winged, and Amboina King Parakeets.

Behavior: Courtship aerobatics, for which the entire flight area of the aviary is utilized. The pupils are contracted so that the iris glows conspicuously from the plumage of the head. Afterwards the male hops once or twice or moves straight up to the female with the feathers retracted smoothly. Subsequently a hurried running in place, accompanied by a slight drumming noise, can be observed. The male makes several bows, pulls himself up to his full height and once more runs in place. The head is swung from side to side, and a ticking sound is produced in the throat.

Superb Parakeet

Polytelis swainsonii (Desmarest)
Characteristics: 40 cm long. Green. Forehead, chin, and throat yellow. This yellow is bordered by a semilunar scarlet shield below. Primaries with blue outer edge. Tail feathers with a blue-green tinge above, underside blackish. Beak orange-red, iris yellow-orange, legs gray-brown. In the female the yellow and red are absent, forehead and throat are gray-green. Remaining body color paler than in the male, under tail coverts having pink borders. Iris brownish. Juveniles similar in coloration, in some males a few red and yellow feathers can already be seen on the throat. At the age of a few months young males start to gurgle and warble; they are easily differentiated from females of the same age. The color change takes 12–18 months.
Range: The interior of New South Wales in

The male Superb Parakeet, *Polytelis swainsonii*, is considerably more colorful than the female.

the range of the River Murrumbidgee, northern regions of Victoria. The range of distribution is very small, but where they do occur Superb Parakeets are very common.

Habitat: In dry areas the narrow wooded strips along the river are inhabited, in the damper savannahs the birds can also be found at a greater distance from the river. Thanks to artificial irrigation the parakeets have spread further during the last few decades.

Habits: Groups of 8–10 animals can also be observed during the breeding season. In the morning and late afternoon even the ground near farmhouses is searched for food. At these times of the day the animals also visit water places. The diet comprises various seeds (e.g., of grasses, alfalfa, stinging nettles, thistles, shepherd's purse, cranesbill), wheat, berries, and flower nectar. Breeding season September to December. The nests are lcoated inside hollow branches, high and out of reach. The males are seen together in small groups during the breeding season as well. Several times a day they leave the group in order to feed their females.

Keeping: 1867, at London Zoo. Eye diseases

were fairly common in imported animals; the lids were very swollen and there was a discharge. It goes without saying that such birds require drug treatment as prescribed by the veterinary surgeon. Animals in need of treatment have to be kept separately in a smallish cage. Under normal circumstances this species is hardy and enduring. Other pleasant attributes are good naturedness and the fact that the birds grow tame very quickly. Unpleasant are the loud and penetrating calls during the mating season. Several pairs can be kept together in the same aviary. Bathing facilities must be provided, even when it rains.

Diet: Fruit and berries, notably elderberries, are very popular. During the breeding season ant pupae and mealworms are accepted.

Breeding: First bred in captivity in 1881, in France. Although sexual maturity is already attained at the age of one, the animals do not normally start breeding until they are two or three years old. For a successful breeding process a slight humidity is of importance. Four to six eggs. Incubation period about 20 days. Nestling period about 30 days. After a further 4 weeks the young are independent. Sometimes the males attack their male progeny. The nests have to be examined with care as some females react badly to the disturbance. Superb Parakeets have proved suitable as foster parents for Red-winged and Australian King Parakeets. Hybridization with the two other species of the genus, with Australian King and Red-winged Parakeets, Eastern Rosella, and Port Lincoln Parakeet.

Behavior: Short courtship flights right round the female. Bowing after landing. The plumage of the head is fluffed, the remaining plumage lying close to the body, the wings are slightly spread. Constantly contracting the pupils, the male runs up and down, calling at the same time. The female responds by squatting, raising the feathers on the head, spreading out the wings (begging position), and emitting quiet begging calls.

Regent Parakeet
Polytelis anthropeplus (Lear)
Characteristics: 40 cm long. As regards body

With adult Regent Parakeets, *Polytelis anthropeplus,* there is little difficulty in distinguishing the sexes.

size and weight, the largest species of the genus. Predominantly yellow. Head, nape, rump yellow-green. Back olive green. Flights blackish. Broad red bar on the inner wing coverts. Greater wing coverts black. Tail feathers black-blue. Beak red, iris reddish brown, legs gray-brown. The coloration may vary slightly; some males are mainly olive green, in others the yellowish green coloration predominates. Females are mostly olive green and look paler than the males. Tip and edge of the lateral tail feathers pink underneath. Beak pale red, iris light yellowish brown. Juveniles are of a dull green color, sometimes the males already show a more intense coloration. In six-month-old males individual yellow feathers can be seen on the head and breast. Full adult plumage after the second autumn molt at the age of about 15 months. Sexual maturity usually not attained until the age of two years, although there have been reports of successful breeding in one-year-old females.

Range: Two separate ranges of distribution, southwestern and southeastern Australia.
Habitat: The eastern populations avoid the proximity of man and inhabit the shrub steppe formed by various *Eucalyptus* species. With progressive cultivation the numbers of these Regent Parakeets continue to diminish. In the west the parakeets have learned to exploit civilization and are usually found in the areas where wheat is grown. Because of the damage incurred by these birds, they are frequently subjected to severe persecution.
Habits: Outside the breeding season in groups of up to about 20 animals. In the highest treetops the birds look for flower nectar and insects, although the bulk of the diet of seeds, grasses and herbs are gathered on the ground. The nest is usually located in the hollows of vertical tree trunks, as opposed to the Superb Parakeet which prefers hollow lateral branches. The bottom of the nesting chamber may be as much as 5 m below the entrance. On rare occasions, the birds will also breed on steep river banks in hollows in the ground covered by vegetation. Breeding season August to January.
Keeping: At London Zoo, in 1864. This species tolerates our climate very well. The flying area should have a length of at least 6 m, particularly if one wants to propagate the birds. Intermingles well with other birds, but accommodation in pairs is recommended during the breeding season. While not shy, Regent Parakeets are very nervous. A shelter inside which the birds can spend the night undisturbed is necessary during the warm season as well. Because of these birds' great flying speed, a collision with the taut wire netting usually has fatal consequences. Prone to inflammations of the eyes and to various forms of paralysis. Paralysis due to sudden shock (for instance, as the result of trapping) is common. In such cases it is best to leave the bird to its own devices. Sometimes, unfortunately, not always will it recover within a few hours.
Breeding: First bred in captivity in 1865, in Australia. First bred in Europe, in 1880 (Belgium). The birds accept nest boxes of various sizes but prefer long natural tree trunks which should be fixed as high as

possible, at an oblique angle. Courtship starts early in the spring. Three to seven (usually four) eggs. Incubation period 22 days. First down feathers white. The young do not leave the nest until they are 6 weeks old and are initially very nervous. The male feeds the incubating hen at the entrance to the nest. Usually just one brood per year. Soft food, egg food, germinated seeds, boiled egg, soaked white bread, ant pupae, and a few mealworms are suitable as rearing food. Hybridization with the other two species of the genus and with Red-winged Parakeets.
Behavior: Courting males take a deep bow and then lift the head up high. Making semicircular movements with the head, they then regurgitate some food.

Parakeets of the genus *Psittacula*

Twelve species, amongst which *Psittacula exsul* is likely to have become extinct and *Psittacula intermedia*'s position as a species in its own right is uncertain. Characteristic are the slender shape caused by the smooth plumage, the long, gradually narrowing tail, the ring round the nape which is present at least in the majority of the males, as well as broad dark moustachial stripes. Males and females usually differ in the color of their plumage and always in the color of their beaks. The juvenile plumage resembles that of the hen, which makes young birds difficult to sex. However, the males start courting at the age of just a few months and this enables one to draw cautious conclusions from the birds' behavior. Although some may feel it inhumane to pluck out a few of the young bird's feathers on body locations which will eventually distinguish a male's adult plumage, it does hasten the sexing process as the regenerated feathers give a clear indication as to the bird's sex. The range of these species extends from China to Sumatra and Borneo. One species occurs in Africa.

Accommodation should consist of aviaries with attached indoor shelters. Danger of frostbite to the feet. Origin and temperature requirements must be taken into account. Long-term, the only suitable type of

A mixed-species group of *Psittacula* parakeets. Photo by Dr. Herbert R. Axelrod.

Rose-ringed Parakeets, *Psittacula krameri,* for sale in a street market in India. Photo by Dr. E. W. Burr.

accommodation for the larger species are all metal aviaries. Only young birds bred in captivity can really be considered for the living room cage. These birds grow tame and usually talk as well. The bonding between a pair comes to an end when the breeding season is over. The female is the dominant partner. Breeding frequently starts in March. Females also spend the night in the nest box outside the breeding season.

Alexandrine Parakeet
Psittacula eupatria (Linne)
Six subspecies, including *P. e. wardi* which has probably already become extinct.
Characteristics: 58 cm long. Green, with a tinge of gray on the front. A black band extending from the chin to the sides of the neck, a red band round the nape. A big reddish brown spot on the shoulders. Beak red, legs gray, iris light yellow. Females without band markings and with a paler shoulder spot. In young birds the shoulder spot appears at 18 months. Complete adult plumage in the third year of life.
Range: Afghanistan, Pakistan, India (at altitudes of up to 8000 m). Also common in the proximity of cities such as Bombay, Calcutta, Karachi. On low ground in Burma, Thailand, southern Vietnam. Common on the Andaman Islands, on the decrease in Ceylon.
Habitat: Damp and dry deciduous forests, dry rocky areas, agricultural land (as a pest, enjoying little popularity), parks, gardens.
Habits: Encountered in small groups during the day, covering distances of several kilometers in search of food. At dusk they gather by the thousands in roosting places in tall trees. Breeding season November to April. The nests are usually located inside hollow tree trunks. Sometimes several pairs breed in the same tree. Occasionally the birds also nest inside chimneys, holes in walls, and under roofs.
Keeping: Has probably already been kept in Europe for centuries. This species and the Rose-ringed Parakeet were the first parrots to reach Europe in the days of Alexander the Great. Although some aviculturists reported that their birds did not destroy any wooden structures of the aviary, this species should only be kept in all metal

Male Alexandrine Parakeet, *Psittacula eupatria.* Females of the species lack the neck band.

enclosures. Wire thickness 1.2 mm. Although, once acclimatized, the animals can tolerate sub-zero temperatures, they are liable to sustain frost damage to the feet. This species does not get along well with other birds.

Diet: In the wild the birds ingest fruit, nuts, grass seeds, bark, buds, ripening corn, wheat, and rice. In captivity their favorite fare includes sunflower seeds, hemp, peanuts, stone pine nuts, figs, bananas, apples, and pears.

Breeding: Nest boxes no smaller than 30 x 30 x 60 cm, diameter of entrance hole 10 cm. Bottom layer of decomposing wood and peat. The birds get into the breeding mood in February, hence the nest box should be hung inside the heated indoor shelter of the aviary, otherwise the hens are prone to egg binding. Two to four eggs, incubation period 28 days, nestling period 6–7 weeks. The female incubates on her own and is fed by the male during this time. A blue

mutation has been in existence since 1929, lutinos since 1935. Hybridization with a subspecies of the Rose-ringed Parakeet (*P. krameri manillensis*) and with the Derbyan Parakeet.

Behavior: Courting males perch close to the female. They turn the head from side to side and flap the wings, uttering soft chattering sounds. At a later stage the male hops round the female with the wings spread out, bows to her and touches her on the upper region of the back with the beak.

Rose-ringed Parakeet
Psittacula krameri (Scopoli)
Six subspecies.

Characteristics: 42 cm long. Green. Back of the head having a tinge of blue. Black neck band starting on the chin, linking up with a pink band on the nape. Narrow black stripe between nares and eye. Upper mandible red, lower mandible blackish. Legs gray, iris light yellow. Females without bands on the neck and nape and without a black stripe. The African subspecies *P. k. krameri* has a black-red or completely black upper mandible. In the males the adult plumage is complete after the second total molt at the age of three years, although sexual maturity is previously attained.

Range: *P. k. krameri*: Western Africa, *P. k. centralis*: Lake Chad to White Nile, *P. k. parvirostris*: Eritrea, northern Ethiopia, Sudan. *P. k. echo* from the island of Mauritius is seriously decreasing in numbers. In 1975 a mere 20 birds were observed. *P. k. borealis* lives in Pakistan, northern India, Assam, Burma, and southeastern China, *P. k. manillensis* in southern India and on Ceylon. Rose-ringed Parakeets have been introduced in Egypt, Oman, Kuwait, Iraq, Iran, Hong Kong, and Singapore as well as on Mauritius and Zanzibar.

Habitat: Originally in sparsely wooded landscapes. Having learned to exploit civilization, now very common in agricultural areas, in gardens, townships, and cities. In search of food, the birds visit cereal fields, coffee plantations, and orchards, forcing the farmers to guard any crop that is particularly at risk.

Habits: Every good opportunity to obtain food is exploited. It has been reported that

The Rose-ringed Parakeet, *Psittacula krameri,* which has become a follower of cultivation, is especially common in Asia. It is one of the three species of parakeets that are not listed in the Appendixes of the CITES treaty.

the birds tear open bags of cereal lying at railway depots. At night huge flocks, often of over a thousand birds, fly off to specific roosting trees. At such times their loud calls drown even the noise of the traffic in the cities. The African forms start breeding in the rainy season, and the Asian races breed between December and April, depending on their range. In India they have been observed breeding in deserted hollows of other birds. One July a female Rose-ringed Parakeet investigated the nesting hollow of a pair of starlings in a jacaranda tree. The parakeet did not move in until the young had fledged, then it widened the hollow. In this case breeding began in February.

Keeping: This species has already been kept in Europe for centuries. An African

An albino Rose-ringed Parakeet, *Psittacula krameri.* Blue and yellow mutations also have been established.

subspecies was successfully bred in captivity for the first time in 1833, in Paris. The birds are so gregarious that several pairs can be kept together. Although Rose-ringed Parakeets in outdoor aviaries without a shelter have survived winter temperatures of as low as -14°C, one should not put their endurance to the test but let them have access to a warm indoor shelter. The Indian Rose-ringed Parakeets adaptability is demonstrated by those birds which settled in the Schlosspark in Wiesbaden-Biebrich a few years ago. Presumably they are animals that have escaped from captivity. In 1980 seven pairs bred there, in the fall of this year the number of birds stood at over 50. For several years now, Rose-ringed Parakeets have also been observed in a park in Vienna. In the winter of 1980/81 there were 8 birds. One African Rose-ringed Parakeet lived in captivity for nearly 50 years; the average life expectancy is about 25 years.

Diet: In the wild the birds consume the seeds of *Acacia arabica*, dates and other fruits, berries, blossoms, and various kinds of cereal grains. In the crop of Nigerian birds the seeds of ficus fruits, millet, and flower particles were found. The devouring of termites was observed. Consequently, when kept in captivity these parakeets should receive above all various types of millet, oats, and wheat, as well as fruit, while seeds with a high fat content should only be given in very small doses.

Breeding: Nest box about 25 x 25 x 35 cm, diameter of entrance hole 8 cm. Bottom layer of decomposing wood. The parakeets already get into the breeding mood in the winter, hence the pairs should already be put together at that time. In unheated aviaries the nest boxes should not be provided until April. Three to six eggs, incubation period 23 days, nestling period 6–7 weeks. The newly hatched young are naked, apart from a few white, thread shaped feathers which disappear after about three days. The eyes of the young are open at 10 days. This is the best time for close ringing the birds. Both parents feed the young. The female spends the night inside the nest until the young fledge. Two weeks after fledging, food is picked up independently for the first time; after a further week the young are no longer

The blue and yellow varieties of the Rose-ringed Parakeet, *Psittacula krameri*. Illustration by R. A. Vowles.

dependent on their parents. Blue and yellow mutations, since 1963 albinos as well. Hybridization with Alexandrine Parakeet (*P. eupatria*), Long-tailed Parakeet (*P. longicauda*), and Moustached Parakeet (*P. alexandri fasciata*).

Behavior: These birds inherently bathe in the rain, which manifests itself in the form of obvious restlessness at the onset of rainfalls. Outside the reproductive period there is no indication of pair bonding. When, during courtship, the male attempts to preen his partner he always approaches her circumspectly, immediately maintaining a distance afterward. Stretched out to his full height, with raised wings and fanned tail feathers, constantly contracting the pupils and calling melodiously, the male trips around the female. Rivals are driven off. After some time the female partner is fed and very soon afterwards issues the invitation to mate. The female crouches, with the body kept in a horizontal position and the wings partially unfolded. During copulation, which may take place several weeks before any eggs are produced, the male perches on the female's back with both feet and hammers in the region of her nape with the beak. The act of copulation may be repeated at hourly intervals. During incubation the male stands on guard. In the event of disturbances the male's warning call induces the female to leave the nest.

Moustached Parakeet
Psittacula alexandri (Linne)
Seven subspecies.
Characteristics: 40 cm long. Green. Head gray with a tinge of blue. A narrow black stripe on the forehead extending to the

Moustached Parakeets, *Psittacula alexandri*. These juveniles are not yet fully colored.

eyes. A broad black stripe begins on the lower mandible and forms the lower boundary of the cheeks. Crop and breast pink. An olive yellow spot on the wings. Red upper mandible, black lower mandible. Legs gray, iris yellowish light gray. In females the upper mandible is also black. Fledged young have pale red beaks which turn black after a month. Plumage showing adult coloration at the age of 4 months, though slightly duller. Upper mandibles of the males red after one year.
Range: From the Himalayan foothills in northern India and Nepal via Assam, Burma, southern China, Indochina to Java, Bali, and the islands off the coast of western Sumatra. Common on the Andaman Islands, in Thailand, and southern Vietnam. On Borneo probably introduced.
Habitat: Plains and mountain regions up to 2000 m. Usually in damp deciduous and bamboo forests. In Burma, along with the Slaty-headed Parakeet, the characteristic parrot of the teak forests.
Habits: Attracts attention by its loud calls. Usually staying in one locality, migrations are influenced by ripening cereal crops. In rice fields in Thailand seen in flocks of over 10,000 animals. Breeding season roughly from December to April, on Java almost at any time of the year. The eggs are laid high up inside hollow trees (often deserted nests of woodpeckers and barbets) on a layer of decomposing wood. Often, several pairs breed in the same tree.
Keeping: In 1832, a Moustached Parakeet was kept in Bavaria. Fairly resistant to low temperatures, hence well-suited for outdoor aviaries (all metal construction). Reluctant to come down to the ground, food and water should be offered at a height of at least 1 m. Acclimatization of young birds is difficult.
Diet: In their natural environment the animals live on various seeds, fruits, nuts, berries, blossoms, and leaf buds and visit rice fields. Newly imported birds will initially consume boiled rice and corn, spray millet, apples, and carrots. It takes some time before they adapt to the usual types of food offered to aviary kept birds. There should be a constant supply of fresh branches. Greenstuff is not always accepted. The following have proved

suitable for rearing: sunflower seeds, hemp, paddy, oats, pine nuts, germinated spray millet, soaked white bread, boiled corn, egg food, apples.

Breeding: Both tall nest boxes (22 x 28 x 50 cm) and horizontal ones (20 x 30 x 20 cm) have proven successful. Diameter of entrance hole 8 cm. A thick bottom layer of soil, peat, sawdust. Breeding starts in March. Three to four eggs, incubation period 22 days, nestling period 6–7 weeks. The eggs are laid at two-day intervals. Only the female incubates. In the event of disturbances she leaves the nest for a short time, which means checks on the clutch or young present no problems. The young are fed exclusively by the female, both in the nest and after fledging. The male supplies the female with food at the flight hole or outside the box. The young are pink at first, with a sparse growth of white fluffy down. Five days after fledging they eat apples and a few days later they are able to cope with spray millet.

Behavior: Courting males perch beside the female and warble while rotating the head. Prior to feeding his partner the male comes closer, nodding the head all the time (regurgitating food) and uttering murmuring sounds. Females that are ready to mate turn the head to the left and right and crouch down. Conspicuous contractions of the pupils, notably during copulation.

Blyth's Parakeet
Psittacula caniceps (Blyth)
Characteristics: 56 cm long. Yellowish green. Head gray, upper parts slightly bluish. A broad black line above the forehead to as far as the eyes. A broad black band going from the lower mandible to below the region of the cheeks and towards the back. Upper mandible red, lower mandible black. Legs gray-brown, iris yellow. Upper mandible black in the females. Juveniles have black beaks, the head is not yet pure gray.
Range: Nicobar Islands.
Habits: Keeps to the green leaves of very tall trees and is difficult to observe. The ripe fruit of *Pandanus* constitute a popular food.

Keeping: A popular pet in its native regions. The only reference that can be found in literature is to an animal kept at London Zoo in 1902.

Newton's Parakeet
Psittacula exsul (A. Newton)
Characteristics: 40 cm long. Greenish blue-gray. A black moustachial stripe extending from the lower mandible towards the back to below the cheeks. A brown-red spot on the shoulders. Upper mandible red, lower mandible black. Legs gray, iris yellow. Females without a shoulder spot, upper mandible black.
Range: Island of Rodriguez (to the east of Madagascar). Last recorded observation in 1875. Probably extinct.

Derbyan Parakeet
Psittacula derbiana (Fraser)
Characteristics: 50 cm long. Green. Head gray-blue, blue at the back with a tinge of lilac. A narrow black line from the forehead to the eyes. A broad black stripe starts at the lower mandible and forms the lower boundary of the cheeks. Breast and belly are a mixture of gray and a bluish ruby color. Nape bright green. Upper mandible

Derbyan Parakeet, *Psittacula derbiana,* a male. Photo by Dieter Hoppe.

Derbyan Parakeets, *Psittacula derbiana.* In this monotypic species bill color is the most obvious way to distinguish the sexes.

red, lower mandible black. Legs gray-black, iris yellowish white. Females with a black upper mandible. In immatures the beak is reddish at first, then black. After the first molt the upper mandibles of the males look red. Full adult coloration in the third year of life.

Range: Southeastern Tibet, northeastern Assam, southwestern China.

Habitat: Mountain forests (conifers, oaks) and areas with rhododendron at altitudes of up to 4000 m.

Habits: Fields with ripening barley and corn are visited by groups of about 50 birds. Breeding season in June. The nests are frequently located inside hollow poplars.

Keeping: First imported into England in 1850. To be housed in aviaries of a firm metal construction. Thanks to its origin not overly sensitive to cold, but frost damage to the legs is possible, particularly after prolonged hanging on the wire (e.g., after

nocturnal disturbances by cats or owls). Not peaceable.

Diet: In their natural habitat the birds eat the buds of poplars early on in the year; later they visit cereal fields and fruit plantations (peaches). In addition to the usual seed mixtures, peanuts, fruit, and fresh twigs should be provided.

Breeding: Nest boxes about 30 x 30 x 60 cm, diameter of entrance hole 10 cm. Bottom layer of sawdust and peat fibers. Two to four eggs, incubation period 26–28 days, nestling period 7 weeks. The young have white down feathers initially; the remaining down feathers are gray and dense. As soon as the young birds are about 10 days old the female leaves the nest from time to time, although continuing to be fed by the male. Suitable rearing foods have turned out to be germinated sunflower seeds, carrots, hemp, white bread soaked in

milk, lettuce, spinach, and apples.

Behavior: Courting males strut about with their legs conspicuously raised. The tail feathers are fanned sideways, there are contractions of the pupil, and bows directed at the female, whereby the lower mandible vibrates. Feeding of the female by the male, but the reverse may also happen.

Long-tailed Parakeet

Psittacula longicauda (Boddaert)
Five subspecies.
Characteristics: 42 cm long. Green with yellowish underside, bluish lower back. Top of the head dark green, sides of the head and nape ruby colored. A broad black moustachial stripe starts at the lower mandible and runs towards the back along the lower edge of the cheeks. Red upper mandible, brownish lower mandible. Legs gray, iris yellow. In females the sides of the head and the nape are of a duller red, green moustachial stripes, black beak. Juveniles similar to females.
Range: Malayan peninsula, Borneo, Sumatra, Andaman Islands, Nicobar Islands.
Habitat: The edges of jungles, dead trees in swampy regions, mangrove and bamboo forests, open terrain.
Habits: Restless birds, forever on the go, calling loudly. At dusk the birds gather in specific places and fly off together to their roosts in clumps of trees or bamboos. On the Andaman and Nicobar Islands the breeding season lasts from February to March, on the Malayan peninsula from February to July.
Keeping: First imported into England in 1864. Regarded as a somewhat delicate bird which does not enjoy a long life span in

Opposite page: A Rose-ringed Parakeet in flight. Photo by Dr. Herbert R. Axelrod.

captivity. Sensitive to cold, should not be kept at below 10°C. Newly imported birds are in need of actual warmth. They are easily unsettled and then do not go near the food. Should, therefore, be kept in a spot as free from disturbances as possible. No great damage is done to wood. With their strongly curved claws they easily get caught in the wire, which can result in injuries.
Diet: In the wild the ingestion of betel nuts (*Areca catechu*), papayas, ripe *Pandanus* fruits, and acacia blossoms was observed along with invasions of coffee and oil palm plantations. During acclimatization these birds should be given plenty of fruit and germinated seeds. Later sunflower seeds, peanuts, apples, berries, figs, and dandelion.
Breeding: In their natural environment the birds breed inside tree hollows lined with strips of bark and rotten bits of wood. Two to three eggs. Reports on successful propagation in captivity do not exist. On the other hand, hybridization was achieved with Rose-ringed Parakeets and Moustached Parakeets.
Behavior: Bathing neither in the rain nor in shallow bowls. Outside the breeding season the female is aggressive towards the male. The male performs his mating ritual on the roof of the nest box or in the immediate vicinity. He walks about in an arrogant manner and gives the impression of being larger than the female. Two to three steps are followed with a jump. The plumage is displayed by moving the tail feathers laterally to and fro. Prior to feeding, the head is moved to the side in a weaving movement, the food being regurgitated at the same time. This looks as if the head were swiveling. Contractions of the pupil.

Plum-headed Parakeet

Psittacula cyanocephala (Linne)
Two subspecies, Including *P. c. rosa.*
Characteristics: 35 cm long. Olive green above, underside yellow-green. Head plum colored, pinkish red in the slightly smaller subspecies *P. c. rosa.* Narrow black neck ring, nape with a light blue-green band. Brownish red shoulder spot. Upper mandible red-yellow, lower mandible blackish. Legs greenish gray, iris yellowish white. Females with a blue-gray head, pale

Long-tailed Parakeets, *Psittacula longicauda.* The tail feathers of the male here have been damaged.

yellow bill, no shoulder spot. Coloration of immature birds similar to that of the females. Males showing full adult coloration after the second complete molt in the third year of life.

Range: A vast part of India, Nepal, Ceylon. *P. c. rosa* in Assam, Burma, Thailand, Cambodia, Vietnam.

Habitat: In India the species has a preference for wooded plains and foothills of up to 1300 m. In Ceylon at up to 1000 m above sea level. *P. c. rosa* is a common woodland bird above all in Thailand.

Habits: In family associations or in small flocks, *P. c. rosa* often seen with *P. alexandri* as well, encountered particularly in forest regions in the proximity of cereal fields. At the time the cereal crops, rice, and fruit ripen they flock together by the hundreds. Breeding season in India from December to April, on Ceylon from February to May. On the market in Bangkok nestlings of *P. c. rosa* are offered for sale from March to May. The birds breed inside the hollows of rotting tree trunks, deserted woodpecker holes and holes in walls. Occasionally several pairs breed in the same tree.

Keeping: At London Zoo in 1862. In 1871, kept by Dr. Russ in Germany and propagated successfully in subsequent years. Does not destroy wood, has not been known to screech, and intermingles well with small birds. Sensitive to frost.

Diet: Apart from various seeds, fruits, blossoms, and buds, the birds are partial to figs in their natural environment. Newly imported specimens must be carefully adapted to the usual aviary foods; mealworms, ant pupae, boiled rice, and plenty of fruit as well as a selection of various seeds should be offered. Acclimatized Plum-headed Parakeets accept the usual seed mixtures, a variety of fruit, dandelion, and chickweed.

Breeding: Nest box about 20 x 20 x 30 cm. Diameter of entrance hole 6 cm. Bottom layer of rotting wood. four to six eggs, incubation period 21–23 days, nestling period 7 weeks. Breeding starts early in the spring. As soon as the female has moved into a nest box the male feeds her. Sensitive to disturbances during incubating. Once the young are about a week old the female starts to forage for her own food again. The male feeds the young until about two weeks

Plum-headed Parakeets, *Psittacula cyanocephala*, are quiet birds that get along well with smaller birds.

after fledging. The feces of the young are removed from the box by the female. Generally speaking, the young are raised without any complications; however, one breeder reported that a male dragged a young bird out of the nest and "hacked it to bits." The rearing food should have a high protein content and include mealworms and ant pupae. One yellow color mutation has been cultivated. Hybridization with Slaty-headed Parakeet (*P. himalayana*).

Behavior: The male begins his courtship song in late winter and displaying his interest in the female by running up and down in front of her on a branch. Further mating behavior includes successive bowing and jerky movements of the tail.

Slaty-headed Parakeet
Psittacula himalayana (Lesson)
Two subspecies.

Characteristics: 40 cm long. Green. Head blackish slate gray. Black band on chin, nape light blue-green. Small brownish red

shoulder spot. Upper mandible red, lower mandible yellowish. Legs gray-green, iris white. Females having a paler head with the shoulder spot absent. Immature birds have a green head and a pale yellow bill.
Range: Eastern Afghanistan, northern India, Nepal to Burma, Thailand, Laos, Vietnam.
Habitat: Predominantly forest dwelling (cedars, oaks). In Nepal found at altitudes of up to 3800 m above sea level in the summer. In the winter between 700 and 1300 m. An observer who spotted a flock in Kashmir in 1974 recorded a nocturnal temperature of 0°C and daytime temperatures of 15°C in this region.
Habits: Birds reside near available food

Head study of a Slaty-headed Parakeet, *Psittacula himalayana*. Photo by J. M. Kenning.

resources. This parakeet can become a pest in corn fields and on fruit plantations. The birds breed very high up inside hollow trees. Sometimes several pairs build their nests in the same tree. In Burma the species breeds from January to March, in India from March to May.
Keeping: At London Zoo in 1879. A quiet voice. Intermingles well with other parrots. Although not sensitive to low temperatures,

The Slaty-headed Parakeet, *Psittacula himalayana*, is seldom imported and even less frequently bred.

the birds should have access to a frost-proof shelter.
Diet: Birds in the wild feed on various seeds and fruits, also on corn, walnuts, apples, and berries. In human care they accept, along with the usual foods, figs, berries, apples, carrots and, with particular relish, grapefruit and millet spray.
Breeding: So far there has only been one report, from England, of these rarely imported parakeets having been successfully propagated in captivity. The eggs were laid at intervals of 5 days (in all other *Psittacula* species egg laying takes place at 2-day intervals) and incubated for 23 days. At 4 weeks the young were feathered and at 7 weeks they fledged. During the first 5 days of life they were fed predominantly on canary seed, white bread soaked in milk, and large quantities of dandelion heads. Later, sunflower seeds were also accepted. Fruit was not fed to the young until they were 4 weeks old.
Hybridization with *P. cyanocephala rosa*.
Behavior: Bathing in the rain with the wings spread out. Courtship, starting around February and lasting for about three weeks, consists of call notes, bowing, and feeding the female.

Emerald-collared Parakeet

Psittacula calthorpae (Blyth)

Characteristics: 30 cm long. Wings and underside green, back blue-gray. Head blue-gray, forehead and orbital ring of a lively green. Lesser wing coverts violet. Upper mandible red, lower mandible brownish. Iris yellowish white, legs greenish gray. Females with a black upper mandible. Juveniles green with a gray-blue rump. Beaks orange-red at first, then dark.

Range: Ceylon, supposedly also on the Maldive Islands.

Habitat: Forest dwelling, up to 1600 m.

Habits: Small flocks, often in association with Black-headed Starlings. How common the birds are depends on food resources.

Keeping: Not kept until 1930, mainly in England. Requirements similar to those of the Plum-headed Parakeet (*P. cyanocephala*).

Diet: No details are available on the foods preferred in the wild. Keepers of this parakeet mention its great appreciation for spinach, above all the leaf stalks.

Breeding: In the wild the breeding season lasts from January to May; sometimes the birds have a second brood between July and September. Nest box as for other parakeets of similar size, with a bottom layer of disintegrating wood or peat. At first the male merely guards the nest, otherwise taking no notice of the female, who is not fed until a later stage.

Malabar Parakeet

Psittacula columboides (Vigors)

Characteristics: 38 cm long. Head, neck, upper back, underparts pigeon gray. Eye region and belly light green. Narrow black neck ring, below it a broad sea green ring. Lower back blue-green. Upper mandible red, lower mandible blackish. Iris yellow, legs gray. Female only possessing the black neck and nape ring without the sea green stripe. Beak blackish. Fledged young have orange-red bills which soon turn black. In the males the upper mandible is already red in the first year of life. Complete adult plumage, in contrast with most other species of the genus, after the first molt.

Range: Southwestern India from Bombay to Kerala.

Habitat: Damp evergreen forests at

The Malabar Parakeet, *Psittacula columboides*—unlike its congeners—shows full adult coloration after the first molt.

altitudes of between 450 and 1000 m. Old clearances, deserted coffee and rubber plantations.

Habits: In some localities seen together with Plum- headed Parakeets (*P. cyanocephala*). Spending almost the whole day searching for food in the treetops. Only coming down to the ground at the time the cereal crops ripen. Also visits orchards. Often nesting in very tall ironwood trees (*Mesua ferrea*). Deserted hollows of woodpeckers and barbets are accepted and widened.

Keeping: 1852, at London Zoo. Pleasant voice. Well suited for garden aviaries but does not get along with other birds.

Diet: In their natural habitat the birds are particularly partial to greenstuff, figs and other fruits, nectar, and buds. Parakeets bought on an Indian market were initially fed mangoes by their owner, later white bread soaked in milk, and gradually adapted to seeds. A cautious approach must be taken when adapting the birds to their new diet. Along with the usual seed mixtures, they should be offered fresh or soaked corn, boiled rice, and most importantly an abundance of fruit.

Breeding: If given a choice, the birds prefer natural hollows. Nest boxes 22 x 22 x 35 cm, diameter of access hole 8 cm. Bottom layer of peat fibers and sawdust (thrown out of the box by some birds). Three to five eggs, incubation period 23 days, nestling period 7–8 weeks. The male remains in the proximity of the nest while the female

A lutino specimen of the Rose-ringed Parakeet, *Psittacula krameri.*

incubates. During the first 6 weeks the young are fed by the female, who in turn is provided with food by the male. At the end of this period the male helps to feed the young. During the rearing period plenty of hemp, Budgerigar food, white bread soaked in milk, hard-boiled egg, and apples were taken. Sunflower seeds were left untouched. According to reports by English aviculturists, there was a great demand for cuttlefish bone.

Intermediate Parakeet

Psittacula intermedia (Rothschild)

Characteristics: 36 cm long. Similar to Slaty-headed Parakeet apart from a pink forehead and eye region. Possibly not a species in its own right but a cross between Slaty-headed Parakeet and Plum-headed Parakeet. So far only carcasses of male birds have been examined.

Range: Himalaya region in north India.

Parrotlets of the genus *Forpus*

Like all subsequent genera, belonging to the tribe of Araini. Small parrots with a thick, light colored bill. Tail feathers short, not extending beyond the wings. Plumage green, usually with blue markings in the males. The sexes can already be differentiated in the juvenile plumage. Females of the individual species very similar in coloration. Sounds uttered are similar to those of sparrows. Distributed from northwestern Mexico to northern Argentina and Paraguay. The exact range of distribution of the species that live in tropical rain forests is not known in every case.

Although reproducing themselves, parrotlets of the genus *Forpus* show little activity when kept in cages. It is better, therefore, to accommodate them in aviaries. Imported animals are initially sensitive to cool temperatures. Acclimatized *Forpus* species who have already had their first molt in captivity can be put into outdoor aviaries from mid-March to mid-September. Cages should only be stocked with one pair at a time. In aviaries the birds usually intermingle well with waxbills; in larger aviaries several pairs may be kept together. Nonetheless, one can never be sure that bickering between the birds may not break out. Males and females continue to be closely attached to each other outside the breeding season.

For all species, nest boxes of the dimensions 14 x 14 x 25 cm with a bottom layer of decomposing wood are suitable. Diameter of entrance hole 5 cm. The cock feeds the incubating hen who seldom leaves the nest. Sensitive to disturbances as a rule. Incubation period 17–20 days, nestling period 5 weeks. The males spend time inside the nest box during the day without doing any of the incubating. During the night they roost in the nest. The newly hatched young are naked, apart from a few light, thread shaped down feathers which disappear after a couple of days. Development proceeds rapidly; the sexes can be differentiated after 20 days. Sometimes seeds are carried into the nest and eaten by the young birds which are almost ready to fledge. After leaving the nest they usually forage for their own food, although the parents may continue to feed them for another two weeks. For a short period the fledged young birds return to the nest to roost. Where conditions are favorable there will be a second brood, occasionally there may even be a third.

The birds are fed on millet, canary seed, niger, hemp, and sunflower seeds. Greenstuff and fruit are less popular. Fresh twigs are readily nibbled. With the exception of species from dry regions, parrotlets of the genus *Forpus* love to bathe in wet leaves or grass. The aviaries should, therefore, be equipped with a few grass tussocks.

Around 1970 these parrotlets were still frequently imported. Today, imports of these species have become rare. Hence there is a necessity for aviculturists and associations to organize the building up of breeding strains and to help preserve these species by their systematic propagation.

Seven species.

Mexican Parrotlet

Forpus cyanopygius (Souance)
Three subspecies.
Characteristics: 13 cm long. Green. Forehead, sides of the head, throat yellowish green. In the males, rump, greater coverts, under wing coverts turquoise blue; secondary covert dark blue. Beak whitish, iris brown, legs gray. In the females all the blue is replaced with yellow-green.
Range: Northwestern Mexico, Islands of Tres Marias.
Habitat: Open dry landscapes up to 1300 m, deciduous forests.
Habits: Birds seen singly, in pairs, or in groups of up to about 40 animals. The periods of main activity are early morning and late afternoon. Sometimes seen in

association with Orange-fronted Conures *(Aratinga canicularis)*. Mexican Parrotlets fly with rapid beats of the wings, without gliding. All turning movements of birds flying in flocks are precisely synchronized. These parrotlets tend to be very cautious on the whole; only when feeding do they permit the observer to come a little closer. Fruit, especially figs, which are still green but already ripening constitutes the favorite fare. The birds search the branches systematically and check whether the fruit is at the right stage of ripeness by sampling it. Breeding season June to July.
Keeping: First imported into Germany in 1924. Acclimatization is not easy. It is advisable only to put birds bred in captivity into outdoor aviaries for the summer months. Such animals are less nervous. If several birds already in the adult plumage are kept together in a limited space, they are liable to start squabbling and cause bite wounds to each other's legs.
Diet: Germinated seeds and millet sprays are particularly appreciated during the period of acclimatization but also remain a popular food later on.
Breeding: In Europe the birds usually breed in August. Egg laying every other day, incubation from the second egg onwards. For rearing, egg food, ant pupae, germinated spray millet, chickweed. After fledging, the young birds are fed for up to another three weeks. A maximum of three successive broods is possible.
Hybridization with Spectacled Parrotlet (*F. conspicillatus*) and Pacific Parrotlet (*F. coelestis*).

Green-rumped Parrotlet

Forpus passerinus (Linne)
Five subspecies.
Characteristics: 12 cm long. Green. Rump region emerald green. Under wing coverts dark blue. Beak of a light horn color, iris dark brown, legs brownish. Females without blue, forehead yellowish green.
Range: Northern Brazil, Guyana, Venezuela. Introduced on Curacao, Trinidad, Barbados, Jamaica.
Habitat: Semi-arid scrubland up to 1800 m, gardens, agricultural land.
Habits: Outside the breeding season in large flocks in search of food. Breeding

season in Surinam February, June, and August; in Venezuela between May and August. The nest is located in hollow branches, hollow tree trunks, and the nests of tree dwelling termites. One nest seen in the natural habitat was 4 m above the ground; the chamber lay 60 cm below the entrance. Nesting material was not present. The natives frequently take these parrots out of the nest and rear them.

Keeping: Although regarded as more peaceable than the blue-rumped species, some degree of caution is required if several parrots are to be kept together. Outside the breeding season they get along with birds of other species as well. In

The Green-rumped Parrotlet, *Forpus passerinus.*

Germany and in England they have been kept as well as bred in free flight conditions during the summer months.

Diet: In the wild they feed on the fruits of tamarinds, on berries and garden fruits.

Greenstuff, apples, pears, and bananas are accepted.

Breeding: Sensitive to disturbances during incubation. The rearing food should consist predominantly of germinated seeds. Fledged young birds are fed for another short period by the parents. At this stage some males start to bite off the feathers of the young. Sometimes young birds are even killed. In many cases, one of the reasons for this aggressive behavior may be cramped accommodations.

Behavior: Very social. Perching close together, the feathers touching. Mutual preening, feeding of the female by the male. Courting males run up and down on a branch in front of the female, delivering a chattering song. The contour feathers are slightly raised, the tail feathers spread out, the wings lifted. During copulation the male stands on the female's back with one foot, clasping the perching branch with the other. Similar sideways copulations are observed in many species of long-tailed parrots. Birds bathing in the rain hang from the branches with the head downwards.

Blue-winged Parrotlet
Forpus xanthopterygius (Spix)
Six subspecies.

Characteristics: 12 cm long. Green. Eye region and ear coverts emerald green. Rump, lower back, wing coverts, and under wing coverts ultramarine. Beak horn colored, iris dark brown, legs blue-gray. Females without blue in the plumage, forehead and cheeks greenish yellow, underside slightly yellowish.

Range: Amazon range of Peru, Bolivia and Paraguay as far as the Atlantic. Northwestern Columbia, northeastern Argentina, eastern and northern Brazil.

Habitat: Scattered, locally common, in open terrain. In Paraguay sometimes seen in areas overgrown with low shrubs, in northwestern Columbia also in cactus thickets. The birds visit fruit plantations and gardens.

Habits: Outside the breeding season in groups, usually of 5–20, sometimes as many as over 50 animals. Always on the move, either searching for grass seeds on the

Hybridization has been extensive among the parrotlets in captivity, making it difficult to obtain pure stock and to identify species with certainty. Photo by Michael Gilroy.

Yellow-faced Parrotlet, *Forpus xanthops,* and Blue-winged Parrotlet, *Forpus xanthopterygius.* Routedale photo.

ground or eating berries in trees and bushes. These parrotlets attract one's attention by their constant twittering. They breed in hollow trees or in the deserted nests of Rufous Horneros (*Furnarius rufus*). In such nests the eggs have been found on a layer of duck's feathers and the green feathers of the brooding female, which does not necessarily mean that the duck's feathers were carried into the nest by the parrotlets.

Keeping: At the beginning of this century Blue-winged Parrotlets were frequently imported and often bred in captivity Imported animals must be carefully acclimatized. Many of them remain shy, which may result in injuries sustained when flying into the aviary wire.

Diet: In the wild the birds feed on seeds, berries, fruit, leaf buds, and probably blossoms as well. English breeders recommend a seed mixture composed of 60% canary seed, 15% white millet, as well

as oats, sunflower seeds, and hemp. Hemp is offered in a germinated state all year round.

Breeding: One pair of the subspecies *F. x. spengeli*, which came into breeding condition in July, was not interested in a nest box for Budgerigars but moved into a hollow birch trunk that had been put up in an oblique position (length 60 cm, internal diameter 15 cm). At first the birds remained inside the hollow for half an hour at the most; a few days later they spent the night inside. After three weeks egg laying began. When the young were being reared, a great deal of hemp was consumed while apples and greenstuff were ignored. The individual subspecies have been bred regularly, mainly in the U.S.A.

Spectacled Parrotlet
Forpus conspicillatus (Lafresnaye)
Three subspecies.

Characteristics: 12 cm long. Green. Rump, secondaries, primaries blue. Orbital ring blue. Beak horn colored, upper mandible darker at the base. Iris gray-brown, legs brown. Female emerald green instead of blue.

Range: Eastern Panama, Colombia, Venezuela.

Habitat: In Colombia, open woodland of the tropical zone. Found at altitudes of up to 1600 m.

Habits: Outside the breeding season in groups searching for food in the trees or on the ground. In Panama laying females and nests are found in the second half of January and in February. One nest was located 2 m above ground level inside a rotten hollow tree trunk. On the bottom of the hollow, which was 50 cm deep, lay 4 eggs on some feathers and bits of wood. The birds also breed inside rotten wooden posts.

Keeping: Imported since 1880. Spectacled Parrotlets, offered for sale at markets in their native countries, are trapped with snares that have been baited with ripe bananas; this demonstrates their special preference for soft fruit. It is, therefore, necessary for imported birds to be adapted to their changed diet very carefully. In many cases, unfortunately, the animals are adapted to totally inadequate foods during

The Spectacled Parrotlet, *Forpus conspicillatus,* in its natural environment exhibits a preference for soft fruit.

their stay at the trapping and quarantine stations. The example of well-acclimatized birds will induce the new arrivals to try other foods in addition to the monotonous diet they have been fed. Sensitive to lower temperatures at first.
Breeding: Successfully bred in captivity on several occasions.

Sclater's Parrotlet
Forpus sclateri (G. R. Gray)
Two subspecies.
Characteristics: 12.5 cm long. Green, back dark olive green. Rump, secondaries, and primaries blue in the male. Upper mandible dark gray, lower mandible horn colored. Iris brown, legs gray-brown. Females yellow-green on the forehead, cheeks, and underside.
Range: Venezuela, northern Brazil, Colombia, Ecuador, Peru, northern Bolivia.
Habitat: Open woods in the tropical zone.
Habits: Rarely observed. It is possible that this species spends more time in the trees than its relatives.

Keeping: In London in 1881. Although imported from time to time, there are no reports on keeping it anywhere.
Breeding: One report gives the following information: breeding begins in June; female inside the nest from the first egg onwards, only coming out to defecate; female fed by the male, who also spends the night inside the box; egg laying every other day; during checks on the nest the female covers the eggs with the wings but does not leave the box; 7 eggs, incubation period 21 days; young covered in yellow down feathers; fledging at 5 weeks, subsequently fed by the parents for a further two weeks, then rejected; niger was particularly popular.

Pacific Parrotlet
Forpus coelestis (Lesson)
Characteristics: 12.5 cm long. Green. Nape gray-blue, back gray-green. Rump, secondaries, greater wing coverts and under wing coverts blue. A tinge of blue above the eyes. Beak horn colored, legs brownish, iris brown. Females without blue on the wings, rump only slightly bluish, only a hint of blue above the eyes. A blue mutation is known to exist in the wild.
Range: Western Ecuador, northwestern Peru.
Habitat: Dry scrubland.
Habits: Towards the end of the breeding season the birds are seen in family groups of about 10 animals. Sometimes they gather in large flocks that attract attention by their calls. The main activities seem to consist of searching for food and social preening. In Ecuador the breeding season starts at the end of January, after the rainy season, and lasts until May. Occasionally there is a second clutch one week after the young have fledged. The birds breed inside hollow tree trunks; hollow rotting branches; holes in fence posts and telegraph poles; deserted woodpecker nests; old nests of Pale-legged Horneros *(Furnarius leucopus)*; the spherical nests (with an entrance tube at the bottom) of Necklaced Spinetails *(Synallaxis stictothorax)*; and the spherical nests (15 cm in diameter, with a lateral entrance tube) of Fasciated Wrens *(Campylorhynchus fasciatus)*. The eggs are laid on the bottom, without nesting

material.

Keeping: Only imported into Europe more frequently after 1962. Until breeding facilities are provided it is possible to keep the animals in groups. It has been reported

Pacific Parrotlets, *Forpus coelestis,* are native to dry regions. They do not bathe and do not enjoy being sprayed.

that the species interacts well with Hanging Parrots. Aggressive during the breeding season; there is the danger of leg injuries. Imported birds remain shy, rarely coming down to the ground. Therefore, water and feeding places must be located at a height of about 1 m. Sensitive to frost.

Diet: Imported birds start off by feeding on germinated spray millet and fresh corn; later they accept millet, canary seed, niger, oats, and sunflower seeds. There should be a constant supply of greenstuff, carrots, apples, and fresh twigs. Rearing food consists of soft food, egg food, and meal worms.

Breeding: Breeding begins in April. Four to six eggs are laid at two-day intervals. Incubation starts from the first or second egg onwards. Incubation periods fluctuate

between 17 and 21 days. Nestling period 30 days. Newly hatched young are naked. The incubating hen leaves the nest briefly once a day in order to drink, feed, preen herself, and deposit her feces (large quantities of a soft consistency). The male is usually found inside the nest, i.e., not far from the entrance. Before the young leave the nest box the parents take millet and hemp to them. A similar phenomenon was observed with regard to Blue-winged Parrotlets *(F. xanthopterygius)* as well. Immediately after fledging the young may be independent and no longer need to rely on parental feeding. Some aviculturists reported, however, that the young were fed by their parents for another two weeks after they had fledged. The pair belonging to a German aviculturist successfully bred inside an open feeding bowl on a layer of litter.

Behavior: In adaptation to their dry habitat, they do not bathe and do not want to be sprayed. Very social, the members of a pair are always very close. Social preening is common. Enemies belonging to a different species are threatened with a raised plumage and an open beak, whereby the birds make swaying movements, bending over backwards. Just before they lose their balance they quickly shoot forward. Despite their shyness, males and females remain inside the nest box during checks. The female raises the plumage and spreads out the tail feathers, thus covering the eggs. With an open beak she pecks upwards. While this is happening the male stands frozen in a corner of the nest box.

Yellow-faced Parrotlet
Forpus xanthops (Salvin)
Characteristics: The largest species, 14.5 cm long. Green. In the male, crown, forehead, cheeks, throat yellow. Otherwise similar to Pacific Parrotlet *(F. coelestis).* In the female, rump feathers of a dull blue, under wing coverts gray with a tinge of blue. Iris light brown, beak of a light horn color, legs brown.
Range: Northern Peru.
Habitat: Dry open scrubland. Has been observed at an altitude of 1720 m.
Keeping: In Germany, W. Heinrich from Mainz obtained a pair by chance in 1975. The animals, which were fairly shy, showed

a preference for sunflower seeds, canary seed, groats, and niger. Spray millet, hemp, apples, and greenstuff were only taken up in small amounts. They roosted inside a nest box for Budgerigars. In the outdoor aviary they got on well with a pair of Blue-winged Parrotlets *(Forpus xanthopterygius)*. Here, they accepted more greenstuff as well. In 1976 the animals were donated to Vogelpark Walsrode (bird park at Walsrode) where, unfortunately, they succumbed to a *Salmonella* infection.
Breeding: In 1981, in Germany, as many as four successful breeding attempts, with two completed broods each, were reported. AZ member Frenger received his pair in October 1981 and accommodated it in a box cage of 100 x 50 x 50 cm. The nest box, hung up in a horizontal position, measured 25 x 12 x 20 cm. The animals were wintered in a bright room at 15°C. The food consisted of large parakeet food, chicken feed, and egg food; sunflower seeds were the most

popular fare. The birds received fresh willow twigs every day and a multivitamin preparation twice a week. In mid-February 1981 they approached the nest box. The first egg was laid on March 8. After an incubation period of 19–21 days, six young hatched; the youngest was suffocated, however. The first down feathers were dense and white, the egg tooth relatively large. After 20 days it was possible to sex the animals. At the age of 32–35 days the young birds left the nest and were fed by their parents for another two weeks. During the rearing period the quantities of spray millet, chicken feed, and egg food used were particularly large.

The Yellow-faced Parrotlet, *Forpus xanthops,* is the largest member of the genus. The extensive yellow indicates that this specimen is a male. Photo courtesy of Vogelpark Walsrode.

Tepui Parrotlet *(Nannopsittaca)*

The most important characteristic is the small, dainty beak not seen in any other genus of Araini.
   One species.

Tepui Parrotlet
Nannopsittaca panychlora (Salvin and Godman)
Characteristics: 14 cm long. Upper parts of a dark green, underside of a slightly lighter green. Slightly yellow in the eye-region. Beak blackish, iris brown, legs pale brown. Sexes identical in color, immature birds probably not deviating in color from the adult animals.
Range: Three regions, far apart from each other, in the higher mountain ranges of eastern Venezuela and in the westernmost part of Guyana. Does not venture into the tropical lowlands that lie between these mountains. Because of this insular distribution, can be regarded as an ancient element of the South American bird world.
Habitat: Damp and cool subtropical mountain forests.
Keeping: Has probably never been kept in captivity. There is no available data on its life in the wild.

Parakeets of the genus *Brotogeris*

Beak laterally compressed, high. Tail progressively narrowing, steplike; varying in length but short in most species. Plumage predominantly green, other colors on chin, forehead, primaries, or under wing coverts. Both sexes and juveniles of the same coloration.

In the wild these parakeets feed mostly on fruits, but also on the green parts of plants, on buds, blossoms, nectar, and various seeds. In captivity they should, therefore, receive not only a variety of seeds but also plenty of fruit and fresh branches. Facilities for daily bathing must be provided. Being tree dwellers, these birds rarely come down to the ground in the aviary either. Food and water must be placed on an elevated table or shelf. All species are sensitive to cold. Nesting facilities should be left in the aviary all the year round as they are used for roosting outside the breeding season as well. They should be affixed as high up as possible. Some species breed in the nests of tree dwelling termites. When attempting to propagate these birds, one can also offer bales of pressed peat or boxes with stamped loamy soil inside. Despite the numerous imports, there have been relatively few reports of successful breeding attempts so far. Birds of the genus *Brotogeris* that are being kept on their own become particularly tame, learning to mimic as well. However, because of their loud screaming they are not very suitable for inside the living area of the house.

Seven species.

Plain Parakeet

Brotogeris tirica (Gmelin)
Characteristics: 25 cm long. Biggest and strongest species. Green. Nape and tail with a bluish tinge. Beak horn colored at the base, otherwise brown. Iris dark brown, legs pink. Juveniles have a shorter tail.
Range: Southern and eastern Brazil.
Habitat: Very common above all in open terrain. In Rio de Janeiro this species lives in the Botanic Gardens and in other parks. They can also be readily observed in a park surrounded by houses in the middle of a shopping center in Sao Paulo. This parakeet, which can justly be said to have learned to exploit civilization, also makes use of the food resources in rice and corn

A Golden-winged Parakeet, *Brotogeris chrysopterus,* is the pet of this Indian child in Brazil. Photo by Dr. Herbert R. Axelrod.

fields.
Habits: Sometimes in association with parakeets of other species. Nesting in hollow trees. In Sao Paulo nestlings were found in January, in Minas Gerais in September.
Keeping: In 1862, at London Zoo. Because it grows tame so quickly, frequently kept in Brazil. Easy to keep, usually gets on well with other parakeets.
Diet: In addition to the usual food, berries are popular. Boiled whole millet has proved suitable as a rearing food. The young birds are also fed on insects.
Breeding: four to five eggs, incubation period 22–23 days, nestling period 6 weeks. Birds in captivity frequently breed in June. Fledged young birds return to the nest box

for some time to roost. In 1912 a blue mutation was cultivated at Schonbrunn Zoo in Vienna. In 1970 there was a report of a blue Plain Parakeet that had been seen in Brazil. Hybridization with Orange-chinned Parakeet (*Brotogeris jugularis*).

Canary-winged Parakeet

Brotogeris versicolorus (P. L. S. Bueller) Three subspecies, among them *B. v. chiriri*.
Characteristics: 22 cm long. Green. First primary black, the next three dark blue, the remainder white. Outer secondaries yellowish white. Greater wing coverts yellow. *B. v. chiriri* with large yellow secondary coverts. Beak of a light horn color, iris dark brown, legs pink with a little gray.
Range: Eastern Ecuador, northeastern Peru, southeastern Colombia, Bolivia, northern Brazil, French Guiana. Introduced in Lima, central Peru, and Puerto Rico. *B. v. chiriri*: eastern and southern Brazil, northern and eastern Bolivia, Paraguay, northern Argentina.
Habitat: Common in the woodland of the tropical zone at up to 1500 m above sea level. River banks; also found in urban areas.
Habits: Usually in groups of up to about 50 birds. In the roosting places on the river banks several thousand of these birds will assemble. Very conspicuous because of their loud voice. In Matto Grosso huge flocks in November, pair formation in January. Nesting in hollow trees or the nests of tree dwelling termites.
Keeping: At London Zoo in 1862. In aviaries it is possible to associate them with small birds. They are too slow to be of any real danger to the latter. During the breeding season each pair should have a separate compartment. No serious damage is done to wooden aviary structures. Avid climbers. Not very sensitive to cold. Near Frankfurt an escaped Canary-winged Parakeet lived free for nine months until it was recaptured unharmed in January; the winter had been a mild one.
Diet: Seed mixtures, plenty of greenstuff and fruit. For rearing, the birds should be supplied with dandelion leaves and flower heads, groundsel, chickweed, apples, pears, bananas.

Canary-winged Parakeet, *Brotogeris versicolorus*. Birds kept singly become closely attached to their keepers.

Breeding: Nest box 18 x 18 x 40 cm, diameter of entrance hole 7 cm. Deep bottom layer of peat fibers. Five to six eggs, incubation period 23 days, nestling period 7–8 weeks. The newly hatched young are naked and develop very slowly. The quills do not burst until more than three weeks have passed. Incubation from the second egg onwards. Only the female incubates; the male spends the night inside the nest. After fledging the young birds return to the nest to roost for a while. They are independent about three weeks after fledging. The beak, white at first, grows darker after about 8 weeks. Breeding season April to June. Both parents feed the young. *B. v. chiriri* has been crossed with the Orange-chinned Parakeet (*Brotogeris jugularis*).
Behavior: During courtship the male feeds his partner. During copulation the two partners perch on a branch side by side. The threat behavior has been described as a lifting and quick dropping of the wings, accompanied by an explosive sound. At the

173

A Canary-winged Parakeet, *Brotogeris versicolorus,* belonging to the subspecies *chiriri.* Photo by Dr. Herbert R. Axelrod.

same time the birds scream. When in a state of excitement the pairs deliver a "shrieking duet." The shrieks uttered by the two animals in turn come out so quickly that one gets the impression they were originating from a single bird.

Grey-cheeked Parakeet

Brotogeris pyrrhopterus (Latham)
Characteristics: 20 cm. Green. Forehead, sides of the head, and chin pale gray. Crown of a light blue-green color. Wing coverts dark blue. Under wing coverts orange. Beak of a light horn color, iris dark brown, legs pale pink. Juveniles paler with a green crown and without blue on the wings.
Range: West of the Andes from Ecuador to southwestern Peru.
Habitat: Dry scrubland in the tropical zone. Banana plantations, gardens.
Habits: Common. Outside the breeding season in large flocks.
Keeping: At London Zoo in 1862. The quietest species of the genus. Outside of the breeding season it intermingles well with other species. Acclimatized animals have been kept in unheated accommodation in the winter.

Grey-cheeked Parakeets, *Brotogeris pyrrhopterus*, are the quietest species of the genus.

It is not possible to distinguish the sexes of the Grey-cheeked Parakeet visually.

Diet: Fruit, especially berries, and greenstuff and corn are all liked by the birds.
Breeding: Nest box 23 x 23 x 50 cm. Courtship starts in May, breeding in June. Three to five eggs, incubation period about 22 days, nestling period 5 weeks. After leaving the nest the young birds are fed by the parents for up to an additional three weeks.

Orange-chinned Parakeet

Brotogeris jugularis (P. L. S. Mueller) four subspecies, among them *B. j. cyanoptera,* which has been described as a species in its own right by some authors.
Characteristics: 18 cm long. Green. Underside yellowish green, head with a tinge of pale blue. Under wing coverts yellow. Orange-red spot on the chin. Beak horn colored, iris dark brown, legs yellowish brown. Over a hundred years ago a blue individual with a white spot on the chin was seen among a flock.
Range: From southwestern Mexico to Colombia, Venezuela, eastern Ecuador, northeastern Peru.

Orange-chinned Parakeets, *Brotogeris jugularis,* are more likely to breed if provided with an artificial termite nest.

Habitat: Open flat landscapes with tall trees. Seen in Honduras at altitudes of up to 1400 m outside the breeding season.
Habits: In many regions of Central America one of the most common and most conspicuous birds. During the breeding season in pairs or in family associations, otherwise in groups of up to 30 birds. In the feeding and roosting places seen by the hundreds. Like staying in flowering trees, where they consume blossoms and nectar. They are exceedingly active when doing this, fluttering from one twig to another, hanging suspended from a branch, and making all sorts of contortions in order to reach a blossom or fruit. In Panama the groups split up into pairs late in the winter. In El Salvador the females lay at the end of January. The favored nesting sites are the hollows of tree dwelling termites, but the Orange-chinned Parakeets often lose these to Green Conures (*Aratinga holochlora*) and other birds. They then excavate holes inside rotting tree trunks and branches or look for deserted woodpecker hollows. Several pairs may be seen to gnaw out nesting hollows in the same tree; on one occasion as many as 12 pairs were observed.
Keeping: First kept at London Zoo in 1872. In 1873, in Vienna, bred in captivity for the first time. Very social, breeding in colonies. Should have a roosting box available to them all year round. While not keen on bathing, Orange-chinned Parakeets allow themselves to be sprayed with water.
Breeding: Crucial to success, these birds must be kept in larger groups and offered artificial termite construction with a short tunnel leading up into the nesting chamber. Up to 9 eggs, incubation period 21 days, nestling period 35 days. Able to reproduce themselves as early as the age of one. While the female incubates, the male stands on guard at the entrance, although often seen inside the nest as well. Hybridization with Plain Parakeet (*Brotogeris tirica*), Canary-winged Parakeet (*Brotogeris versicolorus*), and Grey-cheeked Parakeet (*Brotogeris pyrrhopterus*).

Gustav's Parakeet

Brotogeris gustavi (Berlepsch)
Two subspecies.
Characteristics: 19 cm long. Green. Shoulder and wing margin yellow. Top of head bluish green. Orange-red spot on chin. Under wing coverts green. Beak horn colored, iris dark brown, legs flesh colored.
Range: Eastern Peru, Bolivia.
Habitat: Open terrain.

Golden-winged Parakeet

Brotogeris chrysopterus (Linne)
Five subspecies, among them *B. c. tuipara,* with orange- colored band on forehead and a chin spot of the same color.
Characteristics: 17 cm long. Green. Narrow dark brown band on forehead, orange-brown spot on chin. Head bluish. Foremost large secondary coverts and greater coverts orange-colored. Beak of a pale horn color, iris dark brown, legs yellowish brown.
Range: Amazon range of Brazil, eastern Venezuela, Guyana.
Habitat: Forests and savannahs.
Habits: Restless birds, constantly on the move in search of food. Particularly popular are berries which they ingest in large quantities. Observed were the devouring of blossoms of the *Erythrina* tree and of seeds extracted from the fruits of the

tree *Bombax monguba*. When eating they show little shyness. Towards the evening the birds gather in groups of about 40 animals. Breeding season in Surinam from November to April. The species breeds inside hollow rotting branches, tree hollows, and in the nests of tree dwelling termites.
Keeping: At London Zoo in 1878. Birds kept in isolation grow so tame that they always return to their owner even when allowed to fly free.
Diet: Fruit, soaked white bread and biscuit are readily accepted. Dry pieces of bread are soaked in water by the birds. Special delicacies are the nectar rich blossoms of *Robinia* species.

Tui Parakeet

Brotogeris sanctithomae (P. L. S. Mueller)
Two subspecies.
Characteristics: 17 cm long. Green. Forehead and crown yellow. In *B. s. takatsukasae* a yellow stripe above the eye. Beak chestnut brown, iris gray, legs gray-brown.

Although Tui Parakeets, *Brotogeris sanctithomae*, have from time to time been imported in large numbers, they have seldom been bred.

Range: Amazon range of northern Brazil to eastern Ecuador and northern Bolivia.
Habitat: Forests within the tropical zone. In northwestern Brazil in open terrain, manioc and sugar cane plantations.
Habits: In groups of about 10 animals. In the daytime continuously feeding in the treetops. In northeastern Peru nests were found in July. Breeding inside hollow trees and in the nests of tree dwelling termites at a height of about 5 m.
Keeping: At London Zoo in 1862. Frequently kept in its native range. Although periodically common on the European animal market, there are no detailed reports on the keeping and breeding of this species. Gets along well with small birds.
Breeding: Four to five eggs, incubation period 21 days, nestling period 45 days.

Parakeets of the genus *Bolborhynchus*

Thick bill which looks swollen. Ceres unfeathered, nares open. Unequivocal sexual differential characteristics only in one species (*Bolborhynchus aurifrons*). Because of the small size and the pleasant voice, these parakeets can also be kept inside dwelling houses. Have not been known to destroy wood.
Five species.

Barred Parakeet

Bolborhynchus lineola (Cassin)
Two subspecies.
Characteristics: 17 cm long. Green, underside yellowish. Black transverse bars, with the exception of the underside, on almost the whole body. Beak horn colored, iris dark gray, legs pink. In the females the black markings on the tail and shoulder feathers are less distinct, but with regard to some breeding pairs there were no differences in color between male and female. Immature birds are paler in coloration, beak and legs are lighter.
Range: Southern Mexican mountains to as far as the Andes of Colombia and central Peru.

With the Barred Parakeet, *Bolborhynchus lineola,* breeding is more likely to succeed if the birds are kept in colonies.

Habitat: In southern Mexico in dense forests at altitudes of up to 1600 m. In Honduras these parakeets breed at 1500 m. Later they live in regions at altitudes of about 600 m. Woodland birds, but when the corn ripens they also visit fields.

Habits: Well camouflaged in the forest and difficult to spot, hence presumably regarded as rare. Usually in pairs or in small groups of less than 20 birds. Outside the breeding season in flocks of over 100 animals. Feeding Barred Parakeets allow one to come quite close. No data on reproductive biology in the natural environment. In western Panama one specimen with developed gonads was found in December on one occasion.

Keeping: At London Zoo in 1886. Outside the frosty period, acclimatized animals can be kept in outdoor aviaries. Part of the aviary equipment should consist of branches of a large diameter (at least 4 cm) on which the birds can walk along. Loves shady spots and in planted enclosures hides among the foliage. Nest boxes are occupied for roosting outside the breeding season as

well. Peaceable towards one another, also getting along well with other nonaggressive parakeets and small birds. If kept in association with Zebra Waxbills, there is a possibility that the latter will occupy all the nest boxes and fill them up with nesting material without meeting with any opposition from the Barred Parakeets. Somewhat extraordinary is the excessive growth of the claws in this species. It is necessary to trim the claws every 4 months or so. The birds quickly grow confiding.

Diet: Green and dry panicle millet as well as yellow and red spray millet are readily accepted. If these popular foods are available, the mixture of parakeet and canary food offered in the bowl receives scant attention. Sunflower seeds are liked all year round. Carrots, sliced or whole and affixed to a branch; apples, cut into pieces and affixed to a branch; greenstuff should be supplied every day. For rearing, germinated food, egg food, and soaked white bread have proved suitable.

Breeding: First bred in captivity in 1902, in Germany. Nest box 17 x 17 x 30 cm, diameter of entrance hole 6 cm. Horizontal nest boxes for Budgerigars with a slightly enlarged entrance hole are also accepted. Bottom layer of peat fibers and sawdust. Three to six eggs, incubation period 18–20 days, nestling period 38 days. The incubating hen is fed by the male. Only when the young are about half-grown does the female leave the nest for any length of time. Newly hatched animals are covered in thin, whitish, fluffy down feathers. Good breeding results are achieved where the birds are kept in colonies; some breeders reported three successive broods. A California aviculturist kept a cinnamon colored specimen.

Behavior: Typical is the crouched posture assumed while creeping along the branches, whereby the body is kept in a horizontal position. Often the birds hang vertically from the wire ceiling or from thinner branches. Although the members of a pair like to perch very close together, pressing against one another, social preening is seldom observed and partner feeding during courtship is unlikely at all.

Rufous-fronted Parakeet
Bolborhynchus ferrugineifrons (Lawrence)
Characteristics: 18 cm long. Green, underside yellowish. Plumage round the lower mandible and narrow band on forehead rusty brown. Beak gray, iris dark brown, legs yellowish brown.
Range: So far this species is only known to occur in the central Andes of Colombia.
Habitat: Mountainsides overgrown with shrubs at altitudes of up to 3750 m.
Habits: One male with developed gonads was killed in January.
Keeping: Several specimens which apparently did not survive for long were imported into Germany after 1970. More detailed reports are not available.

The Mountain Parakeet, *Bolborhynchus aurifrons,* is adapted to a high-mountain habitat and finds it difficult to adjust to temperate climates.

Mountain Parakeet
Bolborhynchus aurifrons (Lesson)
Four subspecies.
Characteristics: 17 cm long. Green, underside yellow-green. Forehead and upper cheeks yellow. Females and juveniles without yellow.
Range: Central and southern Peru, central and western Bolivia, the northernmost parts of Chile, northwestern Argentina.
Habitat: High plateaux and slopes of the Andes at altitudes of over 4000 m. During the summer months in northern Chile only in mountains of over 3000 m, in the winter also in regions at lower altitudes. Between September and December they migrate into the mountains of central Chile; in March, after breeding, they move back to their place of origin. In the province of Lima common in steppes and in open terrain where shrubs grow, in fields, woods, gardens, and in the public parks of Lima.
Habits: In addition to various seeds, fruits, and green plants, the seeds of the shrub *Leptophyllum* constitute a popular food. Incubating birds were observed in December in the province of Santiago. The birds breed in rock crevices and on mountain slopes in burrows they have dug themselves. One cave dug into a mound of earth consisted of a tunnel, measuring 2 m in length, which led obliquely upwards into two chambers. The first chamber (with an area of 20 x 30 cm) contained the clutch.
Keeping: Seldom imported. In 1958, one pair at London Zoo; in 1967, one pair kept by an aviculturist in Berlin. Many of the Mountain Parakeets that have been kept so far died within a few months. The cause of death could not be established. It is possible that this bird from the high mountains finds it difficult to adapt to our climate. The parakeets remain shy for a long time, eating, for example, only during the night or when completely undisturbed. Enjoy bathing. Get on well with small birds.
Diet: The animals kept so far accepted hemp, sunflower seeds (also in a germinated condition), grass seeds, millet, oats, niger, apples, bananas, oranges, carrots (including grated ones), and plenty of greenstuff. Soft food and hard-boiled egg were ignored. For rearing, grated carrots and mixed seeds with cod liver oil were taken.

Breeding: First bred in captivity in 1967, in Germany. The birds bred inside a nest box for Budgerigars. Incubation period 23 days. Nine days after the young had fledged the birds started a second brood. A Danish aviculturist, using a natural cave as a model, constructed a nest box (15 x 15 x 30 cm) which had a 90 cm long entrance tube and was divided in two by means of a horizontal plate. A hole in the partition gave access from one chamber to the other. As it turned out, however, Mountain Parakeets are adaptable in their nesting facilities. It is, therefore, perfectly adequate just to offer them Budgerigar nest boxes. Although the fledged young males were slightly paler than the parents, the yellow on the forehead was already quite distinct.

Behavior: Excited Mountain Parakeets rub the upper and lower mandibles against each other, which results in the production of a crunching noise. At the same time the ceres assumes a red color and appears swollen.

Sierra Parakeet

Bolborhynchus aymara (D'Orbigny)
Characteristics: 20 cm long. Long tail feathers. Green. Forehead, crown, and ear coverts of a dark brown-gray color. Cheeks, throat, sides of the neck, and upper breast light gray. Beak horn colored with a tinge of pink. Iris brown, legs brown. In the opinion of some parakeet keepers males possess a darker gray on the crown and light silver gray on the breast, as well as flesh colored legs and a lighter beak.

Range: Mountain slopes in the eastern Andes from central Bolivia to northwestern Argentina.

Habitat: Dry, hilly terrain where shrubs and cacti grow. Up to over 4000 m, in the winter in regions at about 1200 m.

Habits: Often seen in huge flocks, sometimes in association with Mountain Parakeets (*Bolborhynchus aurifrons*). Search for food on berry bearing shrubs or on the ground. Breeding in holes in the rocks, also building caves in the sand or soil (tunnel leading to the nest 2 m, nest chamber 30 cm in diamater). In one locality, about 80 km from La Paz (at an altitude of over 3000 m), 10 Sierra Parakeets were observed in a cactus, 3 m high, where they were obviously nesting.

Keeping: Imported into England in 1959, two years later also available in Germany. A pleasant, quiet voice. Interacts well with small birds such as Budgerigars, Waxbills, and Honeysuckers. A roosting box is required. Tolerating slight, dry frost. In some parts of their native range they are popular pets. They are regularly available at the market in Mendoza.

Diet: Sunflower seeds, hemp, a mixture of

Like the other members of the genus, the Sierra Parakeet, *Bolborhynchus aymara,* is not well known in aviculture. Photo courtesy of Vogelpark Walsrode.

budgerigar and canary food, chickweed, lettuce, spinach, shepherd's purse, fruit, grated carrots, fresh elderberry shoots. Millet sprays are pulled apart but not eaten.

Breeding: Nest box 20 x 20 x 30 cm with a deep bottom layer of peat. The parakeets would, however, prefer to dig their own breeding chamber in an artificial loam wall. One aviculturist stuffed a mixture of wet peat and loam into a box which was open at the front. A pre-dug hole was extended by the birds after 3 days, and it took them an additional 5 days to complete the structure. The eggs are laid at 2-day intervals, up to 10 eggs; incubation period 20 days, nestling period 6 weeks. The female incubates from the third egg

onwards, sometimes not until the clutch is complete. The male feeds the hen and is usually seen just outside the nest, occasionally inside. Newly hatched young are covered in white down at first; after two weeks they have a dense blue gray down plumage. Checks on the nest are tolerated.
Behavior: Perching with physical contact. Partner feeding.

Monk Parakeet
(*Myiopsitta*)

Thick bill with rounded ridge. Long tail. Feathered ceres. Sexes identical in coloration. Large colonial nests of brushwood.
One species.

Monk Parakeet
Myiopsitta monachus (Boddaert)
Four subspecies.
Characteristics: 30 cm long. Green. Forehead, face, lower neck, and breast gray. Beak yellowish brown, iris dark brown, legs gray.
Range: Central Bolivia, southern Brazil to central Argentina. Introduced in Puerto Rico and the northeastern U.S.A.
Habitat: In areas with only a slight rainfall. Rarely above 1000 m. Open forests, trees along watercourses, dry acacia scrubland, palm groves, farmland, orchards. With the spreading of agricultural land the habitat of these parakeets also increased. Secure populations now exist in southeastern New York, New Jersey, and in Connecticut. These are likely to be animals that escaped from captivity originally and were able to survive the winter with bird seed from backyard feeders. Most artificial colonizations in Europe had to be broken up because of the protests from garden owners.
Habits: Gregarious. Groups of 10–100 birds are conspicuous by their loud screaming which becomes louder still when the birds feel threatened. Large colonial nests of twigs, some of them thorny. Inside these nests, each pair has its own breeding chamber and a separate entrance, usually

The Monk Parakeet, *Myiopsitta monachus,* is constantly persecuted because of the damage it does to agriculture.

situated on the underside. Although accepting nest boxes in the aviary, it is unlikely that Monk Parakeets ever breed in tree hollows in the wild. The nest is in occupation all the year round and the birds are constantly extending it. Eventually the construction may weigh up to 200 kg. Jabirus (*Jabiru mycteria*) often breed on the parakeet nests, as do Chimangos (*Milvago chimango*), and Whistling Ducks (*Dendrocygna*). Since Monk Parakeets do a great deal of damage in orchards and corn and millet fields, they are being controlled by drastic methods which include the destruction of the nests by burning. Breeding takes place in October. In some areas one can see mixed flights of Monk Parakeets and Nanday Conures (*Nandayus nenday*).
Keeping: This species has already been on the market at regular intervals and low prices, for a long time. Young animals grow tame but because of their loud voice are not really suitable for keeping inside the dwelling house. Destructive to wood. In

central Europe even the lowest winter temperatures are tolerated without frost damage. It is essential, however, that the animals are given the opportunity to build their protective nest. For this they need a base of sticks or coarse wire into which they can insert the twigs. Each day they must be supplied with large quantities of twigs measuring about half a meter in length. Provided one has tolerant neighbors and lives in a suitable environment, the birds can be allowed free flight without any problems. The most favorable time for liberating the birds is when there are young in the nest. The feeding places have to be supplied regularly and extra food must be allowed for visiting native seed eaters, otherwise the parakeets may move

elsewhere. In most cases, the nest constructed in the aviary will soon be deserted by the liberated animals. They prefer to start a new colony in tall trees nearby. In the display aviaries of zoological gardens, Monk Parakeets get along well with *Agapornis, Psittacula,* and *Aratinga* species (very often because they do not have the opportunity for nest building and breeding); it is safer on the whole not to keep them in association with other species. In smaller enclosures other parakeets tend to get attacked and killed.

Diet: Mixed seeds, notably sunflower seeds; carrots, fruit, greenstuff.

Breeding: First bred in captivity in 1867, in Vienna. If twigs are not available to them, the birds also breed inside ordinary nest boxes (15 x 25 x 40 cm, diameter of entrance hole 7 cm), though still carrying any pieces of twig they can find into the box. Five to eight eggs, incubation period 26 days, nestling period 6 weeks. Two to three broods per year. Able to reproduce at one year. Blue and, more rarely, yellow mutations have been cultivated.

The Monk Parakeet, *Myiopsitta monachus,* has been bred sufficiently in captivity that color mutations have begun to occur, such as the blue individual shown here. Photo by Dieter Hoppe.

The Monk Parakeet, *Myiopsitta monachus,* is unusual among parakeets in that it builds a nest of twigs instead of utilizing a cavity. Photo by Cliff Bickford.

Hybridization with Peach-fronted Conure (*Aratinga aurea*).

Behavior: The bonding between the members of a pair is very deep. Partner feeding outside the breeding season as well, confirming the close relationship. During noisy squabbles between the pairs of a colony, short breaks are taken for ceremonial feeding to express the mutual sympathy of the partners.

Parakeets of the genus *Enicognathus*

In the past, the two species were treated as belonging to two separate genera (*Microsittace* and *Enicognathus*). Because of the correspondence in build and plumage, this does not seem justified. The main difference between the two is the shape of the beak. Long tail, narrowing gradually, step-like. Feathered ceres. No sexual dimorphism. Closely related to the genus *Pyrrhura*. Both species are only rarely imported.

Austral Conure
Enicognathus ferrugineus (P. L. S. Muller) Two subspecies.
Characteristics: 33 cm long. Dark green, underside more olive green. All feathers having a blackish margin. Forehead, belly, cloacal region, tail feathers copper red. Dense plumage. Upper mandible blackish, lower mandible brownish gray. Iris reddish brown, legs gray. In juveniles the copper red color on the belly is less marked.
Range: Chile, southern Argentina, islands in Magellan's Strait. The Austral Conure is the southernmost species of all the parrots.
Habitat: Above all beech forests (*Notophagus*).
Habits: Often seen, probably even on the increase. The southern subspecies remains in one locality whereas the northern one (*E. f. minor*) lives in the Andes at an altitude of 1200 m from September to March, and then descends to regions at lower altitudes. In groups of 10–100. Tree dwelling. When climbing the parakeets press their bodies closely against the twigs, as a result of which they are almost perfectly camouflaged. The favorite food consists of

The Slender-billed Conure, *Enicognathus leptorhynchus*, has a bill adapted to extracting *Araucaria* seeds. Photo by Cliff Bickford.

the seeds of *Araucaria araucana*. In addition, grass seeds, fruits, leaf buds, and bulbous roots are eaten. It goes without saying that when the grain is ripe, cereal fields are visited as well. In December the birds breed inside tree hollows or the deserted cavities of woodpeckers. Very deep holes are filled with bits of twig. On top of these the birds put dry leaves and feathers. If the parakeets are left undisturbed, they occupy their nests over a period of several years. In the absence of suitable hollows the birds apparently build a nest from twigs and grass blades.

E. f. minor first bred in captivity in 1972, at the zoo in East Berlin. However, the young which hatched in September did not survive for long. Several successful breeding attempts in subsequent years. Two to four eggs, incubation period 27 days, nestling period 7–8 weeks.

Slender-billed Conure

Enicognathus leptorhynchus (King)
Characteristics: 40 cm long. Coloration similar to that of the Austral Conure. Beak elongate and narrow and thereby clearly distinct from the beaks of all other araini. Beak blackish, iris red, legs gray. Juveniles have a darker plumage and a shorter upper mandible.
Range: Chile.
Habitat: Forest regions, but also parks (e.g., the Botanical Gardens of Santiago). On the decrease due to deforestation, shooting, and fowl-pest.
Habits: Gregarious, seen in flocks during the breeding season as well. Attract attention by their persistent calling. The Slender-billed Conure has a special preference for the seeds of *Araucaria araucana*, whereby the long bill stands it in good stead. The latter also proves a suitable tool when it comes to digging up roots. The birds love breaking up unripe apples in order to get at the pips. Grass and thistle seeds, leaf buds, and various fruits represent further components of the natural diet. Incubation period November to December. The nests are built inside hollow trees or branches, whereby one tree may accommodate several pairs. Like the Austral Conure, this species also uses twigs to partially fill any hollow that is too deep. Again like the former, the Slender-billed Conure is said to build a nest in dense treetops if there is a shortage of hollows. Other nesting sites are rock crevices and caves dug by the birds themselves.
Keeping: 1840, in London. Sporadically imported again since 1976. Destroys wood, enjoys bathing. The claws must be examined and clipped at regular intervals. Young birds quickly grow tame.
Diet: Sunflower seeds, canary seed, hemp, fresh corn on the cob, boiled corn, various kinds of fruit, carrots, celery. Squeeze mealworms out of their skins and discard the latter. Should be given the opportunity to dig for germinating seeds and roots in the aviary.
Breeding: First bred in captivity in 1913 in Holland. The animals bred inside a spacious hollow tree trunk. In 1978 successful breeding attempts were made in the U.S.A. and in Sweden. In both cases the breeding pairs were kept in relatively small cages (1.2 x 1.2 x 0.6 m). The Swedish aviculturist reported that the hen did not start incubating until 4 days after the first egg had been laid. Three to four eggs, incubation period 26 days, nestling period 8 weeks. The first down feathers are white. Compared with adult birds, fledged young birds have a darker plumage, a shorter bill with a white tip (until the age of about one year), and a light, unfeathered orbital ring. As rearing food the birds accepted bread soaked in milk, hard-boiled egg, and grass roots. Hybridization with Nanday Conure (*Nandayus nenday*).

Conures of the genus *Pyrrhura*

Smaller slender parakeets. The long tail, narrowing in steps, is reddish brown at least on the underside though usually above as well. The reddish brown color also frequently occurs on the belly and on the rump. A naked orbital ring, usually white; naked ceres. Characteristic for this genus is the fact that the feathers on the throat and breast are darker around the edges than in the base, which gives the front a squamate appearance. Beak dark gray to black, in some species of a light horn color. Do not scream, do not destroy wood, are relatively easy to propagate. This means that these species would be ideally suited for the aviary, but in fact only very few of them come on the market with any regularity. Hence the establishment and preservation of breeding strains are urgently recommended. It must be pointed out, however, that the sexes are impossible to distinguish.

185

Keeping presents no problems as long as frost-proof accommodation is provided. Nest boxes (about 25 x 25 x 50 cm, diameter of entrance hole 6 cm) or natural tree trunks are occupied for roosting outside the breeding season as well. Facilities for daily bathing must be provided. Conures of this genus take a lively interest in everything. They sample unfamiliar food without hesitation, which makes it easy to supply them with a wide variety of fruit and greenstuff. On the other hand, they examine their enclosure very carefully. For instance, they immediately slip inside a nest box that has just been hung, and any holes in the wire mesh are spotted very quickly. Birds that have escaped usually choose to return if left unharassed. In favorable weather there may be two broods in one year. From time to time the birds dig caves in the aviary ground and breed in those. The young are slightly duller in coloration and have a lighter bill. Greenstuff, apples, carrots, spray millet (germinated or just soaked), biscuit soaked in a mixture of water and honey with added vitamins have proved suitable as rearing foods. The parents get along with the young, at least until the next clutch is produced.

19 species.

Blue-throated Conure

Pyrrhura cruentata (Wied)
Characteristics: With a total length of 23 cm, the largest species of the genus. Green. Feathers on the crown and nape dark brown with orange colored edges. Lores and ear coverts reddish brown, beyond these an orange colored patch. Rump and middle of belly red. Throat, upper breast, and nape band light blue. Red shoulders. Upper side of tail olive yellow, underside copper red. Beak gray-brown, iris orange-yellow, legs gray.
Range: Eastern Brazil from southern Bahia to northeastern Sao Paulo.
Habitat: Still common in some forest areas but threatened by the increasing number of clearances.
Habits: Usually remaining absolutely quiet. Feeding parakeets only attract one's attention by the noise of falling fruit remnants. Breed inside hollow trees.
Keeping: The natives describe them as

lively and slow to learn and rarely keep them. Imported into Europe around 1850. Nervous at first, trying to hide in the cage. They become acclimatized more quickly if kept in association with birds that are already used to their environment. Get along with parakeets of the species that are similar in size.
Diet: In addition to the usual food, plenty of greenstuff is taken.
Breeding: First bred in captivity in 1937, in England.

Blaze-winged Conure

Pyrrhura devillei (Massena and Souance)
Characteristics: 26 cm long. Green. Breast and sides of neck olive brown with white and brown stripes. Shoulder and lesser under wing coverts scarlet, greater under wing coverts olive yellow. Red spot on belly. Tail olive yellow above, copper red below. Beak gray, iris brown, legs gray.
Range: Eastern Bolivia, northern Paraguay, southwestern Matto Grosso.
Habits: It is possible that in northern Paraguay the species interbreeds with Maroon-bellied Conures (*Pyrrhura frontalis*).

Maroon-bellied Conure

Pyrrhura frontalis (Vieillot)
Three subspecies.
Characteristics: 26 cm long. Green. Sides of neck, throat, breast olive; feathers having yellowish edges. A few red feathers above the ceres. Ear coverts of a pale gray-brown color. A dark red spot on the belly. Tail green above, reddish at the tip, copper red below. Beak black, iris dark brown, legs gray. In juveniles the red colors are slightly duller.
Range: Southeastern Brazil, Uruguay, Paraguay, northern Argentina.
Habitat: All types of forests, apart from eucalyptus plantations, at altitudes of between 800 and 1300 m. Orange plantations, corn fields.
Habits: Groups of 10 to 40. On the wing the parakeets scream very loudly but when consuming food in the treetops they behave quietly. In the Botanic Gardens of Rio de Janeiro they are seen in association with Plain Parakeets (*Brotogeris tirica*) on flowering trees, biting the blossoms open. At the same time they are almost certain to

ingest any insects that live inside the blossoms. Analyses of the gastric contents have, in fact, revealed that these parakeets not only feed on various plant substances but also swallow insects and their larvae. Breeding takes place inside tree cavities.

Keeping: First imported, on the initiative of London Zoo, in 1869. Maroon-bellied Conures behave peaceably towards other parakeets, are easy to keep, and can be recommended to less experienced bird fanciers. Juveniles grow tame if kept in isolation. This species is probably the only one of the genus that is being imported on a regular basis. Bathing facilities must be available at all times. The nest box is used for roosting all the year round. A colony of 4 pairs belonging to an English aviculturist shared a single nest box during the night. Where a sheltered sleeping box of this type had been provided, even temperatures of --20°C were tolerated. Nevertheless, it is not the purpose of bird keeping to test the individual species for their resistance. All birds should be housed in accordance with their natural requirements. Not a single species of the genus *Pyrrhura* occurs naturally in the colder zones.

Diet: Imported birds are frequently accustomed to corn. Hence they have to be gradually adapted to other types of grain food. Fresh twigs, apples, and plenty of greenstuff must be offered at all times.

Breeding: Three to six eggs, incubation period 26–28 days, nestling period 6–8 weeks. Breeding is also possible if the animals are kept in colonies of several pairs. Although the males defend their nest, no injuries result. Often there are two broods. The female incubates, but the male also spends a lot of time inside the nest box. The nestlings are fed by both parents. Once fledged, the young are supplied with food for up to another two weeks by the male. The down plumage of the nestlings is dense and gray. Suitable rearing foods are apples, greenstuff, egg food, and germinated seeds. Hybridization with White-eared Conure (*Pyrrhura leucotis*).

Behavior: Courting males spread out the tail feathers and bow. During copulation the male places one foot on his partner's back; with the other he clasps the perching branch.

The Maroon-bellied Conure, *Pyrrhura frontalis,* is one of the most frequently imported parakeets of this genus. Photo by Isabelle Francais.

Tail coloration is significant in distinguishing the subspecies of the Maroon-bellied Conure; this specimen appears to be *Pyrrhura frontalis frontalis*. Photo by Isabelle Francais.

Pearly Conure
Pyrrhura perlata (Spix)
Four subspecies.
Characteristics: 25 cm long. Green. Upper head brown with a narrow dark brown stripe on the forehead. Ear coverts yellowish. Sides of neck and throat gray, feathers light gray around the edges. Some blue on the upper half of the breast. Cheeks bluish. A reddish brown patch on the belly, green rump. Shoulders and lesser under wing coverts red. Under tail coverts light blue. Tail brown above, blackish below. Beak black, iris reddish brown, legs dark gray.
Habitat: Damp forests.
Habits: Examinations of the gastric contents yielded seeds.
Keeping: At London Zoo in 1884. This species is said to have a particularly great curiosity. Every corner of the enclosure is examined.

Diet: Sunflower seeds, canary seed, millet sprays, some hemp. Apples, grass panicles, chickweed, grapefruit.
Breeding: First bred in captivity in 1963. Three to five eggs, incubation period 23–25 days, nestling period 7 weeks. The incubating is done by the female alone; the male spends the night inside the nest. Checks on the nest do not unduly worry the animals. Young birds have lighter legs and beaks.
Behavior: When the nest is being examined, adult parakeets and fledged young birds threaten the intruder by raising the plumage of the head, extending the neck, and swaying from side to side.

Crimson-bellied Conure
Pyrrhura rhodogaster (Sclater)
Characteristics: 24 cm long. Green. Top of the head and throat pale brown with light feather margins. Forehead, ear coverts, and nape blue. Breast, belly, shoulder, and small under wing coverts red. Tail copper red above, blue at the tip, underside gray. Beak gray-brown, iris dark brown, legs gray.
Range: Northern Brazil south of the Amazon to as far as northern Matto Grosso.
Habits: Undisturbed parakeets in the treetops can only be detected if they give themselves away by uttering their chattering sounds. When alarmed the birds remain absolutely silent and motionless.
Keeping: At London Zoo in 1927. So far this species has only been imported very rarely and is only being kept at a few zoos.
Breeding: First bred in captivity in 1966 and again in subsequent years at Rotterdam Zoo. Propagated at Chester Zoo in 1967.

Green-cheeked Conure
Pyrrhura molinae (Massena and Souance)
Five subspecies.
Characteristics: 27 cm long. Green. Top of the head dark brown. Sides of neck, throat, upper breast pale brown with white and dark brown bands. Cheeks green. A few blue feathers on the nape. A brownish red spot on the belly. Tail reddish brown. Beak gray, iris brown, legs dark gray.
Range: Western, central, and southern Matto Grosso, northern and eastern Bolivia, northwestern Argentina.

Habitat: Forest regions. Observed at altitudes of up to 2000 m.
Habits: In larger groups predominantly in the treetops. In Argentina a clutch was found at the beginning of February inside a hollow tree at a height of 5 m.
Keeping: Easy to acclimatize. In Switzerland this species was kept in an unheated aviary, with a flight hole leading into the outdoor enclosure, all the year round.
Breeding: First bred in 1973 in the enclosures of Dr. Burkard (Switzerland). Two pairs had dug a tunnel to a length of one meter under the floor of the aviary building and bred and raised young inside. The fledged young birds were duller in coloration than their parents and the red spot on the belly was only faintly visible at first. In 1979 Smith in England propagated this species. Two females bred together in the same box and laid 7 eggs between them. The males of the two pairs also got along well together. Incubation period 22-24 days, nestling period 7 weeks.

Yellow-sided Conure

Pyrrhura hypoxantha (Salvadori)
Characteristics: 25 cm long. Green. Forehead and crown brown, ear coverts gray-brown. Sides of neck, throat, and upper breast yellowish white with brown transverse bands. Remaining breast and thighs yellow. Belly orange-red. Tail reddish brown. Beak gray, iris brown, legs brownish.
Range: Western Matto Grosso.

To date only 4 specimens have been collected, some of which were derived from the same flock of birds consisting mostly of Green-cheeked Conures (*Pyrrhura molinae*). It is thought that this is not a species in its own right but a variety of *Pyrrhura molinae phoenicura* that deviates in color.

White-eared Conure

Pyrrhura leucotis (Kuhl)
Five subspecies.
Characteristics: 23 cm long. Top of head gray-brown, nape pale blue. Eye region, lower cheeks, and narrow band on forehead reddish brown. Ear coverts gray-white.

White-eared Conures, *Pyrrhura leucotis,* acclimate quickly and soon become tame.

Sides of neck and throat green with yellowish striations. Brownish red spot on belly. Red shoulders, brownish red rump. Tail reddish brown. Beak gray-brown, iris brown, legs gray. In juveniles the ear coverts are brownish.
Range: Northern Venezuela, eastern Brazil, a colony became established in Rio de Janeiro (Botanic Gardens).
Habits: Living in groups of 15–20 animals and keeping mainly to the highest regions of the trees. It is probable that, in addition to plant substances, the birds also eat insects and their larvae. One analysis of the gastric contents yielded ants.
Keeping: First imported into England in 1871. Quickly become acclimatized and grow tame. Get along well with each other but attack other parakeets and try to injure their legs through a wire partition. Bathe every day. Sensitive to frost.
Diet: Acclimatization by means of soaked corn. Later sunflower seeds, oats, canary seed, millet, hemp, wheat, half-ripened seeds, germinated spray millet, apples.

Breeding: First bred in captivity in 1880, in Vienna. Five to nine eggs, (one egg per day), incubation period 22 days, nestling period 5 weeks. Two broods per year. The bottom of the nest is covered with gnawed off wood shavings by the female, to which she adds a few feathers. Again it is the female alone who does the incubating. The male provides her with food. She stays in the box from the time the eggs are laid until the young leave the nest; the male spends the night inside the nest. Before the young hatch, some hens bathe frequently and then return to the nesting hollow with wet abdominal plumage. Humidity and warmth are regarded as essential for successful breeding. A natural tree trunk with thick walls affords better protection from temperature fluctuations than do nest boxes made of wooden boards. Boiled rice

One of the more colorful subspecies of the White-eared Conure, *Pyrrhura leucotis.* Routedale photo.

and hard-boiled egg, mixed with grated carrots, proved suitable as rearing foods. Soft food and ant pupae are rarely accepted. White-eared Conures are probably not able to reproduce themselves until the second year of life. Hybridization with Maroon-bellied Conure (*Pyrrhura frontalis*).

Painted Conure
  Pyrrhura picta (P. L. S. Muller)
Seven subspecies.
Characteristics: 24 cm long. Green. Top of the head and nape brown. Upper cheeks and lores reddish brown. Forehead, lower cheek regions, and nape band gray-blue. Nape, throat, and upper breast brown with light feather margins, resulting in squamations. Ear coverts brownish to whitish, depending on the subspecies. Reddish brown patch on belly. Lower back, upper tail coverts, and tail brown. Shoulders red, in juveniles green with a few individual red feathers. Beak gray-brown, iris brown, legs gray.
Range: Guyana, Venezuela, northern Colombia, southeastern Peru, northern Bolivia, northern Brazil.
Habitat: Near rivers, in forest regions.
Habits: In addition to seeds, fruits, berries, and nuts the birds are likely to feed on insects and their larvae as well. The nest is located in hollow trees. In Surinam, eggs were found in February; in Colombia, this species breeds in June; in Bolivia, in August.
Keeping: At London Zoo in 1870. Like virtually all representatives of this genus, the species needs a roosting box and the opportunity for a daily bath.
Diet: In addition to seeds, plenty of fruit, greenstuff, and soft food.
Breeding: The subspecies *P. p. lucianii* was propagated in France, in 1866. Incubation period 21 days. The female does all the incubating and is supplied with food by the male. He spends most of his time guarding the entrance to the breeding hollow and utters a warning call in the event of any disturbance, moving the top part of the body to and fro at the same time. The legs of young birds are initially pink.

Santa Marta Conure
Pyrrhura viridicata (Todd)
Characteristics: 25 cm long. Green. Ear coverts brown. A narrow red stripe on the forehead. Part of the underside shows irregular patches of orange red. In contrast with the other species, there are no squamations on the throat and breast. Shoulders and under wing coverts yellow and orange red. Tail green above, reddish brown below. Beak horn colored, iris brown, legs gray.
Habitat: Mountain forests and mountain slopes overgrown with grass and shrubs at altitudes of between 2100–2400 m.
Habits: Breeding season probably September, since at that time males with developed gonads have been collected.
Range: Only seen in the Santa Marta Mountains in northern Colombia.

Fiery-shouldered Conure
Pyrrhura egregia (Sclater)
Two subspecies.
Characteristics: 25 cm long. Green. A narrow brown band on the forehead. Ear coverts reddish brown. The green feathers on the throat, sides of the neck, and upper breast are yellowish white around the edges. Red shoulders. Under wing coverts yellow and orange. Tail dark reddish brown above, gray below. Beak horn colored, iris brown, legs gray.
Range: Southeastern Venezuela, western Guyana, northeastern Brazil.
Habitat: Forest regions.

Maroon-tailed Conure
Pyrrhura melanura (Spix)
Four subspecies.
Characteristics: 24 cm long. Green. Forehead reddish brown. Sides of neck, throat, and breast greenish brown with lighter feather margins. Primaries red with yellow tips. Tail black above with a green base, dark brown below. Beak gray, iris dark brown, legs gray.
Range: Colombia, southern Venezuela, northwest Brazil, Ecuador, northeastern Peru.
Habitat: At altitudes of between 1600–2800 m.
Habits: Groups of 6–12 animals or more have been observed frequently. They prefer to keep to the taller trees, coming down lower when searching for food. In open terrain they fly just above the ground. In eastern Ecuador the breeding season lasts from April to June.
Keeping: Until 1967 only imported sporadically, then slightly more often. These parakeets do not grow confiding as quickly as other species of the genus. They need warmth and a higher humidity and the opportunity for a daily bath. Little damage is done to wooden constructions. The pairs get along well together, one indication of this being the social preening that can frequently be observed.
Diet: The birds' favorite seeds are sunflower seeds, oats, and millet sprays; the preferred high water content foods are carrots, apples, berries, and rosehips.
Breeding: Incubation period 22–25 days, nestling period 7 weeks. The bottom of the nest box should be covered with a deep layer of peat fibers or wood shavings. The birds usually start breeding between November and January. Breeding has also been successful in room aviaries, where the parakeets are allowed to fly free inside the apartment. By the age of 4 weeks the young have a dark gray down plumage. The first signs of independent feeding were observed 4 days after fledging. Accepted rearing foods consisted of greenstuff, germinated sunflower seeds, parakeet biscuits, berries, and apples. On the other hand, hard-boiled egg and soft food were left untouched.

Berlepsch's Conure
Pyrrhura berlepschi (Salvadori)
Characteristics: 24 cm long. Green. Forehead brownish. Throat and breast with broad white-gray feather margins. A reddish brown spot on the belly. Primaries blue. Beak gray, iris dark brown, legs gray. Adult animals look very similar to *Pyrrhura melanura souancei*. Some authors refer to it as a subspecies of *Pyrrhura melanura*; others regard it as nothing more than a slightly deviating form of *Pyrrhura melanura souancei*.
Range: Only known from the Huallaga Valley in eastern Peru.
Breeding: 1977, in Holland.

Black-capped Conure
Pyrrhura rupicola (Tschudi)
Two subspecies.
Characteristics: 25 cm long. Green. Top of the head brown, sides of the head green. Sides of neck, throat, upper breast dark brown with whitish edges, and on the upper breast with yellowish edges around the feathers. Shoulders green. Primary coverts red. Tail green above, dark gray below. Beak gray, iris brown, legs dark gray.
Range: Central and southeastern Peru, northern Brazil, extreme northwest of Brazil.
Habitat: Has been observed at altitudes of between 170–300 m.
Habits: Said to breed in rock crevices.

White-necked Conure
Pyrrhura albipectus (Chapman)
Characteristics: 24 cm long. Green. Top of head brown. Ear coverts orange-yellow. Whitish band on nape. Throat and upper breast white with a tinge of pink, changing to yellow on the lower breast. No squamations. Primary coverts red. Tail reddish brown. Beak gray-brown, iris brown, legs dark gray.
Range: Southeastern Ecuador.
Habitat: Subtropical forests.
Keeping: First imported into Belgium in 1928. Since then only rarely on the market.

Brown-breasted Conure
Pyrrhura calliptera (Massena and Souance)
Characteristics: 25 cm long. Green. Top of head brown with a tinge of blue. Ear coverts and a patch on the belly red-brown. Sides of neck, throat, and upper breast reddish brown, feathers with a light margin. Primary coverts yellow. Tail red-brown. Beak horn colored, iris yellow brown, legs brownish. The primary coverts of juveniles are said to be green.
Range: Central Colombia.
Habitat: Forests and moorlands at high altitudes in regions with a relatively cool climate.

Rose-crowned Conure
Pyrrhura rhodocephala (Sclater and Salvin)
Characteristics: 24 cm long. Green. Top of the head rose red. Ear coverts and spot on belly brownish red. White primary coverts. Tail red-brown. Beak horn colored, iris brown, legs dark gray.
Range: Western Venezuela.
Habitat: Forest regions.

Hoffmann's Conure
Pyrrhura hoffmanni (Cabanis)
Two subspecies.
Characteristics: 25 cm long. Green. Top of the head and throat green, partly with yellow feather margins. Red ear coverts. Yellow wing coverts with green tips. Tail reddish olive above, red-brown below. Beak horn colored, iris brown, legs gray.
Range: Southern Costa Rica, western Panama.
Habitat: Mountain forests between 1000 and 3000 m.
Habits: In pairs or in small groups. Very wary. The calls do not sound parrot-like but are similar to those uttered by songbirds. Breeding season probably May.

Yellow-eared Conure (*Ognorhynchus*)

Very similar in appearance to the Macaws. In contrast with the latter, however, the lores and cheeks are feathered.
One species.

Yellow-eared Conure
Ognorhynchus icterotis (Massena and Souance)
Characteristics: 42 cm long. Green. Back dark green, belly more yellowish green. Forehead, lores, and cheeks yellow. A gray bald orbital ring. Beak black with a lighter tip, iris red-brown, legs gray. Feathers on forehead not lying smooth but bushy as in some Macaws.
Range: The Andes of Colombia and northern Ecuador.
Habitat: Subtropical and temperate zones where the wax palm (*Ceroxylon andicola*) can be found. Has also been observed at altitudes of between 2500–3200 m.

Habits: Breeding season probably between March and May. Nesting hollows under the palm fronds at a height of 25 m. In some areas one breeding pair can be found in every palm tree.

Keeping: Very seldom imported. In 1871 there was a report of a tame pair being kept in Stettin. Two Yellow-eared Conures were offered for sale by a dealer in London, in 1965. One animal, observed by Rosemary Low for several months, spoke a few words and was very aggressive towards women. In the aviary this parakeet got along well with a Yellow-collared Macaw (*Ara auricollis*).

Diet: The parakeet mentioned above was particularly partial to stone pine nuts and rose hips.

Golden-plumed Conure (*Leptosittaca*)

Very similar in appearance to Conures of the genus *Aratinga*. Differs from these mainly by having feather tufts in the ear region.

One species.

Golden-plumed Conure

Leptosittaca branickii (Berlepsch and Stolzmann)

Characteristics: 35 cm long. Green. Narrow, orange colored band on forehead. Extended yellow feathers above the ear coverts. Lores and stripes under the eyes yellow. Belly olive yellow with red speckles. White naked orbital ring. Beak horn colored, iris orange, legs gray.

Range: Central Andes of Colombia, southwestern Ecuador, and central Peru.

Habitat: Forests at altitudes of above 3000 m.

Nanday Conure (*Nandayus)*

Like the Conures of the genus *Aratinga* in its appearance, behavior, and keeping requirements.

Nanday Conure

Nandayus nenday (Vieillot)

Characteristics: 33 cm long. Green. Top of head, anterior sides of head, and chin brown-black. Throat and upper breast of a faded blue. Thighs red. White naked orbital ring. Beak black, iris dark brown, legs pink. In juveniles the blue is less distinct.

Range: Southeastern Bolivia, southern Matto Grosso, Paraguay, northern Argentina.

Habitat: Savannahs, forest regions, palm groves, agricultural land.

The Nanday Conure, *Nandayus nenday,* is not sexually dimorphic. Photo by Harald Schultz.

Like many of their relatives, Nanday Conures, *Nandayus nenday,* are very noisy and also are persistent gnawers.

Habits: Nanday Conures exploit the food resources offered by grain fields, rice fields, and fruit plantations. In Paraguay they are frequent visitors of sunflower and corn fields when the crops are ripening. In such localities these birds often assemble in huge flocks, sometimes together with Monk Parakeets (*Myiopsitta monachus*). In Matto Grosso the breeding season starts in November. The nest is located in hollow trees or in hollow wooden posts.

Keeping: 1870, at London Zoo. The loud voice and the tendency to destroy wooden constructions in the aviaries mean that only few parakeet fanciers are able to keep this species, which is frequently on the market. Hand reared birds grow very tame, however, and are less loud as well. A roosting box and bathing facilities must be provided; Nanday Conures also like bathing in the rain. Keeping in free flight conditions is possible.

Diet: Sunflower and other seeds, carrots, various kinds of fruit, greenstuff, fresh branches.

Breeding: First bred in captivity in 1881, in France; since then animals raised in captivity have been propagated on a regular basis. Nest box about 30 x 30 x 40 cm. The eggs (4–5) are laid at 2-day intervals. Incubation period 25 days, nestling period 7 weeks. The hen does all the incubating on her own. The male spends the night in the nest. Checks on the nest are tolerated. Where the birds are kept in colonies breeding presents no problems either. Hybridization with Jandaya Conure (*Aratinga jandaya*).

Conures of the genus *Aratinga*

The powerful and, in some species, thick bill possesses a distinct dental notch. Narrow ceres partially feathered. Naked, light orbital rings. The wedge-shaped tail, which narrows step-like, extends beyond the folded wings. With the exception of two species a green plumage color predominates. Contrasting colors are found mainly in the region of the head. There is no difference in color between the sexes. The females are generally somewhat daintier than the males and also differ from the latter in the shape of the head and by having a slightly more slender bill. Where breeding is to be attempted it is advisable, because of the uncertain sexual differentiation, to either keep the birds in groups in larger enclosures or to observe the members of a group; once the animals have selected their own partners, put each pair into a smaller, separate aviary (of about 4 x 1 x 2 m).

Nearly all species have a very loud voice and destroy wood and wire mesh of insufficient thickness. The nest boxes must be checked constantly and repaired. Average dimensions of the boxes 30 x 30 x 45 cm, diameter of entrance 7 cm. Natural tree trunks are preferred. The nesting hollows are occupied for roosting all the year round. Bathing facilities are required.

Feeding on sunflower seeds, canary seed, millet, hemp, oats, niger, buckwheat, millet sprays, fresh or boiled corn, spray and panicle millet, greenstuff, and various kinds of fruit. For rearing, plenty of greenstuff and germinated food should be provided. The *Aratinga* species need a constant supply of fresh twigs.

Two to seven eggs; only the Golden Conure (*Aratinga guarouba*) lays fewer. Incubation period 26 days, nestling period 7–8 weeks. After fledging the young birds are fed by their parents for another two weeks or so. Specimens raised individually grow tame and are able to mimic a few words.

20 species

Blue-crowned Conure
Aratinga acuticaudata (Vieillot)
Four subspecies.
Characteristics: 37 cm long. Green. Forehead, crown, lores, cheeks, and ear

Blue-crowned Conure, *Aratinga acuticaudata,* the subspecies *haemorrhous.*

coverts blue. White orbital ring. Upper mandible horn colored, lower mandible blackish, iris yellow, legs pink. Juveniles have horn colored beaks and less blue.
Range: Eastern Colombia and northern Venezuela to Paraguay, Uruguay, and northern Argentina.

Habitat: Dry regions of the tropical zone. In northern Colombia grass steppes in the proximity of scrub and woodland.
Habits: In some areas only common at certain times of the year. The migrations are usually determined by the ripening of specific berries. In addition to these, Blue-crowned Conures feed on a variety of seeds, nuts, mangoes, and cactus fruits. In Paraguay they cause damage to millet fields while on the other hand proving themselves beneficial to agriculture by devouring the seeds of weeds. The nest is located in tree cavities. In Chaco, clutches have been found in December.
Keeping: In 1864 the subspecies *A. a. haemorrhous* was kept in London. These parakeets are not shy in the wild, growing quickly confiding in the aviary. Peaceable towards other species outside the breeding season.
Diet: Food to be offered on a table or shelf. Apples, rowanberries, and rose hips are very popular.
Breeding: Two broods. The down plumage of the young is dense and gray. Nestling period 8 weeks. The fledged young are fed by the male. Hybridization with Finsch's Conure (*Aratinga finschi*) and Peach-fronted Conure (*Aratinga aurea*).
Behavior: The pairs form a close attachment, which is expressed by perching close together and social preening.

Golden Conure
Aratinga guarouba (Gmelin)
Characteristics: 38 cm long. This species cannot be confused with any other. Animals in adult plumage are golden yellow with green primaries and secondaries. Narrow white orbital ring. The strong beak is horn colored, iris brown, legs pink. The juvenile plumage (up to the age of about 15 months) includes individual green feathers on the upper wing coverts and on the cheeks. The sexes can be differentiated by the slightly bigger upper mandible of the males.
Range: Northeastern Brazil south of the Amazon.
Habitat: Tropical rain forests.
Habits: A decline in numbers, largely due to the destruction of the habitat, has been noted since 1946. Today the Golden Conure is strictly protected.

However, this can do little to prevent the natives from keeping the animals or using their feathers. Flying about in pairs or in small groups. Searching for food in the treetops.

Keeping: At London Zoo in 1871. Has always been the best known and the most sought after of all the *Aratinga* species. Today, imports from Brazil are no longer possible. Golden Conures can only be accommodated in aviaries of indestructible material. Only after an acclimatization period of about a year can they be kept in outdoor aviaries during the summer. In England, acclimatized animals were kept in unheated enclosures all year round; however, one must not forget that they originate from regions close to the equator. The feather plucking which is often observed is probably due to the birds being kept at too low a humidity. Golden Conures get along well with each other but do not tolerate other species. As the Duke of Bedford reported, his free-flying animals attacked Amazons and Crimson Rosellas.

Diet: Particularly popular are half-ripe cereal grains, peanuts, berries, apples, oranges, melons, mangoes, and various kinds of greenstuff.

Breeding: Both nest boxes and hollow tree trunks (about 60 cm deep, the bottom covered with rotting wood and dry leaves) are accepted. The first published report of successful propagation in captivity came from Colombia and dates back to 1939. Here the young birds stayed in the nest for 43 days. Other breeding reports would suggest that the nestling period spans 60–70 days. Usually 2–3 eggs, only very rarely 5. Incubation period 28–30 days. A nest box is not accepted until several weeks have elapsed; some aviculturists have to wait for 2 years before the birds start to breed. Only the hen incubates; the male spends the night in the nest. The aggressiveness of the breeding birds is also vented on their keeper. The California aviculturist, West, noticed an increased water requirement during the rearing of the young. In this case, the wings and tail feathers were developed at 35 days of age and the animals were completely feathered at 6 weeks. Both parents fed their offspring. Three days after fledging, at the end of the 10th week of life, the young birds picked up food independently for the first time.

Behavior: As with the preceding species, the partners form a close attachment to one another. During courtship feeding, one wing is laid over the partner. Those who have kept these parakeets regard them as the most intelligent of the genus. While this assessment is not based on scientific research, it is confirmed solely by the strongly marked play behavior, during which the parakeets roll about on the ground like human children and engage in mock fights.

The Golden Conure, *Aratinga guarouba,* is one of the most seriously endangered parakeets. Photo by Harald Schultz.

Golden Conure, *Aratinga guarouba,* with clipped wings.

The Green Conure, *Aratinga holochlora,* is too plainly colored to attract the attention of fanciers. Photo courtesy of San Diego Zoo.

Golden Conure, *Aratinga guarouba.* Special efforts are now being made to breed the birds currently in captivity.

Green Conure

Aratinga holochlora (Sclater)

Five subspecies.

Characteristics: 32 cm long. Green. A few individual feathers on or below the throat red. Gray-brown orbital ring. Beak of a light horn color, iris orange-red, legs brownish. From a lateral aspect, the male's head appears large, elongate, and angular. The breast is broad, the bird looks stocky. In comparison, the female's breast is narrow, the head smaller.

Range: Island of Socorro off the western coast of Mexico, northwestern Mexico to northern Nicaragua.

Habitat: On the island of Socorro forest regions, in Mexico tropical dry regions as well as stone pine forests up to 2200 m. The countryside surrounding Mexico City.

Habits: Green Conures are often seen roaming the countryside in flocks, screaming loudly—the size of these flocks depending on the available food resources. Popular are the seeds of acacias, half-ripe seeds of *Mimosa* trees, as well as ripening rice and corn. Breeding season in Mexico April and May, in El Salvador from January to March. At the end of January pairs of these birds were seen to excavate termite constructions. They also breed inside hollow trees, however, and in deserted woodpecker cavities.

Keeping: At London Zoo in 1886. Rarely imported, probably often confused with similar species. Peaceable towards other birds, aggressive during the breeding season.

Breeding: First bred in captivity in 1934, in the U.S.A. Incubation period 23 days, nestling period 50 days, independent feeding 14 days later. First down whitish gray, plumage development complete at 45 days. Until just before the young fledges, the parents spend nearly all their time in the nest.

Finsch's Conure
Aratinga finschi (Salvin)

Characteristics: 28 cm long. Green. Forehead, crown, shoulder, and thighs red. White orbital ring. Beak horn colored, iris orange, legs gray-brown. Juveniles have less red or no red at all on the forehead and less réd on the shoulders.

Range: Tropical Central America from southern Nicaragua to western Panama.

Habitat: Open terrain with shrubs, as well as fields and pasture land.

Habits: Flocks of varying size. At the roosting places on palm trees, up to 500 parakeets assemble in the evenings. Within the flock, the individual pairs stick visibly close together. The flock takes off in the morning depending on how light it is; when the sky is overcast the departure is delayed by over an hour. This species visits the grain fields when the crop is ripening. In Panama, the birds breed in July.

Red-fronted Conure
Aratinga wagleri (G. R. Gray)
Four subspecies.

Characteristics: 36 cm long. Green. Forehead and crown red, a red band or at least a few individual red feathers on the throat. Orbital ring white-gray. In the subspecies *A. w. frontata* and *A. w. minor*, shoulders and thighs are red. Beak horn colored, iris yellow, legs brownish. In juveniles only the edge of the forehead is red and there are very few red feathers on

Finsch's Conure, *Aratinga finschi*, occupies a restricted range in Central America. Photo by Cliff Bickford.

the throat.

Range: Northern Venezuela, Colombia, western Ecuador to southern Peru.

Habitat: Subtropical forests to above 3000 m. The subspecies *A. w. frontata* inhabits trees and cacti in open steppes and from there ventures forth into fields and orchards.

Habits: Common, in the Rancho Grande

The Red-fronted Conure, *Aratinga wagleri,*
comprises several subspecies distributed along the
Pacific and Caribbean coasts of South America.

area the most frequently represented
species of parrot. Roosting places and
feeding places are often separated by vast
distances. In southern Peru the parakeets
roost on the high mountainsides and
descend into the valley in the mornings. In
Venezuela breeding takes place from April
to June. In western Colombia the birds nest
in groups on rock crevices so high as to be
virtually inaccessible to human beings.
Keeping: At London Zoo in 1873. Since this
first import, these birds have been brought
to Europe only occasionally, despite the
fact that these birds are so common.
Diet: Sunflower seeds, millet, corn, wheat,
stone pine nuts, shrimps, lettuce,
cucumbers, carrots, plenty of fruit,
dandelion, chickweed.
Breeding: At Chester Zoo in England three
generations of Red-fronted Conures have
already been bred in captivity. A detailed
report is provided by Klossner about the
birds bred on his premises in 1977 and 1978.
Nest boxes 50 x 25 x 25 cm, diameter of
entrance hole 10 cm. First egg in 1977 on
May 27th, in 1978 on June 20th. Egg laying
every other day. Each clutch consisted of
three eggs. Incubation period 24 days.
During the day the male incubated, during
the night the female, which in *Aratinga*
species is particularly remarkable. The
young from the 1977 clutch were not fed by
the parents; the young birds that hatched in
1978 were hand reared. Presumably
because of the absent parental example,
they did not start picking up seeds
independently until the 14th week of life.
Hybridization with Jandaya Conure
(*Aratinga jandaya*).

Mitred Conure
Aratinga mitrata (Tschudi)
Two subspecies.
Characteristics: 38 cm long. Green. Very
similar to the preceding species, but the
red on the head more extensive and also
extending to lores, cheeks, and sometimes
ear coverts. In some cases a few scattered
red feathers on the whole body with the
exception of the wings. Orbital ring white.
Beak horn colored. Iris orange-yellow, legs
brownish. In juveniles only the edge of the
forehead and the lores are red; sometimes
a few red feathers can be seen on the neck.

Above and left: The Mitred Conure, *Aratinga mitrata,* is the largest member of the genus *Aratinga.* Upper photo by Fred Harris.

Range: Central Peru, eastern Bolivia, northwestern Argentina.
Habitat: Forests between 1000 and 2600 m. In southern Peru this species occurs in the same areas as the Red-fronted Conure (*Aratinga wagleri*). The subspecies *A. m. alticola* can be found at altitudes of up to 3400 m.
Habits: Breeds inside hollow trees. Breeding season in northwestern Argentina in December.
Keeping: According to Dr. Burkard (Switzerland), resistant to winter temperatures. These parakeets scream loudly only on occasion.
Behavior: The members of a pair are inseparable. They play together, engage in mock fighting, and scratch one another, sometimes so vigorously that the plumage gets damaged as a result.

Red-masked Conure
Aratinga erythrogenys (Lesson)
Characteristics: 34 cm long. Green.
Forehead, cheeks, eye region, shoulder,
small and medium under wing coverts as
well as thighs red. Orbital ring white. Beak
horn colored, iris yellow, legs gray.
Juveniles have less red on the head.
Range: Dry regions of the tropical zone in
western Ecuador and northwestern Peru.
Habitat: Not found in forests.
Habits: Conspicuous by their loud voice.
Also nesting in rock crevices.
Keeping: At London Zoo in 1854. Well suited
for keeping in the aviary but very loud. One
pair was kept in free flight conditions by
Delacour in Cleres. Juveniles grow very
tame and learn to speak a few words.
Diet: Sunflower seeds, canary seed, millet,
groats, paddy, some hemp, fresh or soaked

Breeding pair of Red-masked Conures, *Aratinga erythrogenys.* Photo by Fred Harris.

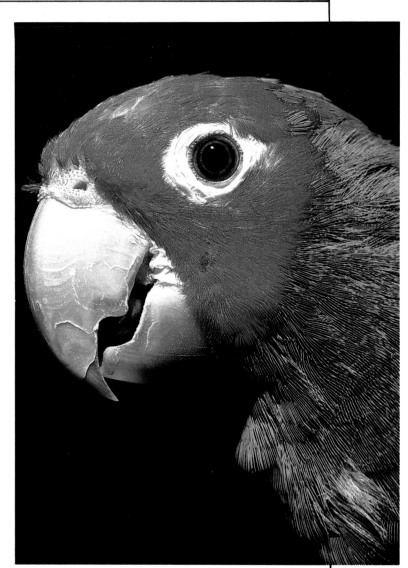

Head study of a Red-masked Conure, *Aratinga erythrogenys.* Photo by K. T. Nemuras.

corn, millet sprays, green panicle millet
and half-ripe grass seeds, peanuts, fruit,
carrots, fresh twigs. The birds like drinking
sweet fruit juice.
Breeding: Although larger nest boxes were
available to them, one pair chose a box (of
the dimensions 35 x 20 x 20 cm) intended for
Lovebirds. The access hole was widened,
however. The eggs were laid at two-day
intervals. Incubation period 28 days,
nestling period 50 days. The female, who
does all the incubating, immediately leaves
the nest if there are any disturbances. In
this case reported by Harton, both parents
fed the young for three months.

White-eyed Conure
Aratinga leucophthalmus (P.L.S. Muller)
Three subspecies.
Characteristics: 35 cm long. Green. A few red feathers on the head, neck, and thighs. Wing edges, shoulders, and lesser wing coverts red, greater under wing coverts golden yellow. White orbital ring. Beak horn colored, iris orange, legs gray-brown. In juveniles the under wing coverts are green. There are striking differences in size even among animals found in the same locality.
Range: Guyana, Venezuela, eastern Colombia to northern Argentina and northern Uruguay.
Habitat: In the open forests of central Brazil this species is one of the most common parrots. In Surinam, White-eyed Conures can be found in mangrove forests.
Habits: In pairs or in flocks of 10–30 birds. In northeastern Venezuela seen in association with Blue-crowned Conures (*Aratinga acuticaudata*), from whom they can readily be distinguished by their calls. Food is foraged for on the ground or in the trees. The stomach contents consisted mainly of grass seeds, but cactus fruits, insects, and insect larvae are also consumed. When the crop is ripening the corn fields are visited. Breeding season in northern Argentina in November, in Guyana in February. The birds nest in the cavities of palm trees.
Keeping: At London Zoo in 1871, but there is one breeding report that dates from 1822. Seldom imported nowadays. Once acclimatized, the animals are very hardy. Wooden constructions and wire netting up to 1 mm in thickness are destroyed. White-eyed Conures are particularly watchful. If anything unusual happens, all the birds in the establishment are alerted by their calls.
Diet: Sometimes adapted exclusively to sunflower seeds. Then it takes a long time before any other foods are accepted as well. Apples, spinach, groundsel, chickweed.
Breeding: First bred in captivity in 1934 in the U.S.A. Breeding started in January, a second brood was produced in the fall. Three to six eggs, a nestling period of 9 weeks. The bottom of the nest box was lined with peat fibers; to these the birds added some wood shavings they had gnawed off. All the incubating is done by the female. A

White-eyed Conures, *Aratinga leucophthalmus,* are among the most common parrots in the open forests of the Brazilian interior.

clutch with young that had died inside the eggs was deserted after 26 days. Checks on the nest were reacted to with noisy calls and attacks. The young developed normally without any special rearing foods.

Hispaniolan Conure
Aratinga chloroptera (Souance)
Two subspecies.
Characteristics: 32 cm long. Green. White orbital ring. Large under wing coverts grayish yellow, others partly red. Beak horn colored, iris yellow, legs brownish.
Range: Numerous on Haiti. The subspecies *A. ch. maugei* from the island of Mona near Puerto Rico is said to have already become extinct.
Habitat: Everywhere, even in dry plains, but particularly common in the mountains.
Habits: Leaf buds, figs, ripening corn. Feeding birds allow the observer to

The Hispaniolan Conure, *Aratinga chloroptera,* is now found only on the island of Haiti. Photo courtesy of Vogelpark Walsrode.

approach. The birds nest inside hollow trees and in deserted woodpecker cavities which may be located as high as 25 m. Three to seven eggs.
Breeding: In 1935, in the U.S.A.

Cuban Conure

Aratinga euops (Wagler)
Characteristics: 26 cm long. Green. Individual red feathers on the head, neck, belly, and thighs. Small under wing coverts red, large ones yellowish blue. White orbital ring. Beak horn colored, iris yellow, legs brownish.
Range: Cuba; at one time on the Isla de Pinos as well, but here the species became extinct at the beginning of our century.
Habitat: Mainly forest regions, but occasionally in open terrain. Deforestation is causing a gradual decline in the numbers of this species.
Habits: Family groups or small flocks seen feeding in the treetops, when they allow one to come fairly close. Occasionally in association with Cuban Amazons (*Amazona leucocephala*). Nesting inside hollow trees, especially palm trees, or in deserted cavities of Cuban Green Woodpeckers (*Xiphidiopicus percussus*). Breeding season May to August.
Keeping: In 1893 first exhibited at a bird show in Berlin. Seldom imported, recently only seen at a few zoos in East Germany. Gets along with other parakeets until the breeding season. Destroys wood; very loud.
Diet: The few people who have kept this species report that the birds accepted mainly sunflower seeds, some canary seed, and apples.
Breeding: Two to five eggs, incubation period 23 days, nestling period 48 days. The male spends a lot of time in the nest with the female and feeds her, but is unlikely to take an active part in the incubating. Nestlings were fed on soaked spray millet, half-ripe seeds, and apples.

Sun Conure

Aratinga solstitialis (Linne)
Characteristics: 30 cm long. Orange-yellow. Forehead, cheeks, belly, lower back, and rump orange-red. Wings yellow, secondaries with some green, primaries dark blue. Under tail coverts green with a

Few specimens of the Cuban Conure, *Aratinga euops,* are in the hands of private fanciers. Photo courtesy of San Diego Zoo.

trace of yellow, underside of tail dark olive. Orbital ring whitish. Beak dark gray, iris dark brown, legs gray. In juveniles the orange on the head and underside is less pronounced or, rather, these areas are yellow instead. There is more green on the wings. The latter change color at 7–9 months.

Range: Guyana, southeastern Venezuela, northeastern Brazil.

Habitat: Open forests, palm groves, savannahs.

Habits: Huge flocks on trees with ripening fruit. Breeding season in Surinam in February. Nests have been found inside hollow palm trees.

Keeping: At London Zoo in 1862. Because these birds originate from regions near the equator, Sun Conures that have arrived only recently should not be kept at temperatures of below 20°C. The well-

Sun Conures, *Aratinga solstitialis,* will require elevated temperatures during the early stages of acclimation.

known unpleasant characteristics of the Sun Conure and most representatives of this genus are its loud voice and delight in destroying wood.

Diet: Sunflower seeds are popular, as are canary seed, apples, and greenstuff.

Breeding: First bred in captivity in 1883, in France. Three to six eggs, laid at two day intervals; incubation period about 27 days, nestling period 6–8 weeks. Two broods per year. Newly hatched chicks are sparsely covered in white first down feathers; later the down plumage is gray white. One pair, which bred inside a natural tree trunk (40 cm high, internal diameter 20 cm, diameter of entrance 6 cm), removed the layer of sawdust and peat fibers that had been used to cover the bottom of the hollow. The male only spends the night in the nest. Checks on the nest are tolerated without great anxiety. Both parents feed the young, which tend to be completely independent by the time they are 8 weeks old. The fledged young return to the nest in the evening. Suitable rearing foods proved to be commercial canary raising food, white bread soaked in milk, dog biscuit, apples, and during the first three weeks of life egg biscuit. Sun Conures can be very prolific, as reported by a Rhodesian aviculturist. Within eighteen months 17 young from a total of 4 clutches were raised. Hybridization with Peach-fronted Conure (*Aratinga aurea*).

Behavior: The members of a pair are very close and preen each other's plumage. Hence Sun Conures that have been raised in isolation form a close attachment to their keeper.

Jandaya Conure
Aratinga jandaya (Gmelin)

Characteristics: 30 cm long. Head, nape, and parts of the upper breast bright yellow. Underside orange-red. Thighs olive green. Wings and upper parts green, lower back orange-red. Flights and tip of tail blue, tail feathers olive green, blackish underneath. Orbital ring off-white. Beak black, iris gray-brown, legs gray. In juveniles the yellow and orange are slightly paler and interspersed with individual green feathers.

Range: Northeastern Brazil.

Habitat: Forest clearings, among coconut palms.

Keeping: Kept at the Viennese Zoo in Schonbrunn around 1850. Seldom imported in recent years. Very loud, destructive to wood. Acclimatized animals can be kept in the outdoor aviaries at temperatures of 0°C

In recent years the Jandaya Conure, *Aratinga jandaya,* has been imported less often.

Jandaya Conures, *Aratinga jandaya*. Increased captive breeding has helped to keep this handsome species available to fanciers. Photo by Ron & Val Moat.

and above. Gets along well with small birds, Budgerigars, and pheasants. Where the aviaries are larger it is possible to keep several pairs together. Even during the breeding season the pairs do not disturb each other. A bird fancier from Lisbon granted partial liberty to a pair of this species. The birds were able to leave the enclosure, through a basket-type opening in the morning and returned voluntarily at night.

Breeding: First bred in captivity in 1891, in England. Three to four eggs. Egg laying at 2-day, sometimes longer intervals. Incubation period about 26 days, nestling period 8 weeks. The first down feathers are long and white-yellow. Some aviculturists report that the males share the incubating. All that is known for certain, however, is that the males are often inside the nest during the day and invariably spend the night there. In June the Jandaya Conures belonging to a German aviculturist carried small twigs into the nest box and broke them into pieces. Both parents feed the young, in some cases still doing so as late as 5 weeks after fledging. Checks on the nest must be carried out with great care, as the females leave the nest box at the slightest

Jandaya Conures, *Aratinga jandaya.* Photo by Dieter Hoppe.

disturbance. Two broods per annum are possible. An especially popular rearing food is soaked corn. Hybridization with Nanday Conure (*Nandayus nenday*), Red-fronted Conure (*Aratinga wagleri*), Peach-fronted Conure (*Aratinga aurea*), Brown-

Jandaya Conures in a nesting cavity. Photo by Dieter Hoppe.

throated Conure (*Aratinga pertinax*), and Sun Conure (*Aratinga solstitialis*).
Behavior: Courting males dance about in front of the female and bow to her. Partner feeding.

Golden-capped Conure
Aratinga auricapilla (Kuhl)
Two subspecies.
Characteristics: 31 cm long. Green. Red lores, red forehead, top of the head yellow. Lower breast, belly, and flanks dark red. Orbital ring light gray. Beak black, iris brown, legs gray.
Range: Eastern Brazil.

The Dusky-headed Conure, *Aratinga weddellii.* Photo courtesy of the San Diego Zoo.

Numbers of the Golden-capped Conure, *Aratinga auricapilla,* have diminished as a result of deforestation.

Habitat: Enclosed and open woodland, savannahs. South of the Rio de Janeiro the species has become rare due to deforestation.
Keeping: It is likely that this species was kept at London Zoo after 1860. After 1975 imported into Europe and the U.S.A. on several occasions.
Breeding: First bred in captivity in 1883, in France. In recent years there have been several reports on its propagation from the U.S.A. and Holland.

Dusky-headed Conure
Aratinga weddellii (Deville)
Characteristics: 28 cm long. Green. Head gray-blue. White orbital ring. Beak black, iris yellowish white, legs gray.
Range: Southeastern Colombia, eastern Ecuador, eastern Peru, northeastern Bolivia, western Brazil.
Habitat: Forests, as well as smaller woodland areas in savannahs, coffee plantations adjoining forests.
Habits: Groups of 6–20 birds. In Bolivia, males in breeding condition were encountered in August.
Keeping: At London Zoo in 1923. First imported into Germany in 1976. Since then very rarely on the market. Quiet, not very active.
Breeding: Incubation period 25 days, nestling period 43 days. Incubation may start after the second or third egg. Parents still feeding the young 6 weeks after fledging. Nest boxes are soon occupied and retreated into for roosting and during disturbances. Dusky-headed Conures may start breeding in the winter. Newly hatched birds are covered in white fluffy down. The later down feathers are also white. Rearing foods that proved suitable are soaked corn, carrots, apples, and a mixture of semolina (baby food), rolled oats, squashed linseed, soft food, calcium, and hard-boiled egg. Checks on the nest are tolerated by the parents.
Behavior: Courting males dance around the female with drooping wings. The hen indicates her readiness to mate by crouching down. The copulating male supports himself by putting one foot on the hen's back and clasping the perching branch with the other. Copulation takes place two to three times a day; duration about two minutes in each case.

Aztec Conure
Aratinga astec (Souance)
Three subspecies.
Characteristics: 24 cm long. Green. Throat and upper breast brownish olive. Underside yellowish olive green. Tail yellowish beneath. The ceres covered by a narrow band of orange-yellow feathers. Orbital ring white. Beak horn colored, iris orange, legs gray.
Range: Mexico, Honduras, western Panama.
Habitat: The edges of forests, partially cleared forests, up to 1000 m. Ripening grain fields.
Habits: Tends to keep to the lower regions of the trees rather than the tops. Breeding season in Honduras from April to May. The nest is located inside the constructions of tree dwelling termites and in loamy walls.
Keeping: Seldom imported. In comparison with its relatives, a quiet bird.
Breeding: First bred in captivity in 1903, in Jamaica, in a cage of a mere 90 cm.

The Olive-throated Conure, *Aratinga nana,* is the only conure that occurs on Jamaica. Photo courtesy of Vogelpark Walsrode.

Olive-throated Conure

Aratinga nana (Vigors)

Characteristics: 26 cm long. Green. Throat, breast, and center of abdomen olive brown. Ceres at the nostrils with yellow feathers. White orbital ring. Beak horn colored, iris orange, legs gray.

Range: Jamaica.

Habitat: Mountainsides, hilly terrain with trees.

Habits: Groups of 5–30 birds, larger units when the fruit is ripening. Especially popular are the seeds and flesh of the guavas. The nest is located in termite structures.

Orange-fronted Conure

Aratinga canicularis (Linne)

Characteristics: 25 cm long. Green. Forehead orange- red, crown gray blue. Sides of head and the throat olive brown. Breast, belly, and under wing coverts yellowish green. Orbital ring light orange-yellow. Beak horn colored, iris pale yellow, legs gray-brown. Juveniles possess a brown iris and less orange on the forehead.

Range: Western Central America from Sinaloa in Mexico to western Costa Rica. The range of distribution would appear to be the same as that of the termite *Nasutitermes nigriceps,* in whose structures the Orange-fronted Conures build their nests.

Habitat: Above all deciduous woods. In Honduras at altitudes of up to 1500 m.

Habits: Outside the breeding season in flocks of over 200 animals. The favorite food of the species consists of juicy and sticky fruit, so the head and beak are often quite messy. Wild figs, the small juicy fruits of a balsam tree (*Bursera* sp.), and mangoes are consumed. About an hour before dusk the birds fly to their specific roosting trees. Breeding season in Mexico from March to April, in El Salvador from January to February. Where there is a shortage of termite nests the parakeets also breed inside hollow trees and in deserted woodpecker holes. Deserted termite constructions grow dry and eventually disintegrate; they are unsuitable as nesting sites for the Orange-fronted Conures. Often the birds start building a breeding chamber but do not complete it. The entrance, with a diameter of 7 cm, is near the base of the termite nest. A tunnel with a length of 30 cm leads steeply upwards and after a sharp bend terminates in the nesting chamber (15 to 20 cm in diameter). Males and females do the digging together, but the male is the slightly more active partner. After one week the building process has been completed. Then there is a pause of a further week, during which the termites add the finishing touch.

Keeping: At London Zoo in 1869. Easy to keep. Not very loud, peaceable. Wooden structures are gnawed but not destroyed. In the U.S.A. this species has become a popular pet. Juveniles readily grow tame, learn to speak a few words, and are very playful.

Breeding: First propagated in captivity in 1929, in the U.S.A. Three to five eggs (one egg a day), incubation period approximately 30 days, incubation from the first egg onwards. Only the hen incubates; the male spends the night inside the nest and accompanies the hen when the latter leaves the box in search of food. Newly hatched

young are covered in fluffy white down. In most cases the young are fed by both parents. It has, however, also been reported that the female looked after the newly hatched on her own. Immatures are distinguished from adult birds mainly by the dark iris. Hybridization with Nanday Conure (*Nandayus nenday*).
Behavior: Social preening can be observed

Found in Mexico and Central America, the Orange-fronted Conure, *Aratinga canicularis,* has been for many years particularly popular as a pet.

all the year round. This would indicate that the pair bonding is long-term. By raising the wings or lifting the tail the partner is requested to scratch the wing or tail region.

Brown-throated Conure
Aratinga pertinax (Linne)
11 subspecies, among them *A. p. pertinax* and *A. p. aeruginosa.*
Characteristics: 26 cm long. Green. Forehead, sides of head, throat golden yellow. Crown with a tinge of blue. Center of abdomen orange. Underside of tail golden olive. Gray-white orbital ring. Beak gray-brown, iris yellow, legs gray. In the subspecies *A. p. aeruginosa* the cheeks and forehead are brown.

Range: Panama, northern South America, islands off the northern coast of Venezuela. Prior to 1860 introduced on the island of St. Thomas (Virgin Islands).
Habitat: Predominantly dry areas. Savannahs, agricultural land. Very rarely in mangrove forests.
Habits: Usually in smaller groups, but on fruit plantations and millet and corn fields flocks of over 100 animals congregate. Sometimes in association with Yellow-crowned Amazons (*Amazona ochrocephala*). In search of food the birds also visit acacias and cacti (*Cereus repandus*). The subspecies *A. p. xanthogenia* from Bonaire Island was seen to feed on blossoms rich in nectar. Like most other members of the genus,

The Brown-throated Conure, *Aratinga pertinax,* occurs in northern South America and many of the adjacent islands. Photo courtesy of the San Diego Zoo.

Brown-throated Conure, *Aratinga pertinax*. This is the subspecies *aeruginosa,* one of the more distinctively colored of the forms of this parakeet. Routedale photo.

these parakeets are very noisy. They are not particularly nervous with human beings; in fact they are frequently seen in towns and villages. In Curacao the natives take young St. Thomas Conures out of the nest and keep them in cages as tame pets. On the island of St. Thomas eggs have been found in March, in northern Venezuela between February and April, in Surinam and its neighborhood the birds do not seem to have any specific breeding season. The birds breed inside the nests of tree dwelling termites, in hollow trees, in the cavities of calcareous rock or in the ground on slopes. Often 4–5 nests are seen close together. The access tunnels to the nests located inside termite structures have a diameter of 7–10 cm. Length of tunnel about 50 cm, diameter of nesting chamber 25 cm. While no soft nesting material was found inside these nests or in hollow trees, the nests inside rock cavities are lined with a few feathers.

Keeping: To date only a few subspecies (*A. p. pertinax, A. p. ocularis, A. p. aeruginosa,* and *A. p. chrysophrys*) have been imported, and these fairly seldom. The birds are noisy, have to be accommodated in secure enclosures with strong wire netting, and do not tolerate low temperatures. During the breeding season they are aggressive.

Breeding: A. p. chrysophrys was propagated in England in 1955. The animals bred inside a nest box (23 x 17 x 38 cm), the bottom of which had been lined with a layer of peat fibers. Every day one egg was laid; incubating started with the second egg. Incubation period 25–26 days, nestling period 6–7 weeks. The male spent the night inside the nest; during the day it guarded the nest and drove off other aviary residents that came too close to the box. For rearing, the birds selected seeds, soaked spray millet, and apples. Greenstuff was not readily consumed. A few other subspecies have also been successfully propagated.

Cactus Conure

Aratinga cactorum (Kuhl)

Two subspecies.

Characteristics: 25 cm long. Green. Forehead pale olive brown. Crown of a faded bluish color. Lores, cheeks, neck, and upper breast pale brown. Breast and belly orange. A yellow line below the eye. White orbital ring. Beak horn colored, iris orange, legs gray-brown.

Range: Northeastern Brazil.

Habitat: Dry terrain where the vegetation consists of cacti, shrubs, and succulents. Open forests, savannahs.

Cactus Conure, *Aratinga cactorum*. Captive breeding of this species has been undertaken only recently. Photo by Fred Harris.

Habits: In pairs or small flocks. Searching for food in bushes or on the ground. Feeding on cactus fruits and berries. Breed inside holes in cacti excavated by themselves.

Keeping: At London Zoo in 1862. Frequently kept in its country of origin. Less noisy and liable to gnaw than related species. Frost is not tolerated. The enclosure must be furnished with plenty of branches for the Cactus Conures to climb on.

Diet: Consisting mainly of sunflower seeds, abundant greenstuff.

Breeding: First bred in captivity in 1883, in France. Three to six eggs. Some reports say the eggs were laid daily, others at two-day intervals. Incubation from the second egg onwards. During the first three days of life the young were fed on soaked rusks, then with white sunflower seeds, hemp, groats, millet, rowanberries, and greenstuff. Hybridization with Brown-throated Conure (*Aratinga pertinax aeruginosa*).

Peach-fronted Conure
Aratinga aurea (Gmelin)
Two subspecies.

Characteristics: 28 cm long. Green. Large orange- yellow spot on the forehead. Crown and lores blue. Neck and breast olive brown. Orbital ring with yellow feathers. Beak black, iris yellow-orange, legs gray. Juveniles have less orange and blue on the head, beak horn colored, iris gray.

Range: Brazil, mainly south of the Amazon, eastern Bolivia, northern Paraguay, northwestern Argentina.

Habitat: Found above all in open terrain. The Peach-fronted Conure is one of the few species that have been extending their habitat as a result of forest clearances.

Habits: In pairs or in flocks of 10–30 birds. Food is searched for on trees and on the ground. In addition to plant food the birds also feed on insects. Not particularly shy. The nest is located inside hollow trees.

Keeping: At London Zoo in 1869. These parakeets are popular pets in their native range. In Germany they are the most widely kept birds of the genus. Little damage is done to wooden constructions. Bathing facilities and a roosting box must be provided. Outside the breeding season the birds get on well with other species. Birds kept on their own grow tame and learn a few words. Peach-fronted Conures have been known to survive in captivity for over 20 years.

Breeding: First bred in captivity in 1880, in Danzig. Two to six eggs, incubation period 26 days, nestling period 50 days. While leaving the nest during checks, the birds quickly return. The bottom of the nest box needs to be covered with a layer of peat fibers or sawdust. In addition to the usual

The Peach-fronted Conure, *Aratinga aurea,* is perhaps the most widely kept of all the *Aratinga* parakeets. Photo by Dr. Herbert R. Axelrod.

food, soft food and apples should be provided for rearing. Greenstuff tends to be left untouched. The nest is defended against the keeper as well. As soon as the young have attained the age of 4 weeks they are fed exclusively by the male. Two weeks after fledging they are independent. Two broods per annum. Hybridization with Orange-fronted Conure (*Aratinga canicularis*), Brown-throated Conure (*Aratinga pertinax aeruginosa*), Sun Conure (*Aratinga solstitialis*), Jandaya Conure (*Aratinga jandaya*), and Monk Parakeet (*Myiopsitta monachus*).

Attempts at breeding the Peach-fronted Conure, *Aratinga aurea,* have been hampered by the fact that the sexes look alike.

Patagonian Conure
(*Cyanoliseus*)

Similar to the genus *Aratinga* but upper mandible only having a slight dental notch. Ceres feathered, nares covered by feathers. The two sexes are identical in color.
One species.

Patagonian Conure
Cyanoliseus patagonus (Vieillot)
Three subspecies.
Characteristics: 43–53 cm long. Olive brown with a tinge of green. Head and wings more greenish, back more brownish. Forehead black-brown. Throat and breast gray-brown with a little white on the upper breast. Belly yellow, centrally red. Thighs red. White orbital ring. Beak black, iris white, legs flesh colored. In immature birds the iris is gray, the upper mandible white. Lesser Patagonian Conure (*C. p. patagonus*): White only along the sides of the upper breast. 43–46 cm long. Greater Patagonian Conure (*C. p. byroni*): The white extended into a band. The yellow and red on the abdomen more intense. 53 cm long. *C. p. andinus*: No white; no or very little yellow, less red on the abdomen. 43–46 cm long.
Range: C. c. patagonus: Southern Argentina, in the winter migrating northward to as far as Mendoza and Buenos Aires, sometimes as far as Uruguay. *C. p. byroni*: Just a few regions in the central provinces of Chile. *C. p. andinus*: Mountains in northwestern Argentina.
Habitat: Treeless grass steppe with bushes, sometimes also in forests, where Patagonian Conures have been observed in the tops of the trees. In Chile at an altitude of 1900 m during the summer, returning to Tallagen after the first snowfalls in May.
Habits: Undoubtedly on the decline. In Chile, adult animals were hunted and the barely feathered young taken out of the breeding chambers by means of hooks at the end of November for consumption at a feast in honor of a saint. Today the Greater Patagonian Conure is protected in Chile, but there are some doubts as to the effectiveness of this measure. In Argentina the Patagonian Conures are being severely persecuted as agricultural pests. The

Patagonian Conure, *Cyanoliseus patagonus*, the nominate subspecies.

important to furnish the enclosure with thick perching rods and, if possible, with an artificial rock face. Bathing facilities must be available to the birds. It is possible to keep several pairs together, but the birds do not get along with other species. Because of the loud voice, it is hardly feasible to keep the animals in the aviary in well populated areas. Patagonian Conures kept on their own quickly grow tame.

Diet: Sunflower seeds, oats, millet, fresh or soaked corn, canary seed, peanuts, apples,

Patagonian Conures require an ample supply of wood for gnawing. Photo by P. Leysen.

parakeets roost either on specific trees, where they gather into large flocks from all directions (Lesser Patagonian Conure), or inside their breeding hollows in the sandstone walls (Greater Patagonian Conures). They feed on a variety of seeds including grain, fruits, berries, thistle seeds (*Carduus mariana*), and on green plants. Breeding season in Chile from September to November, in Argentina starting in December. Breeding hollows inside sandstone or loamy walls, often on steep water banks. Entrances (8–18 cm in diameter) high above the ground. Tunnels up to 3 m long, nesting chamber 40 cm in diameter, height 15 cm. Breeding in colonies, so that individual tunnels often cut across each other.

Keeping: 1868, at London Zoo. Tolerate cold and damp. Wooden constructions and weak wire netting are destroyed. Instead of a nest box, which also tends to be destroyed very quickly, it is better to provide a natural tree trunk of hard wood. Patagonian Conures do not do a lot of climbing, hence it is more

carrots, greenstuff, fresh twigs.

Breeding: Two to three eggs, incubation period of 25 days, nestling period of 55–60 days. The eggs may be laid at intervals of up to 7 days. Bred comparatively often. Three weeks after fledging the young are independent and do not return to the nest. The birds belonging to an English aviculturist bred inside a natural tree trunk with a height of 75 cm and an internal diameter of 23 cm. Diameter of the entrance hole 10 cm. It has been observed on several occasions that the male does not go into the nest until the young have hatched. He then helps to feed them. In another case the female started incubating after the second egg had been laid; after the third egg had been produced the male also spent most of his time inside the box, only coming out in search of food. The light upper mandibles of the young start to grow dark after about 8 months. At Chester Zoo, Lesser Patagonian Conures dug a cave in the hard aviary

The Patagonian Conure, *Cyanoliseus patagonus,* is able to withstand cold and damp. Photo by Dieter Hoppe.

ground, although a nest box and a natural tree trunk were at their disposal. The material was loosened with the bill and thrown a meter and a half towards the back with the feet. When completed, the cave had a diameter of 29 cm and had been lined with small feathers. As the birds were molting, it is not certain whether the feathers were in the nest coincidentally. In addition to the normal food, the birds were given shrimp, germinated seeds, seeding weeds, white bread with a sweetened pap, spinach, dandelion, liquid vitamins, and pigeon grit when rearing their young.
Behavior: Courting males stretch out to their full height and open and shut the beak loudly. They "strut" up and down on their perching branch. The female can be heard to make the same noise with the bill.

Thick-billed Parakeet
(*Rhynchopsitta*)

Long wings, almost extending to the tip of the tail. Strong bill. Ceres and cheeks feathered. Sexes identical in color.
   One species.

Thick-billed Parakeet
Rhynchopsitta pachyrhyncha (Swainson)
Two subspecies.
Characteristics: 40 cm long. Green. Forehead, stripe above and behind the eye, as well as shoulder and thigh red. Under wing coverts yellow. Beak black, iris orange-yellow, legs gray. In the subspecies *R. p. terrisi* the red has been replaced by chestnut brown. In the males the bill is broader and therefore appears larger. In juveniles the beak is horn colored, the red eye stripe is absent, the shoulders are green.
Range: Mexican highlands. In the past, large numbers of these birds occasionally migrated as far as the mountains of southern Arizona and southwestern New Mexico.
Habitat: Stone pine forests at altitudes of between 1500 and 3400 m. A decline in numbers due to deforestation; the subspecies *R. p. terrisi* is close to extinction.
Habits: Since the deforestation of the stone pine forests in the south of the U.S.A. the autumnal migrations of these parakeets have ceased. In addition to the pine seeds, the birds also consumed acorns as part of their staple diet during the cold season. Seasonal migrations also occur within Mexico itself. Breeding takes place between May and August. The breeding hollows are located high up in the pine trunks, usually in dead trees. Sometimes the parakeets breed inside the deserted nests of the Imperial Woodpecker (*Campephilus imperialis*). Diameter of entrance hole 15–18 cm, depth of the hollow 45–60 cm, internal diameter of the breeding chamber 20–25 cm. Bottom layer of decaying wood.
Keeping: 1920, at Washington Zoo. A few imports prior to 1970 but today under strict protection of the International Agreement on Species Preservation. Hardy in regard to

The Thick-billed Parakeet, *Rhynchopsitta pachyrhyncha,* is now strictly protected and no longer freely traded.

weather conditions; destructive to wood. The animals like to forage for food on the ground, which means there is a possibility of worm infestation. Worming at regular intervals is advisable.

Diet: Sunflower seeds, hemp, peanuts, stone pine nuts and other conifer seeds, canary seed, fresh twigs. The parakeets prefer the apples and carrots to be attached to the perching rods.

Breeding: One to two eggs, incubation period 28 days, nestling period 60 days. First bred in captivity in 1965 at San Diego Zoo. Nest box 35 x 35 x 60 cm, a bottom layer of soil and sawdust. Diameter of entrance hole 15 cm. The box had been put up at a height of 3 m. Only the hen incubates; the male feeds her. During the first 11 days the female was on her own in the nest; subsequently both parents fed the young. Breeding does not usually start until August or September.

Head study of a Thick-billed Parakeet. Routedale photo.

Index

Page numbers in **boldface** refer to illustrations.

Index